Essentials of
Enterprise Networks

Essentials of Enterprise Networks

Kian Bennett

Larsen & Keller
www.larsen-keller.com

Essentials of Enterprise Networks
Kian Bennett
ISBN: 978-1-64172-108-0 (Hardback)

Larsen & Keller
Published by Larsen and Keller Education,
5 Penn Plaza,
19th Floor,
New York, NY 10001, USA

Cataloging-in-Publication Data

Essentials of enterprise networks / Kian Bennett.
      p. cm.
Includes bibliographical references and index.
ISBN 978-1-64172-108-0
1. Business enterprises--Computer networks. 2. Computer networks.
3. Business networks. I. Bennett, Kian.
HD30.37 .E87 2019
004.6--dc23

For more information regarding Larsen and Keller Education and its products, please visit the publisher's website www.larsen-keller.com

Table of Contents

Preface

Enterprise networks are networks that org nizations build to interconnect its office locations for the easy sharing of computer resources. Private enterprise networks may have a combination of intranets and extranets. An intranet is a set of networks under the control of a single administrator. It uses IP protocol and IP-based tools like file transfer applications and web browsers. An extranet is the network that is administered by a single organization but supports access to an external network. The concept of the internetwork is of significance to enterprise networks. An internetwork refers to the connection of multiple computer networks through a common routing technology. The largest example of an internetwork is the Internet. Network traffic is carried out through network paths by routing. It is done for packet switched networks and circuit switching networks. This textbook is a compilation of chapters that discuss the most vital concepts in the field of enterprise networks. The topics included herein are of the utmost significance and bound to provide incredible insights to readers. It aims to serve as a resource guide for students and experts alike and contribute to the growth of the discipline.

A short introduction to every chapter is written below to provide an overview of the content of the book:

Chapter 1, An enterprise network is the communications channel that allows the connection of computers and other devices across different functional divisions in an organization for the facilitation of data accessibility. The aim of this chapter is to provide an introduction to enterprise networks and its classification such as personal area network, local area network, metropolitan area network and wide area network, among others; **Chapter 2**, Study of enterprise networks requires an understanding of the different elements of a network, such as network host, network link, network protocols, network topology and intermediary network device. All such topics have been elaborately discussed in this chapter for an extensive understanding; **Chapter 3**, The measure of the service quality of a network is referred to as network performance. Many different techniques of measuring the performance of a network exist. The following chapter elucidates the varied aspects of network performance, such as network performance management, network capacity, network capacity planning, network delay and network quality of service; **Chapter 4**, In a telecommunication network, a network address is the identifier for a host or a node. It is a unique identifier across the network. This chapter has been carefully written to provide an extensive understanding of network address through the elucidation of topics such as IP address, virtual IP address, private IP address, unicast address, etc.; **Chapter 5**, The selection of a path for traffic in a single network or multiple networks is possible through the process of routing. It works on the assumption that network addresses are structured in a way that similarity in addresses implies proximity within that network. This chapter explores the fundamentals of routing and elucidates its central concepts like routing table, IP routing, routing algorithms, route selection, etc.; **Chapter 6**, Ethernet refers to a computer networking technology that is used in LAN, MAN and WAN. In order to completely understand ethernet technology, it is necessary to understand the chief aspects of ethernet physical layer, ethernet frame, power over ethernet, ethernet over PDH, ethernet over SDH, etc. which have been extensively detailed in this chapter.

Finally, I would like to thank my fellow scholars who gave constructive feedback and my family members who supported me at every step.

Kian Bennett

Introduction to Enterprise Networks

An enterprise network is the communications channel that allows the connection of computers and other devices across different functional divisions in an organization for the facilitation of data accessibility. The aim of this chapter is to provide an introduction to enterprise networks and its classification such as personal area network, local area network, metropolitan area network and wide area network, among others.

An enterprise network is an enterprise's communications backbone that helps connect computers and related devices across departments and workgroup networks, facilitating insight and data accessibility.

During the 1980s, organizations began to install local area networks to connect computers in departments and workgroups. Department-level managers usually made decisions about what type of computers and networks they wanted to install.

Eventually, organizations saw benefits in building enterprise networks that would let people throughout the organization exchange e-mail and work together using collaborative software. An enterprise network would connect all the isolated departmental or workgroup networks into an intracompany network, with the potential for allowing all computer users in a company to access any data or computing resource. It would provide interoperability among autonomous and heterogeneous systems and have the eventual goal of reducing the number of communication protocols in use. Toward this goal, industry organizations were formed to create open standards, and vendors developed their own strategies.

An enterprise network is both local and wide area in scope. It integrates all the systems within an organization, whether they are Windows computers, Apple Macintoshes, UNIX workstations, minicomputers, or mainframes.

An enterprise network can be thought of as a "plug-and-play" platform for connecting many different computing devices. In this platform scenario, no user or group is an island. All systems can potentially communicate with all other systems while maintaining reasonable performance, security, and reliability.

This has largely been achieved with Internet protocols and web technologies that provide better results at lower cost and fewer configuration problems than the enterprise computing models. TCP/IP is a unifying internetwork protocol that lets organizations tie together workgroup and division LANs, and connect with the Internet. Web protocols (HTTP, HTML, and XML) unify user interfaces, applications, and data, letting organizations build intranets (internal internets). A web browser is like a universal client, and Web servers can provide data to any of those clients. Web servers are distributed throughout the enterprise, following distributed computing models. Multitiered architectures are used, in which a Web client accesses a Web server and a Web server accesses back-end data sources, such as mainframes and server farms.

Trends in Enterprise Networking

At one point, there was a trend toward building networks with stripped-down diskless clients and huge servers. This NC (Network Computer) strategy, championed by Oracle, never took off because full-function desktop and portable PCs became very cheap. But the number of handheld devices, smart phones, network appliances, and other devices that connect to networks, either directly or wirelessly, is increasing.

An interesting 3Com paper called "Massively Distributed Systems," by Dan Nessett, discusses the growth of distributed computer networks to billions of nodes, many of which will be embedded systems. While these embedded systems will handle some computing and communication tasks on their own, many will need to off-load heavy computations to more capable systems. The paper discusses the potential architecture of distributed systems that include such embedded system devices.

New wireless Ethernet LAN protocols (IEEE 802.11a) support data rates over 50 Mbits/sec.

As interest in Voice Over IP (VOIP) increases, the need for higher-capacity networks, QoS, bandwidth management, and policy management will increase.

Another trend reduces the need for enterprise networks. If users can connect to the Internet with high-speed pipes (DSL, cable-or wireless), then the Internet-or at least a local service provider-can become the enterprise network. This becomes a reality when the bandwidth constraints of local access are lifted. An enterprise may provide connections to its application servers via the Internet, so that users go out on the Internet and then back in to the enterprise Web site. Alternatively, an enterprise may have an ASP (application service provider) host its applications. As more users become mobile and use wireless devices, a traditional enterprise network becomes a platform that ties them to the locations where they can connect to that network.

Classification of Networks

In the today world, two devices are in network if a process in one device is able to exchange information with a process in another device. Networks are known as a medium of connections between nodes (set of devices) or computers. A network is consist of group of computer systems, servers, networking devices are linked together to share resources, including a printer or a file server. The connection is established by using either cable media or wireless media.

Personal Area Network (PAN) - The interconnection of devices within the range of an individual person, typically within a range of 10 meters. For example, a wireless network connecting a computer with its keyboard, mouse or printer is a PAN. Also, a PDA that controls the user's hearing aid or pacemaker fits in this category. Another example of PAN is a Bluetooth. Typically, this kind of network could also be interconnected without wires to the Internet or other networks.

Local Area Network (LAN) - Privately-owned networks covering a small geographic area, like a home, office, building or group of buildings (e.g. campus). They are widely used to connect computers in company offices and factories to share resources (e.g., printers) and exchange information. LANs are restricted in size, which means that the worst-case transmission time is bounded and known in advance. Knowing this bound makes it possible to use certain kinds of designs that would not otherwise be possible. It also simplifies network management. Traditional LANs run at speeds of 10 Mbps to 100 Mbps, have low delay (microseconds or nanoseconds), and make very few errors. Newer LANs operate at up to 10 Gbps.

Metropolitan Area Network (MAN) - Covers a larger geographical area than is a LAN, ranging from several blocks of buildings to entire cities. MANs can also depend on communications channels of moderate-to-high data rates. A MAN might be owned and operated by a single organization, but it usually will be used by many individuals and organizations. MANs might also be owned and operated as public utilities. They will often provide means for internetworking of LANs. Metropolitan Area Networks can span up to 50km, devices used are modem and wire/cable.

Wide Area Networks (WAN) - Computer network that covers a large geographical area, often a country or continent. (Any network whose communications links cross metropolitan, regional, or national boundaries).

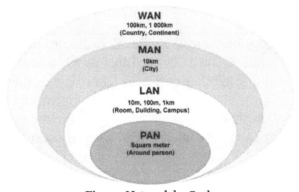

Figure: Network by Scale

Personal Area Network

A personal area network, or PAN, is a computer network that enables communication between computer devices near a person. PANs can be wired, such as USB or Fire-Wire, or they can be wireless, such as infrared, ZigBee, Bluetooth and ultrawideband, or UWB. The range of a PAN typically is a few meters. Examples of wireless PAN, or WPAN, devices include cell phone headsets, wireless keyboards, wireless mice, printers, bar code scanners and game consoles.

Wireless PANs feature battery-operated devices that draw very little current. Sleep modes commonly are used to further extend battery life. Network protocols tend be simpler than Wi-Fi or WiMAX (to reduce required processor power), and the transmit power is typically less than 1 milliwatt.

In the United States, PANs for the most part operate in two unlicensed bands: 902-928 MHz and 2.4-2.4835 GHz. Ultrawideband devices also can operate in the 3.1-10.6 GHz band, coexisting with other radio services by employing low overall power and ultra-low power densities (watts/Hz).

Let's examine three of the most popular PAN technologies: ZigBee, Bluetooth and ultrawideband.

ZigBee is a short-range, low-power computer networking protocol that complies with the IEEE 802.15.4 standard. In the U.S., ZigBee devices operate in the 902-928 MHz and 2.4 GHz unlicensed bands. The technology is intended to be less complex and less expensive than other WPANs such as Bluetooth. Although ZigBee is a WPAN protocol, it also is used for telemetry applications such as automatic meter reading and building automation.

ZigBee employs direct-sequence spread spectrum modulation with a gross data rate of 40 kb/s in the 900 MHz band and 250 kb/s in the 2.4 GHz band. Advertised transmission range is from 10 to 75 meters, but like any radio system, the actual range depends on the environment.

There are three types of ZigBee devices: ZigBee Coordinator (ZC), ZigBee Router (ZR), and ZigBee End Device (ZED). The ZC is the most capable device, forming the root of the network tree and bridging to other networks. There is only one ZC per network. The ZR can run an application function as well as act as an intermediate router, passing data from other devices. A ZED contains just enough functionality to talk to its parent node, which is a coordinator or a router. It can sleep most of the time, extending its battery life.

The ZigBee Alliance is a trade organization charged with developing and publishing the Zigbee standard and promoting its use.

Bluetooth is a computer networking protocol designed for short-range, low-power communications in the 2.4 GHz unlicensed band. It was named after King Harald Bluetooth, ruler of Denmark and Norway in the late 10th century. Sven Mattison and Jaap Haartsen, both employees of Ericsson Mobile Platforms in Lund, Sweden, published the first Bluetooth standard in 1994. The current version of the standard is 2.1 and specifies gross data rates up to 3 Mb/s.

Bluetooth employs frequency-hopping spread spectrum modulation with a rate of up to 1600 hops per second using 79 different channels, each 1 MHz wide. Because the technology uses a spread spectrum signal and low power, it is less likely to cause harmful interference to other 2.4 GHz devices, such as Wi-Fi radios, that often exist in the same personal computer. There are three classes of Bluetooth devices corresponding to different transmit power levels. Class 1, 2 and 3 devices operate at up to 100 mW, 2.5 mW and 1 mW, respectively.

Bluetooth networks normally operate in a master-slave configuration. A master device can communicate with up to seven active slave devices, and this network of up to eight devices is called a piconet. Up to 255 additional devices can be inactive or parked, waiting for wakeup instructions from the master.

The technology implements confidentiality, authentication and key derivation using algorithms based on the SAFER+ block cipher.

The Bluetooth Special Interest Group is a privately held, nonprofit trade association organized to promote Bluetooth in the marketplace and to develop Bluetooth standards.

Ultrawideband is a radio technology useful for short-range, high-bandwidth communications that does not create harmful interference to users sharing the same band. By FCC definition, a UWB signal has a bandwidth that exceeds the lesser of 500 MHz or 20% of the arithmetic center frequency. Such a bandwidth exceeds all conventional spread spectrum radio systems, and the resulting low power density ensures the signal does not cause harmful interference.

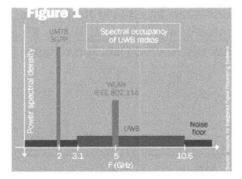

The FCC allows UWB devices to operate in the 3.1-10.6 GHz band. In this band, the emission limit is -41.3 dBm per MHz, which is the Part 15 limit for unintentional emissions in this band. Unlike conventional radios, which continuously modulate a sinusoidal carrier, UWB radios are short-duration pulse generators. The occupied bandwidth is roughly equal to the inverse of the pulse duration. The duty cycle of UWB signals is usually quite low, but the net throughput is still high because the burst information rate during the pulse can be more than 100 Mb/s.

A pulse-based UWB method is the basis of the IEEE 802.15.4a draft standard and working group, which has proposed UWB as an alternative physical layer protocol to ZigBee.

The WiMedia Alliance is a trade association organized to promote UWB and develop standards.

In addition to these three, other WPANs include Wibree, an ultra-low-power complement to Bluetooth; Wireless USB; EnOcean, composed of self-powered devices; and 6LoWPAN, which allows IPv6 packets to ride 802.15.4 networks.

Local Area Network

The local area network (LAN) is a network which is designed to operate over a small physical area such as an office, factory or a group of buildings. LANs are very widely used in a variety of applications.

The personal computers and workstations in the offices are interconnected via LAN to share resources. The resources to be shared can be hardware like a printer or softwares or data. A LAN is a form of local (limited-distance), shared packet network for computer communications. In LAN all the machines are connected to a single cable. The data rates for LAN range from 4 to 16 Mbps with the maximum of 100 Mbps.

The term LAN can also refer just to the hardware and software that allows you to connect all the devices together. In this sense, Local Talk is one kind of LAN, Ethernet is another.

The components used by LANs can be divided into cabling standards, hardware, and protocols. Various LAN protocols are Ethernet, Token Ring: TCP/IP, 5MB, NetBIOS and NetBeui, IPX/SPX, Fiber Distributed Data Interchange (FDDI) and Asynchronous Transfer Mode (ATM).

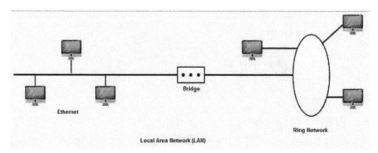

Local Area Network (LAN)

Types of LAN

Ethernet is the most common type of LAN. Different LAN can be differentiated on the behalf of following characteristics.

- Topology: The topology is the geometric arrangement of network elements. For example, Network devices can be interconnected in a ring topology or in a bus topology or linear bus.

- Protocols: It is a guideline for communicating data between two devices. The protocols also determine type of error and data compression.

- Media: The cables used in LAN to connect devices are twisted-pair wire, coaxial cables, or fiber optic.

Example of LAN Topologies

Various topologies are possible for the broadcast LANs such as bus topology or ring topology.

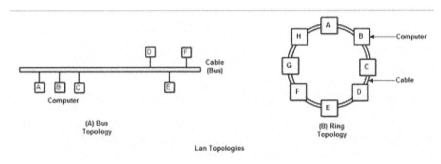

Lan Topologies

Bus Topology

- Bus topology is shown in the above figure. In this topology at any instant only one computer acts as master and it is allowed to transmit (broadcast). The others are supposed to listen.

- If two or more machines want to transmit simultaneously then an arbitration mechanism has to be used for resolving the conflict.

- It is possible to have a centralized or distributed type arbitration mechanism.

- The most popular example of bus topology is Ethernet (IEEE 802.3). It has a decentralized control and it operates at 10 or 100 Mbps.

- Computers on Ethernet can transmit whenever they want. If collision of their packets takes place, then they wait for a random time and retransmit their packets.

Ring Topology

- This is another broadcast topology.

- In a ring each bit propagates around on its own without waiting for the rest of the packet to which it belongs.

- Since it is a broadcast system, some rules are essential for arbitrating the simultaneous access to the ring.

- An example of ring based LAN is IEEE 802.5 (IBM token ring) operating at 4 and 16 Mbps.

Static and Dynamic Broadcast Networks

The broadcast networks are further classified into two types namely,

1. Static networks and

2. Dynamic networks.

- This classification is based on how the channel is allocated.

- In static allocation, each machine is allowed to broadcast only in its allotted time slot.

- But static allocation wastes the channel capacity when a machine does not want to transmit in its allotted time slot.

- Hence most of the systems try to allocate the channel dynamically i.e. on demand.

LAN Applications and Benefits

LANs are used almost exclusively for data communications over relatively short distances such as within an office, office building or campus environment. LANs allow multiple workstations to share access to multiple host computers, other workstations, printers and other peripherals, and connections to other networks. LANs are also being utilized for imaging applications, as well. They are also being used for video and voice communications, although currently on a very limited basis.

LAN applications include communications between the workstation and host computers, other workstations, and servers. The servers may allow sharing of resources. Resources could be information, data files, e-mail, voice mail, software, hardware (hard disk, printer, fax, etc.) and other networks.

LAN benefits include the fact that a high-speed transmission system can be shared among multiple devices in support of large number of active terminals and a large number of active applications in the form of a multi-user, multi-tasking computer network. LAN-connected workstations realize the benefit of decentralized access to very substantial centralized processors, perhaps in the form of mainframe host computer and storage capabilities (information repositories). Additionally, current technology allows multiple LANs to be inter-networked through the use of LAN switches, routers and the like.

Metropolitan Area Network

A large computer network which extends to a city or to a large university campus is termed as metropolitan area network or MAN. The purpose of MAN (Metropolitan Area Network) is to provide the link to the internet in the long run. A MAN (Metropolitan Area Network) usually incorporates a number of LANs to form a network. This large network MANs (Metropolitan Area Network) backbone comprises of an optical fiber set-up.

Most widely used technologies to develop a MAN (Metropolitan Area Network) network are FDDI (fiber distribution data interface), ATM (Asynchronous Transfer Mode) and SMDS (switched multi megabit data service).ATM (Asynchronous Transfer Mode) is the most frequently used of all. ATM (Asynchronous Transfer Mode) is a digital data transfer technology. It was developed in 1980 to improve the transportation of real time data over a single network. ATM (Asynchronous Transfer Mode) works just like cell relay system, where data is separated in the form of fixed equal sized packets and is transferred overtime. The purpose of ATM (Asynchronous Transfer Mode) was to access clear audio and video results during a video conferencing. The attributes of ATM has enabled it to become a base of wide area data networking.

ATM (Asynchronous Transfer Mode) combines the characteristics of circuit switching and packet switching, which allows it to transfer even the real time data. FDDI is a standard for data transfer over LAN, which can be extended to the range of approximately 200kms. FDDI can help support the data transmission of many thousand users. This is the reason why it is referred to as the MAN (Metropolitan Area Network) technology. FDDI uses optical fiber for its basic infrastructure that is why it is referred to as fiber distribution data interface. When data is transferred through a connectionless service we use the technology named as SMDS. Connectionless service implies that data is transferred by storing the information in the header and it reaches its destination independently through any network. When the data is transferred using the technology of SMDS, it also forms small data packets just like in ATM. However SMDS allows the transmission of data over large geographical areas in the form of datagrams (the data packets of an unreliable data service provider). Nowadays MAN (Metropolitan Area Network) links are established using infrared and microwave signals.

Working of Metropolitan Area Networks (MAN)

MAN (Metropolitan Area Network) usually falls between LAN and WAN. It is generally applied to connect geographically dispersed LANs. Therefore the goal of MAN is to develop a communication link between two independent LAN nodes. A MAN (Metropolitan Area Network) is usually established using optical fiber. The network is established using routers and switches. A switch is a port which is active in handling the filtration of data usually coming in the form of frames. Any switch acts as a dual port, at one end it is handling filtration of data and at the other end managing connections. Router is another device for facilitating the network connection. Router helps the data packets to identify the path to be taken. Hence in other words it keeps an eye on the data transfer. MAN (Metropolitan Area Network) is usually operated over an area of up to 50kms.

Advantages of MAN (Metropolitan Area Network)

MAN (Metropolitan Area Network) falls in between the LAN and WAN. It therefore increases the efficiency of handling data while at the same time saves the cost attached to establish a wide area network. MAN (Metropolitan Area Network) offers centralized management of data. It enables you to connect many fast LANs together. Telephone companies worldwide have facilitated the transfer of data with the help of an underground optical fiber network. These optical fibers increase the efficiency and speed of data transfer. The optical fibers enable you to access a speed of almost 1000mbps. If you develop a WAN of 1.45 mbps its cost is more than what it gives you. Whereas when you establish metropolitan area network it offers you the speed of 1000mbps as a whole with the lowest cost involved.

Wide Area Network

A WAN (wide area network) is a communications network that spans a large geographic area such as across cities, states, or countries. They can be private to connect parts of a business or they can be more public to connect smaller networks together.

The easiest way to understand what a WAN is to think of the internet as a whole, which is the world's largest WAN. The internet is a WAN because, through the use of ISPs, it connects lots of smaller local area networks (LANs) or metro area networks (MANs).

On a smaller scale, a business may have a WAN that's comprised of cloud services, its headquarters, and smaller branch offices. The WAN, in this case, would be used to connect all of those sections of the business together.

No matter what the WAN joins together or how far apart the networks are, the end result is always intended to allow different smaller networks from different locations to communicate with one another.

WANS Types

A company that has an office in London and another office in Manchester and need these offices to be connected to each other so as to be on the same network even though they are miles away, The following WAN options or types and the protocols used are available to use.

Leased Line

Point-to-point connection between two Local Area Networks LANs.

Advantages

Very if not most secure.

Disadvantage

Very Expensive to run.

Protocols used

PPP, HDLC, SDLC.

Circuit Switching

A dedicated circuit path is created between endpoints. Good example is dialup connections (telephone system) which links together wire segments to create a single unbroken line for each telephone call.

Advantages

Less expensive.

Disadvantages

Call Setup.

Protocols used

PPP, ISDN.

Packet Switch

Network devices transport packets via a shared single point-to-point or point-to-multi-point medium across. Variable length packets are transmitted over PVCs or SVCs

Advantages

Highly efficient use of bandwidth.

Disadvantages

Shared media across link.

Protocols used

X.25, Frame Relay.

Cell Relay

Same as packet switching but uses fixed-length packets. Data is divided into fixed length cells and then transported across virtual circuits.

Advantages

Best for simultaneous use of voice and data.

Disadvantages

Overhead can be considerable.

Protocols used

ATM.

Internet

Wireless packet switching using the Internet as the WAN infrastructure. Uses network addressing to deliver packets. Because of security issues VPN technology must be used.

Advantages

Least expensive, globally available.

Disadvantages

Least secure.

Protocols used

VPN, DSL, cable modem, wireless.

Ways to Connect WANs

Since WANs, by definition, cover a larger distance than LANs, it makes sense to connect the various parts of the WAN using a virtual private network (VPN). This provides protected communications between sites, which is necessary given that the data transfers are happening over the internet.

Although VPNs provide reasonable levels of security for business uses, a public internet connection does not always provide the predictable levels of performance that a dedicated WAN link can. This is why fiber optic cables are sometimes used to facilitate communication between the WAN links.

X.25, Frame Relay and MPLS

Since the 1970s, many WANs were built using a technology standard called X.25. These types of networks supported automated teller machines, credit card transaction systems, and some of the early online information services such as CompuServe. Older X.25 networks ran using 56 Kbps dial-up modem connections.

Frame Relay technology was created to simplify X.25 protocols and provide a less expensive solution for wide area networks that needed to run at higher speeds. Frame Relay became a popular choice for telecommunications companies in the United States during the 1990s, particularly AT&T.

Multiprotocol Label Switching (MPLS) was built to replace Frame Relay by improving protocol support for handling voice and video traffic in addition to normal data traffic. The Quality of Service (QoS) features of MPLS was key to its success. So-called "triple play" network services built on MPLS increased in popularity during the 2000s and eventually replaced Frame Relay.

Leased Lines and Metro Ethernet

Many businesses started using leased line WANs in the mid-1990s as the web and internet exploded in popularity. T1 and T3 lines are often used to support MPLS or internet VPN communications.

Long-distance, point-to-point Ethernet links can also be used to build dedicated wide area networks. While much more expensive than internet VPNs or MPLS solutions, private Ethernet WANs offer very high performance, with links typically rated at 1 Gbps compared to the 45 Mbps of a traditional T1.

If a WAN combines two or more connection types like if it uses MPLS circuits as well as T3 lines, it can be considered a hybrid WAN. These are useful if the organization wants to provide a cost-effective method to connect their branches together but also have a faster method of transferring important data if needed.

Problems with Wide Area Networks

WAN networks are much more expensive than home or corporate intranets.

WANs that cross international and other territorial boundaries fall under different legal jurisdictions. Disputes can arise between governments over ownership rights and network usage restrictions.

Global WANs require the use of undersea network cables to communicate across continents. Undersea cables are subject to sabotage and also unintentional breaks from ships and weather conditions. Compared to underground landlines, undersea cables tend to take much longer and cost much more to repair.

Rise of Internet of Things

In all walks of life, we are becoming more and more dependent on machines and data. Equipment that was once analogue is now shiny machines packed full of sophisticated electronics, generating a constant flow of data. Just look at your watch for instance. The old ticking of the second hand has been replaced by streams of data showing heart rate and all manner of environmental factors. It seems like we are finding reasons to connect just about anything and everything to the internet. The recent rise in the internet of things (IoT) has ushered in what has been dubbed the "fourth industrial revolution". Gartner estimates that 20 billion connected devices will be in use worldwide in the next 18 months.

When it comes to commercial applications, IoT is already delivering radical and sometimes disruptive transformation. Most progressive organizations are seriously exploring how IoT can give them their next competitive advantage. As with all these things, there is a cost versus return exercise that needs to be worked through. Organizations that manage to find ways of getting the best ratio between cost and return will obviously see the greatest success.

The range of IoT hardware available is vast, including everything from smart meters and smart watches, to connected children's toys, and the market is still growing. What's more, IoT sensors are being increasingly used by businesses of all sizes across numerous industries, especially in retail and manufacturing. With total spending on endpoints in 2017 worth £2 trillion alone, it's safe to say that IoT has become big business for those capable of unlocking its potential.

IoT provides businesses with a powerful data resource gathered from devices traditionally difficult to derive data from. For instance, data on where delivery vehicles are and their ETA at any given moment can be mixed with other contextual data, like traffic and weather, to show when a given component will be available to a consumer in store and thus improve customer service, trust and loyalty.

IoT has also seen widespread adoption in manufacturing, with IDC forecasting that this will be where the most investment will be made in 2018. The primary use of IoT in manufacturing is for predictive maintenance, where IoT sensors monitor various inputs and outputs to track the wear-and-tear of machinery. This allows manufacturers to repair or replace parts before they break, avoiding critical failure, which causes unplanned disruptions to production and incurs significant costs for manufacturers. The data from IoT sensors is also often used to track performance, allowing manufacturers to understand what is normal for that piece of machinery and create an automated system that will halt production if an abnormal circumstance arises, preventing mistakes and the waste of valuable raw materials.

Whatever your business does, there's most likely an opportunity for IoT to transform it for the better, and channel partners are there to guide businesses through the process successfully.

It's Not Easy Being Green

It was recently World Environment Day, where many organizations and government bodies paid homage to 'greener' legislations and business solutions. Surprisingly, one of the most notable attempts to reduce the negative environmental impact of urbanization is to make cities smarter with the help of IoT. Smart cities, theoretically, will be able to monitor and adjust the population's consumption behavior based on data derived from smart devices. By recording and analyzing data with the help of IoT and AI, it is possible to determine the most efficient and greenest ways to use and manage our cities.

As businesses come under increasing pressure to encourage and implement environmentally-friendly solutions for their employees and customers alike, investment in IoT will give them the ability to implement greener strategies across their whole organization and fast.

Barriers to IoT Entry

Research conducted earlier this year by satellite communications company Inmarsat revealed that many organizations lack the skills to develop, manage and deploy IoT solutions, especially in areas such as data analytics and cyber security. IoT demands a broad range of very different IT skills. In order to take full advantage of the opportunities that IoT offers, it's important to build or have access to a dedicated IoT team and not just shift the lion's share of responsibility onto an already stretched IT department. For businesses in the channel, the answer to filling this burgeoning IoT skills gap – and quickly – lies in partnering with an IoT aggregator that already has the appropriate skillset in place to accelerate IoT deployment across the whole enterprise on their behalf.

Role of the IT Channel

Data is a new business staple, and as the technology behind IoT has matured, so has the thinking around how to put this data to good use. Sensors are now being deployed more strategically and more effectively or to solve particular problems. Helping businesses to do this is where savvy channel partners come to the fore to take the mounting pressure away from in-house IT teams, and into the hands of a team of specially designated IoT experts who can guide an organization on its way to IoT success.

Channel partners and distributors are increasingly funneling more and more funding into IoT solutions, as well as into IoT-specific training to educate vendors and customers on how to deploy IoT effectively, in a bid to raise awareness around the possibilities IoT offers the channel, and maximize ROI. Businesses in the channel have, as a result, more opportunities than ever before to learn how IoT can benefit their organizations and make the most of the opportunities that IoT offers with the help of the distributor's expertise.

References

- Enterprise-network-7044: techopedia.com, Retrieved 19 June 2018

- How-many-type-of-computer-networking, computer-network, computer networking notes: ecomputernotes.com, Retrieved 29 March 2018

- Connecting-personal-level, personal-area: urgentcomm.com, Retrieved 14 May 2018

- Wide-area-network-816383: lifewire.com, Retrieved 10 July 2018

- Wide-area-network-wan-2: orbit-computer-solutions.com, Retrieved 30 March 2018

Elements of a Network

Study of enterprise networks requires an understanding of the different elements of a network, such as network host, network link, network protocols, network topology and intermediary network device. All such topics have been elaborately discussed in this chapter for an extensive understanding.

Network Host

A host (also known as "network host") is a computer or other device that communicates with other hosts on a network. Hosts on a network include clients and servers that send or receive data, services or applications.

Hosts typically do not include intermediary network devices like switches and routers, which are instead often categorized as nodes. A node is also a broader term that includes anything connected to a network, while a host requires an IP address. In other words, all hosts are nodes, but network nodes are not hosts unless they require an IP address to function.

On a TCP/IP network, each host has a host number that, together with a network identity, forms its own unique IP address. In the Open Systems Interconnection (OSI) model, protocols in the transport layer, also known as Layer 4, are responsible for communication between hosts. Hosts use various protocols to communicate, including transmission control protocol (TCP) and User Datagram Protocol (UDP).

Types of IT Hosts

The term host is used in several other areas within information technology (IT), carrying a slightly different meaning depending on the context.

Web Host

For companies or individuals with a website, a host is a web server that stores and transmits the data for one or more websites. Host can also refer to the service provider that leases this infrastructure, which is known as hosting.

Cloud Host

A cloud host is based on cloud computing technologies that allow a number of servers to act as one system in which website performance can be guaranteed by multiple machines. It often includes a network of servers pulling from different data centers in different locations. Cloud hosts operate as a service that allows clients to buy as much of the service as they need. Cloud hosting is an alternative to hosting a website on a single server. Cloud hosting can be considered both infrastructure as a service (IaaS) and platform as a service (PaaS). Using a public cloud model, a public network transmits data that is physically stored on virtual servers and uses public networks to transmit the data that is physically stored on shared servers that make up the cloud resource.

Virtual Host

The term virtual host has two uses. One refers to the technology used to run multiple domains or applications on a single physical server, and the second refers to companies that sell virtual infrastructure services.

Remote Host

In this context, a remote host is in a different physical location than the user accessed using a private network or the Internet, which provides users with remote access. Examples include servers that can be logged into remotely or a host computer for a remote desktop.

Host virtual machine. This refers to the hardware that is, the physical server that provides the computing resources to support virtual machines (also known as server virtualization).

Mainframe Computer Environments

In this context, a mainframe computer can be the host provider of services for the workstations attached to it. This does not mean that the host only has "servers" and that the workstations only have "clients." The server-client relationship is a programming model independent of this contextual usage of "host."

Hostname

A hostname is a plaintext name identifying a host in a given domain. On a local area network (LAN), a server's hostname might be a nickname like mailserver 1. On the internet, a hostname makes up part of a web address and has three parts: the subdomain, domain name and top-level domain. For example, the hostname whatis.techtarget.com consists of the subdomain whatis, the domain techtarget and the top-level domain.com.

Client-server Model

In client-server model, any process can act as Server or Client. It is not the type of machine, size of the machine, or its computing power which makes it server; it is the ability of serving request that makes a machine a server.

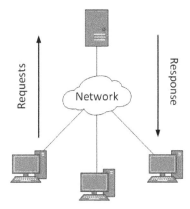

A system can act as server and client simultaneously. That is, one process is acting as Server and another is acting as a client. This may also happen that both client and server processes reside on the same machine.

Communication

Two processes in client-server model can interact in various ways:

- Sockets
- Remote Procedure Calls (RPC)

Sockets

In this paradigm, the process acting as Server opens a socket using a well-known (or known by client) port and waits until some client request comes. The second process acting as a Client also opens a socket but instead of waiting for an incoming request, the client processes 'requests first'.

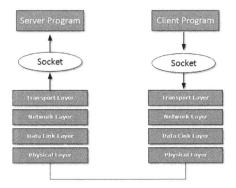

When the request is reached to server, it is served. It can either be an information sharing or resource request.

Remote Procedure Call

This is a mechanism where one process interacts with another by means of procedure calls. One process (client) calls the procedure lying on remote host. The process on remote host is said to be Server. Both processes are allocated stubs. This communication happens in the following way:

- The client process calls the client stub. It passes all the parameters pertaining to program local to it.

- All parameters are then packed (marshalled) and a system call is made to send them to other side of the network.

- Kernel sends the data over the network and the other end receives it.

- The remote host passes data to the server stub where it is unmarshalled.

- The parameters are passed to the procedure and the procedure is then executed.

- The result is sent back to the client in the same manner.

Peer-to-peer Networking

Peer-to-peer, or P2P in its abbreviated form, refers to computer networks that use a distributed architecture. That means that all the computers or devices that are part of it share the workloads in the network. The computers or devices that are part of a peer-to-peer network are called peers. Each peer from a peer-to-peer network is equal to the other peers. There are no privileged peers, and there is no central administrator device in the center of the network.

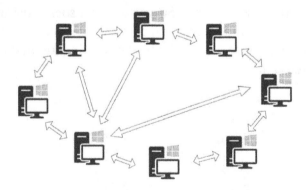

In a way, peer-to-peer networks are the socialist networks in the world of computing. Each peer is equal to the others, and each peer has the same rights and duties as the others. Peers are both clients and servers at the same time.

Furthermore, every resource available in a peer-to-peer network is shared among the peers, without any central server being involved. The shared resources in a P2P network can be things such as processor usage, disk storage space or network bandwidth.

Purpose of P2P Networks

The primary purpose of peer-to-peer networks is to share resources and help computers and devices work collaboratively, to deliver a specific service or perform a particular task. As we mentioned earlier, P2P is used for sharing all kinds of computing resources such as processing power, network bandwidth or disk storage space. However, the most common use case for peer-to-peer networks is for sharing files on the internet. Peer-to-peer networks are ideal for file-sharing because they allow the computers connected to them to receive files and send files simultaneously.

Consider this situation: you open your web browser and visit a website from where you download a file. In this case, the website works as a server, and your computer acts as a client which receives the file. You can compare it to a one-way road: the file that you download is a car that goes from point A (the website) to point B (your computer).

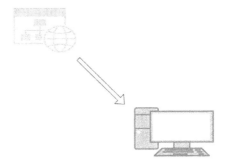

If you download the same file through a peer-to-peer network, using a BitTorrent website as a starting point, the download is performed differently. The file is downloaded to your computer in bits and parts that come from many other computers in the P2P network that already have that file. At the same time, the file is also sent (uploaded) from your computer to others which ask for it. This situation is similar to a two-way road: the file is like multiple small cars that come to your PC but also leave to others when they are requested.

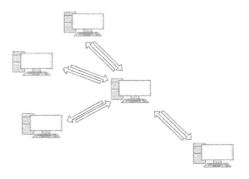

Usefulness of Peer-to-peer Networks

P2P networks have a few characteristics that make them useful:

- They are difficult to take down. Even if you shut down one of the peers, the others continue to work and communicate. You have to close down all the peers for the network to stop working.

- Peer-to-peer networks are extremely scalable. Adding new peers is easy, as you do not need to do any central configuration on a central server.

- When it comes to file sharing, the larger a peer-to-peer network is, the faster it is. Having the same file stored on many of the peers in a P2P network means that when someone needs to download it, the file is downloaded from many locations simultaneously.

Need of P2P Networks

We need peer-to-peer networks to connect computers and devices without having to configure a server. Having to create a server for everything is very expensive and difficult to manage, and people use cheaper alternatives like P2P. Here are a few examples of common use cases for P2P networks:

- When you connect the Windows computers in your home to a Homegroup, you create a peer-to-peer network between them. The Homegroup is a small group of computers that are connected between them to share storage and printers. This is one of the most common uses for peer-to-peer technology. Some people might say that Homegroups can't be peer-to-peer because the computers in the network are connected to a router. However, keep in mind that the router has nothing in common with managing what the computers from the Homegroup share among them. The router does not work as a server but merely as an interface or gate between the local network and the internet.

- When you create an ad-hoc network between two computers, you create a peer-to-peer network between them.

- Sharing large files over the Internet is often done using P2P network architecture. For example, some online gaming platforms use P2P for downloading games between users. Blizzard Entertainment distributes Diablo III, StarCraft II and World of Warcraft using P2P. Another large publisher, Wargaming, does the same with their World of Tanks, World of Warships and World of Warplanes games. Others, like Steam or GOG, choose not to use P2P and prefer maintaining dedicated download servers around the world.

- Windows 10 updates are delivered both from Microsoft's servers and through P2P Many Linux operating systems are distributed via BitTorrent downloads that use P2P transfers. Such examples are Ubuntu, Linux Mint, and Manjaro.

P2P networks are the cheapest method of distributing content because they use the bandwidth of peers, not the bandwidth of the content's creator.

The precursor of peer-to-peer networks appears to be USENET, which was developed in 1979. It was a system that allowed users to read and post messages/news. It was a network system similar to the online forums today, but with the difference that USENET did not rely on a central server or administrator. USENET copied the same message/news to all the servers found in the network. Similarly, P2P networks distribute and use all the resources available to them.

The next big thing in the history of P2P was the year 1999 when Napster came to life. Napster was file-sharing software that was used by people to distribute and download music. The music shared on Napster was usually copyrighted and thus illegal to distribute. However, that did not stop people from getting it. Although Napster was the one that got P2P into the mainstream, Napster ultimately failed and was shut down by authorities because of all the content that was shared illegally on it. Nowadays, P2P remains one of the most popular technologies for sharing files over the internet, both lawfully and unlawfully.

Illegal uses of Peer-to-peer Networks

P2P is a controversial technology because it is widely used for piracy. There are many websites on the web that offer access to copyrighted content like movies, music, software or games, through P2P networks, due to the advantages of this technology. While the technology itself is not illegal and it has many legitimate use cases that don't involve piracy, the way some people use P2P is illegal. When using P2P, make sure not to engage yourself in piracy or other use cases that are punished by law.

Network Interface Card

NIC is short for network interface card. It's network adapter hardware in the form of an add-in card that fits in an expansion slot on a computer's motherboard. Most computers have them built-in (in which case they're just a part of the circuit board) but you can also add your own NIC to expand the functionality of the system.

The NIC is what provides the hardware interface between a computer and a network. This is true whether the network is wired or wirelesses since the NIC can be used for Ethernet networks as well as Wi-Fi ones, as well as whether it's a desktop or laptop.

"Network cards" that connect over USB are not actually cards but instead regular USB devices that enable network connections through the USB port. These are called network adapters.

Working of NIC

Put simply, a network interface card enables a device to network with other devices. This is true whether the devices are connected to a central network (like in infrastructure mode) or even if they're paired together, directly from one device to the other (i.e. ad-hoc mode).

However, a NIC isn't always the only component needed to interface with other devices. For example, if the device is part of a larger network and you want it to have access to the internet, like at home or in a business, a router is required too. The device, then, uses the network interface card to connect to the router, which is connected to the internet.

NIC Physical Description

Network cards come in many different forms but the two main ones are wired and wireless.

Wireless NICs need to use wireless technologies to access the network, so they have one or more antennas sticking out of the card. You can see an example of this with the TP-Link PCI Express Adapter.

Wired NICs just use an RJ45 port since they have an Ethernet cable attached to the end. This makes them much flatter than wireless network cards. The TP-Link Gigabit Ethernet PCI Express Network Adapter is one example.

No matter which is used, the NIC protrudes from the back of the computer next to the other plugs, like for the monitor. If the NIC is plugged into a laptop, it's most likely attached to the side.

Speed of Network Cards

All NICs feature a speed rating, such as 11 Mbps, 54 Mbps or 100 Mbps, that suggest the general performance of the unit. You can find this information in Windows by right-clicking the network connection from the Network and Sharing Center > Change adapter settings section of Control Panel.

It's important to keep in mind that the speed of the NIC does not necessarily determine the speed of the internet connection. This is due to reasons like available bandwidth and the speed you're paying for.

For example, if you're only paying for 20 Mbps download speeds, using a 100 Mbps NIC will not increase your speeds to 100 Mbps, or even to anything over 20 Mbps. However, if you're paying for 20 Mbps but your NIC only supports 11 Mbps, you will suffer from slower download speeds since the installed hardware can only work as fast as it's rated to work.

In other words, the speed of the network, when just these two factors are considered, is determined by the slower of the two.

Another major player in network speeds is bandwidth. If you're supposed to be getting 100 Mbps and your card supports it, but you have three computers on the network that are downloading simultaneously, that 100 Mbps will be split in three, which will really only serve each client around 33 Mbps.

Getting Drivers for Network Cards

All hardware devices need device drivers in order to work with the software on the computer. If your network card isn't working, it's likely that the driver is missing, corrupted or outdated.

Updating network card drivers can be tricky since you usually need the internet in order to download the driver, but the driver issue is precisely what's preventing you from accessing the internet! In these cases, you should download the network driver on a computer that works and then transfer it to the problem system with a flash drive or CD.

The easiest way to do this is to use a driver updater tool that can scan for updates even when the computer is offline. Run the program on the PC that needs the driver and then save the information to a file. Open the file in the same driver updater program on a working computer, download the drivers and then transfer them to the non-working computer to update the drivers there.

Network Address

A network address serves as a unique identifier for a computer or other device on a network. When setting up correctly, computers can determine the addresses of other computers and devices on the network and use these addresses to communicate with one another.

Physical Addresses vs. Virtual Addresses

Most network devices have several different addresses.

Physical addresses belong to individual network interfaces attached to a device. For example, the Wi-Fi radio and the Bluetooth radio of a mobile device possess their own physical network addresses.

Virtual addresses are assigned to devices according to the kind of network they are attached to. The virtual addresses of a mobile device, for example, change as it migrates from one network to another, while its physical addresses remain fixed.

IP Addressing Versions

The most popular type of virtual network address is the Internet Protocol (IP) address. The current IP address (IP version 6, IPv6) consists of 16 bytes (128 bits) that uniquely identify connected devices. The design of IPv6 incorporates a much larger IP address space than its predecessor IPv4 to scale up support for many billions of devices.

Much of the IPv4 address space was allocated to Internet service providers and other large organizations to assign to their customers and to Internet servers—these are called public IP addresses. Certain private IP address ranges were established to support internal networks like home networks with devices that did not need to be directly connected to the Internet.

MAC Addresses

A well-known form of physical addressing is based on Media Access Control (MAC) technology. MAC addresses, also known as physical addresses, are six bytes (48 bits) that manufacturers of network adapters embed in their products to uniquely identify them. IP and other protocols rely on physical addresses to identify devices on a network.

Address Assignment

Network addresses are associated with network devices through several different methods:

- Networks can be configured to assign IP addresses automatically in a process called dynamic address assignment.

- Network administrators can choose specific IP addresses and assign them to devices manually in a process called static address assignment.

- Network adapter vendors set a unique MAC address in the read-only memory (ROM) of each unit manufactured in a process sometimes called "burning."

Home and business networks commonly use Dynamic Host Configuration Protocol (DHCP) servers for automatic IP address assignment.

Network Address Translation

Routers commonly use a technology called Network Address Translation (NAT) to help direct Internet Protocol traffic to its intended destination. NAT works with the virtual addresses contained inside IP network traffic.

Problems with IP Addresses

An IP address conflict occurs when two or more devices on a network both are assigned the same address number. These conflicts can occur either due to human errors in static address assignment or— less commonly—from technical glitches in automatic assignment systems.

Port (Computer Networking)

In network technology, the port (Port) generally has two meanings: one is the physical meaning of the port, for example, ADSL Modem, hubs, switches, routers used to connect other network equipment interfaces, such as RJ-45 port, SC port and many more. Second, the logical meaning of the port, generally refers to the TCP / IP protocol port, port number range from 0 to 65535, such as for browsing Web services port 80, 21 ports for FTP services and so on. Ports act as logical communications endpoints for computers and are used on the Transport layer of the OSI model by protocol. There are 65536 port altogether, numbering between 0 and 65535.

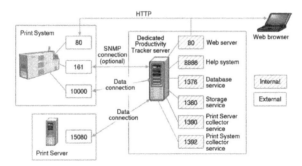

Port logical sense for a variety of classification criteria, the following describes two common classifications:

1. Distribution division by port number

   • Well-known port

Well-known port known as the port number, range from 0 to 1023, these port numbers are generally fixed for some services. For example, port 21 is assigned to the FTP service, port 25 is assigned to the SMTP (Simple Mail Transfer Protocol) service, port 80 is assigned to the HTTP service, port 135 is assigned to the RPC (remote procedure call) service.

- Registered Ports

Ports used by vendors for proprietary applications, range from 1024-49,151. These must be registered with the IANA. For example, Microsoft registered 3389 for use with the Remote Desktop Protocol.

- Dynamic port (Dynamic Ports)

Dynamic port range from 1024 to 65535, these numbers are generally not assigned to a fixed service, that many services can use these ports. Just run the program to the system application to access the network, the system can be allocated from a number of these ports for the program. For example, 1024 port is assigned to the first system to apply for the program. After closing the program process, it will release the occupied port number.

However, the dynamic port is also often used by the virus Trojans, such as the glacial default connection port is 7626.

2. Classification by protocol

By protocol type division, can be divided into TCP, UDP, IP and ICMP (Internet Control Message Protocol) port. The following describes the TCP and UDP port:

- TCP port

TCP port that Transmission Control Protocol ports required establishing a connection between the client and the server, which can provide reliable data transmission. Commonly, FTP port 21, Telnet 23, SMTP 25, HTTP 80, and so on.

- UDP port

UDP port that the user datagram protocol port, without the need to establish a connection, security cannot be guaranteed between the client and the server. Common DNS services are 53 ports.

Intermediary Network Device

Computer networks vary in scale from small work groups, local area networks (LANs) to some of the largest networks like the Internet. They are all created from connections between computers. These devices make the data transfer and regulation of these networks possible. They are designed to serve many functions like making data flow control decisions, encryption, modulation, and demodulation, provide network security, and most importantly, provide point-to-point connectivity. Here are some of the prime examples.

Switches

Network switches or packet switches are devices that connect the various segments of a network, and their main function is switching packets of data. Also known as a network bridge, they switch processes and direct data at the level of the data link layer, which is second of the OSI model layers (concerned with physical addressing of data). A switch may also operate at the level of other OSI layers like the physical, network, or transport layer. Multilayer switches act at different OSI layers simultaneously. Network switches play a vital role in the functioning of local area networks.

Routers

As its name suggests, a router is an intermediary device that regulates and directs data traffic between computer networks. It forwards data to various network destinations and controls its flow between two or more logical subnets, which do not have the same network address in a large network. It selects the optimum path for data transfer between two points in a network. Routers are one of the most vital network devices that make data transmission possible.

Modem

A modem (modulator - demodulator) is an intermediary device that converts analog signals transferred over networks into digital signals and digital signals back to analog. They enable the transmission of digital data over analog mediums like telephone lines and optic fiber cables.

Wireless Access Points

A wireless access point (WAP) is an intermediary device in a network that connects various types of wireless communication devices with wireless networks. The connectivity is made possible through 'Bluetooth' and 'Wi-Fi' technologies. It acts as an intermediary between wireless and wired devices that are part of a network.

Hub

Working at the physical layer of the OSI model, a hub is basically a connector between Ethernet segments, which also control the bandwidth sharing among connected computer terminals.

Repeater

Repeaters are network devices that carry out the task of maintaining signal strength during transmission through a network. They regenerate data signals and amplify them for further transmission.

Firewall

A firewall is any hardware appliance or software designed to filter network traffic that passes through it, according to certain criteria and trust levels set by the network administrator.

These were some of the most common devices that are part of every computer network at any scale. Some other examples of intermediary network devices are proxy servers, gateways, and digital media receivers. Without them, the working of a computer network would be next to impossible.

Network Link

Network links allow you to tell more complex and dynamic stories with your KML files. They allow you to do many more things, from keeping content updated to changing content in response to what the user does.

Using KML as a Bookmark

In the most generic sense, a KML file with a network link acts as a gateway into the content on your server. Your users download your KML file just once, but they will always see the most updated content, even if you updated it after they download your KML.

In fact, many content owners choose to have users download a KML file that includes only a network link. The KML file is similar in some ways to a bookmark in a web browser, allowing users to quickly get back to content that they like while allowing the content owner to update content at will. As a side benefit, the initial download of your KML file is always small and fast.

Loading Large Data Sets

Along with regions, network links introduce a powerful mechanism for downloading small parts of large multimedia files only when they're absolutely needed.

Example: 3D Models

3D models can bring more realistic representations of structures and objects to your KML files. However, they can also be quite large in size, resulting in slow downloads, if you include them all in a single KMZ file.

One solution is to include links to your 3D models in your placemark balloons. However, that requires users to open placemarks and click on links. You might want models to just appear in their geospatial context as the user is flying around.

A network link using the on Region value for view Refresh Mode is the best solution, because it allow users to download models on-demand, based on where they are flying in Google Earth.

Example: Superoverlays

A similar challenge occurs with very large images. If you have large image overlays you'd like to include, you can use a variant of the region-based technique for 3D models. When the user is zoomed out, you can show lower-resolution imagery, and as the user zooms into a particular region, you can show the higher-resolution image for that particular region. By using network links you can load the image parts you need on the fly.

Using Real-time Data

After a user downloads your KML file, even if the user doesn't fly to a specific region, you might want to update your content simply because it has changed. Perhaps you have real-time data from sensors, or maybe you're monitoring exit-poll results on election night.

Network links allow you to update content based on the passage of time. Using refreshMode and refreshInterval or expires, you can choose to refresh after a few seconds or when a deadline passes.

What does refreshing allow you to do? You could simply reload the entire file behind the original network link. Alternatively, you could change only the parts of the KML that have actually changed. Perhaps you only update sensor placemarks where you have new data, or only update districts where new votes have been counted.

Network Protocols

Network protocols are formal standards and policies comprised of rules, procedures and formats that define communication between two or more devices over a network. Network protocols govern the end-to-end processes of timely, secure and managed data or network communication.

Network protocols incorporate all the processes, requirements and constraints of initiating and accomplishing communication between computers, servers, routers and other network-enabled devices. Network protocols must be confirmed and installed by the sender and receiver to ensure network/data communication and apply to software and hardware nodes that communicate on a network.

There are several broad types of networking protocols, including:

- Network communication protocols: Basic data communication protocols, such as TCP/IP and HTTP.

- Network security protocols: Implement security over network communications and include HTTPS, SSL and SFTP.

- Network management protocols: Provide network governance and maintenance and include SNMP and ICMP.

Network Protocols: Basic Layers

Network protocols are broken up into categories called layers, but suffice it to say that the first layer is closest to the electrical components, like the network cable of a computer. The last layer is closest to what a person interacts with, such as reading your email on the screen.

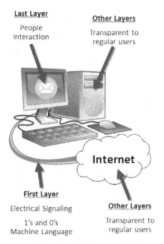

Figure: The Basic Network Layers

Standard vs. Proprietary Network Protocols

Standard Protocols are some of the most commonly used protocols. Standard protocols are vetted by organizations such as the Internet Society, who's mission it is 'to promote the open development, evolution, and use of the Internet for the benefit of all people throughout the world'.

Standard Protocols are freely usable by people who make gadgets that communicate on a network. They don't have to worry about acquiring permission or paying royalties to use them. It's like driving your car on public roads. You don't have to pay for the framework (at least not directly) that supports traffic laws, such as traffic lights, signs, or painted traffic markings on the road.

Occasionally companies will create their own private network protocols. These are called proprietary protocols. These protocols are usually owned by a company or individual, and become the intellectual property of the creator. If you wanted to use one you would have to obtain permission and pay a royalty.

Types of Network Protocols

The most common network protocols are:

- Ethernet
- Local Talk
- Token Ring
- FDDI
- ATM

The followings are some commonly used network symbols to draw different kinds of network protocols.

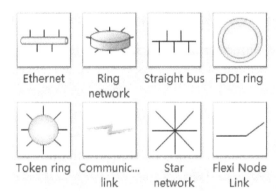

Ethernet

The Ethernet protocol is by far the most widely used one. Ethernet uses an access method called CSMA/CD (Carrier Sense Multiple Access/Collision Detection). This is a system where each computer listens to the cable before sending anything through the network. If the network is clear, the computer will transmit. If some other nodes have already transmitted on the cable, the computer will wait and try again when the line is clear. Sometimes, two computers attempt to transmit at the same instant. A collision occurs when this happens. Each computer then backs off and waits a random amount of time before attempting to retransmit. With this access method, it is normal to have collisions. However, the delay caused by collisions and retransmitting is very small and does not normally effect the speed of transmission on the network.

The Ethernet protocol allows for linear bus, star, or tree topologies. Data can be transmitted over wireless access points, twisted pair, coaxial, or fiber optic cable at a speed of 10 Mbps up to 1000 Mbps.

Fast Ethernet

To allow for an increased speed of transmission, the Ethernet protocol has developed a new standard that supports 100 Mbps. This is commonly called Fast Ethernet. Fast Ethernet requires the application of different, more expensive network concentrators/hubs and network interface cards. In addition, category 5 twisted pair or fiber optic cable is necessary. Fast Ethernet is becoming common in schools that have been recently wired.

Local Talk

Local Talk is a network protocol that was developed by Apple Computer, Inc. for Macintosh computers. The method used by Local Talk is called CSMA/CA (Carrier Sense Multiple Access with Collision Avoidance). It is similar to CSMA/CD except that a computer signals its intent to transmit before it actually does so. Local Talk adapters and special twisted pair cable can be used to connect a series of computers through the serial port. The Macintosh operating system allows the establishment of a peer-to-peer network without the need for additional software. With the addition of the server version of AppleShare software, a client/server network can be established.

The Local Talk protocol allows for linear bus, star, or tree topologies using twisted pair cable. A primary disadvantage of Local Talk is low speed. Its speed of transmission is only 230 Kbps.

Token Ring

The Token Ring protocol was developed by IBM in the mid-1980s. The access method used involves token-passing. In Token Ring, the computers are connected so that the signal travels around the network from one computer to another in a logical ring. A single electronic token moves around the ring from one computer to the next. If a computer does not have information to transmit, it simply passes the token on to the next workstation. If a computer wishes to transmit and receives an empty token, it attaches data to the token. The token then proceeds around the ring until it comes to the computer for which the data is meant. At this point, the data is captured by the receiving computer. The Token Ring protocol requires a star-wired ring using twisted pair or fiber optic cable. It can operate at transmission speeds of 4 Mbps or 16 Mbps. Due to the increasing popularity of Ethernet, the use of Token Ring in school environments has decreased.

FDDI

Fiber Distributed Data Interface (FDDI) is a network protocol that is used primarily to interconnect two or more local area networks, often over large distances. The access method used by FDDI involves token-passing. FDDI uses a dual ring physical topology. Transmission normally occurs on one of the rings; however, if a break occurs, the system keeps information moving by automatically using portions of the second ring to create a new complete ring. A major advantage of FDDI is high speed. It operates over fiber optic cable at 100 Mbps.

ATM

Asynchronous Transfer Mode (ATM) is a network protocol that transmits data at a speed of 155 Mbps and higher. ATM works by transmitting all data in small packets of a fixed size; whereas, other protocols transfer variable length packets. ATM supports a variety of media such as video, CD-quality audio, and imaging. ATM employs a star topology, which can work with fiber optic as well as twisted pair cable.

ATM is most often used to interconnect two or more local area networks. It is also frequently used by Internet Service Providers to utilize high-speed access to the Internet for their clients. As ATM technology becomes more cost-effective, it will provide another solution for constructing faster local area networks.

Gigabit Ethernet

The latest development in the Ethernet standard is a protocol that has a transmission speed of 1 Gbps. Gigabit Ethernet is primarily used for backbones on a network at this time. In the future, it will probably also be used for workstation and server connections. It can be used with both fiber optic cabling and copper. The 1000BaseTX, the copper cable used for Gigabit Ethernet, became the formal standard in 1999.

Network Topology

A Network Topology is the arrangement with which computer systems or network devices are connected to each other. Topologies may define both physical and logical aspect of the network. Both logical and physical topologies could be same or different in a same network.

Point-to-point

Point-to-point networks contains exactly two hosts such as computer, switches or routers, servers connected back to back using a single piece of cable. Often, the receiving end of one host is connected to sending end of the other and vice-versa.

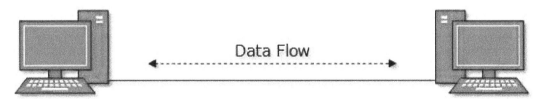

Data Flow

If the hosts are connected point-to-point logically, then may have multiple intermediate devices. But the end hosts are unaware of underlying network and see each other as if they are connected directly.

Bus Topology

In case of Bus topology, all devices share single communication line or cable. Bus topology may have problem while multiple hosts sending data at the same time. Therefore, Bus topology either uses CSMA/CD technology or recognizes one host as Bus Master to solve the issue. It is one of the simple forms of networking where a failure of a device does not affect the other devices. But failure of the shared communication line can make all other devices stop functioning.

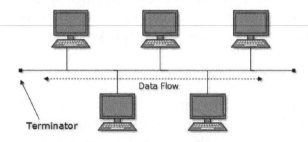

Both ends of the shared channel have line terminator. The data is sent in only one direction and as soon as it reaches the extreme end, the terminator removes the data from the line.

Star Topology

All hosts in Star topology are connected to a central device, known as hub device, using a point-to-point connection. That is, there exists a point to point connection between hosts and hub. The hub device can be any of the following:

- Layer-1 device such as hub or repeater
- Layer-2 device such as switch or bridge
- Layer-3 device such as router or gateway.

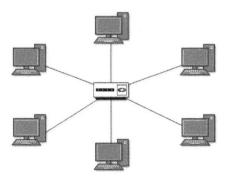

As in Bus topology, hub acts as single point of failure. If hub fails, connectivity of all hosts to all other hosts fails. Every communication between hosts, takes place through only the hub. Star topology is not expensive as to connect one more host, only one cable is required and configuration is simple.

Ring Topology

In ring topology, each host machine connects to exactly two other machines, creating a circular network structure. When one host tries to communicate or send message to a host which is not adjacent to it, the data travels through all intermediate hosts. To connect one more host in the existing structure, the administrator may need only one more extra cable.

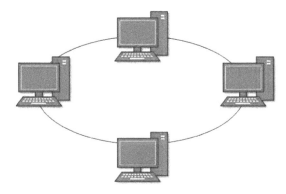

Failure of any host results in failure of the whole ring. Thus, every connection in the ring is a point of failure. There are methods which employ one more backup ring.

Mesh Topology

In this type of topology, a host is connected to one or multiple hosts. This topology has hosts in point-to-point connection with every other host or may also have hosts which are in point-to-point connection to few hosts only.

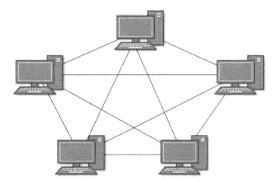

Hosts in Mesh topology also work as relay for other hosts which do not have direct point-to-point links. Mesh technology comes into two types:

- Full Mesh: All hosts have a point-to-point connection to every other host in the network. Thus for every new host n(n-1)/2 connections are required. It provides the most reliable network structure among all network topologies.

- Partially Mesh: Not all hosts have point-to-point connection to every other host. Hosts connect to each other in some arbitrarily fashion. This topology exists where we need to provide reliability to some hosts out of all.

Tree Topology

Also known as Hierarchical Topology, this is the most common form of network topology in use presently. This topology imitates as extended Star topology and inherits properties of bus topology.

This topology divides the network in to multiple levels/layers of network. Mainly in LANs, a network is bifurcated into three types of network devices. The lowermost is access-layer where computers are attached. The middle layer is known as distribution layer, which works as mediator between upper layer and lower layer. The highest layer is known as core layer, and is central point of the network, i.e. root of the tree from which all nodes fork.

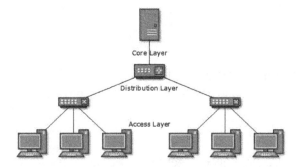

All neighboring hosts have point-to-point connection between them. Similar to the Bus topology, if the root goes down, then the entire network suffers even. Though it is not the single point of failure. Every connection serves as point of failure, failing of which divides the network into unreachable segment.

Daisy Chain

This topology connects all the hosts in a linear fashion. Similar to Ring topology, all hosts are connected to two hosts only, except the end hosts. Means, if the end hosts in daisy chain are connected then it represents Ring topology.

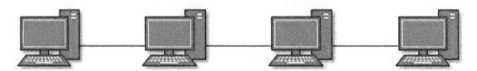

Each link in daisy chain topology represents single point of failure. Every link failure splits the network into two segments. Every intermediate host works as relay for its immediate hosts.

Hybrid Topology

A network structure whose design contains more than one topology is said to be hybrid topology. Hybrid topology inherits merits and demerits of all the incorporating topologies.

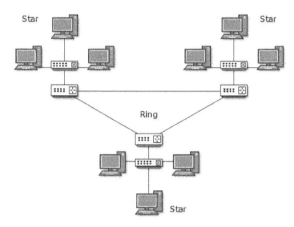

The above picture represents an arbitrarily hybrid topology. The combining topologies may contain attributes of Star, Ring, Bus, and Daisy-chain topologies. Most WANs are connected by means of Dual-Ring topology and networks connected to them are mostly Star topology networks. Internet is the best example of largest Hybrid topology.

References

- Introduction-to-network-addresses-817378: lifewire.com, Retrieved 19 June 2018
- Port-computer-networkingport-numberport-networktcp-portudp-portdestination-port-source-porthttp-port: securityonline.info, Retrieved 11 July 2018
- Intermediary-devices: techspirited.com, Retrieved 18 May 2018
- Network-protocols-12938: techopedia.com, Retrieved 14 March 2018
- What-is-a-network-protocol-types-list: study.com, Retrieved 10 June 2018
- Computer-network-topologies, data-communication-computer-network: tutorialspoint.com, Retrieved 15 April 2018

Network Performance

The measure of the service quality of a network is referred to as network performance. Many different techniques of measuring the performance of a network exist. The following chapter elucidates the varied aspects of network performance, such as network performance management, network capacity, network capacity planning, network delay and network quality of service.

Network performance is the analysis and review of collective network statistics, to define the quality of services offered by the underlying computer network.

It is a qualitative and quantitative process that measures and defines the performance level of a given network. It guides a network administrator in the review, measure and improvement of network services.

Network performance is primarily measured from an end-user perspective (i.e. quality of network services delivered to the user). Broadly, network performance is measured by reviewing the statistics and metrics from the following network components:

- Network bandwidth or capacity - Available data transfer
- Network throughput - Amount of data successfully transferred over the network in a given time
- Network delay, latency and jittering - Any network issue causing packet transfer to be slower than usual
- Data loss and network errors - Packets dropped or lost in transmission and delivery.

Factors that Impact Network Performance

A network's limitations are critical areas of concern when performing capacity and performance management. These limitations primarily include the following:

- Errors: Network errors can generally be categorized into problems with queuing, latency, and jitter. The data queue can affect network performance in several ways. For example, larger queues increase the wait time, while smaller queues increase the probability of dropped data.
- Speed: Pipe size is the amount of data the network can send simultaneously on a single connection. It's often confused with connection speed, although pipe size doesn't actually affect the speed at which data travels between nodes. While

hardware capabilities determine the maximum bandwidth that is theoretically available, software mechanisms typically allocate a lower bandwidth for each network service.

- Memory: Memory is a computing resource that has requirements in both the data and control planes. The performance of the entire network can degrade when control plane processes fail, as is the case when routing convergence requires additional memory.

- Distance: Distance can have a dramatic impact on network performance, especially when the applications haven't been optimized. The maximum speed at which data can be forwarded is the speed of light, which is 186,000 miles per second or 186 miles per millisecond. This packet forwarding delay becomes significant when an enterprise is running an international client/server application.

- Central Processing Unit (CPU): A node's central processing unit (CPU) is typically used by both the control and data planes. Capacity and performance management requires a network and its nodes to have insufficient processing capability at all times. A single node with an inadequate CPU can impact the entire network due to the high degree of interdependence between the nodes in the modern network. Insufficient processing can also increase latency if a node's CPU is unable to keep up with network traffic.

- Applications: Applications can also affect a network's capacity and performance, with issues such as the amount of data the application is able to transmit compared to what it needs to transmit. This factor is especially critical for the performance of Wide Area Networks (WANs). Additional application characteristics that affect capacity and performance include application keep-alives and window sizes.

- Input/Output (I/O): Input/Output (I/O) capability on a network is also known as the network's back plane and is usually measured in terms of bus size. An inadequate back plane can cause the network to drop packets, thus increasing the network traffic due to retransmitted data.

Management of a network's availability, capacity, and performance is therefore crucial for achieving an organization's business objectives.

Measuring Network Performance

When troubleshooting network degradation or outage, measuring network performance is critical to determining when the network is slow and what is the root cause (e.g., saturation, bandwidth outage, misconfiguration, network device defect, etc.).

Whatever the approach you take to the problem (traffic capture with network analyzers like Wireshark, SNMP polling with tools such as PRTG or Cacti or generating traffic and active testing with tools such as SmokePing or simple ping or traceroute to track network response times), you need indicators: these are usually called metrics and are aimed at producing tangible figures when measuring network performance.

Measuring Network Performance: UDP

UDP throughput is not Impacted By Latency

UDP is a protocol used to carry data over IP networks. One of the principles of UDP is that we assume that all packets sent are received by the other party (or such kind of controls is executed at a different layer, for example by the application itself).

In theory or for some specific protocols (where no control is undertaken at a different layer; e.g., one-way transmissions), the rate at which packets can be sent by the sender is not impacted by the time required to deliver the packets to the other party (= latency). Whatever that time is, the sender will send a given number of packets per second, which depends on other factors (application, operating system, resources,).

Measuring Networks Performance: TCP

TCP is Directly Impacted by Latency

TCP is a more complex protocol as it integrates a mechanism, which checks that all packets are correctly delivered. This mechanism is called acknowledgment: it consists of having the receiver transmit a specific packet or flag to the sender to confirm the proper reception of a packet.

TCP Congestion Window

For efficiency purposes, not all packets will be acknowledged one by one; the sender does not wait for each acknowledgment before sending new packets. Indeed, the number of packets that may be sent before receiving the corresponding acknowledgement packet is managed by a value called TCP congestion window.

Impacts of TCP Congestion Window on Throughput

If we make the hypothesis that no packet gets lost; the sender will send the first quota of packets (corresponding to the TCP congestion window) and when it will receive the acknowledgment packet, it will increase the TCP congestion window; progressively the number of packets that can be sent in a given period of time will increase (throughput). The delay before acknowledgment packets are received (= latency) will have an impact on how fast the TCP congestion window increases (hence the throughput).

When latency is high, it means that the sender spends more time idle (not sending any new packets), which reduces how fast throughput grows.

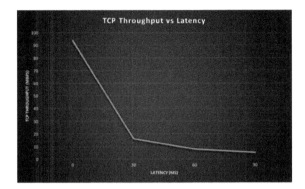

Round trip latency	TCP throughput
0ms	93.5 Mbps
30ms	16.2 Mbps
60ms	8.07 Mbps
90ms	5.32 Mbps

TCP is Impacted by Retransmission and Packet Loss

Handling of Missing Acknowledgment Packets by TCP Congestion

The TCP congestion window mechanism deals with missing acknowledgment packets as follows: if an acknowledgement packet is missing after a period of time, the packet is considered as lost and the TCP congestion window is reduced by half (hence the throughput too – which corresponds to the perception of limited capacity on the route by the sender); the TCP congestion window size can then restart increasing if acknowledgment packets are received properly.

Packet loss will have two effects on the speed of transmission of data:

- Packets will need to be retransmitted (even if only the acknowledgment packet got lost and the packets got delivered)
- The TCP congestion window size will not permit an optimal throughput.

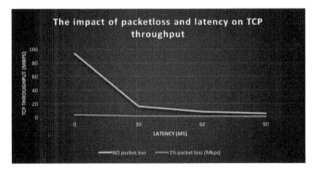

With 2% packet loss, TCP throughput is between 6 and 25 times lower than with no packet loss.

Round trip latency	TCP throughput with no packet loss	TCP throughput with 2% packet loss
0 ms	93.5 Mbps	3.72 Mbps
30 ms	16.2 Mbps	1.63 Mbps
60 ms	8.7 Mbps	1.33 Mbps
90 ms	5.32 Mbps	0.85 Mbps

This will apply irrespective of the reason for losing acknowledgment packets (i.e., genuine congestion, server issue, packet shaping.

Network Performance Baseline

In the simplest terms, a network performance baseline is a set of metrics used in network performance monitoring to define the normal working conditions of an enterprise network infrastructure. Engineers use network performance baselines for comparison to catch changes in traffic that could indicate a problem.

Setting a network baseline also provides early indicators that application and network demands are pushing near the available capacity, giving the networking team the opportunity to plan for upgrades. Aligning network performance baselines with existing network service-level agreements (SLAs) can help the IT organization stay within capacity parameters and identify problem areas that are falling out of compliance.

The network monitoring challenge for engineers, however, is to define what is normal for their organization's infrastructure.

No Industry Standard for Network Monitoring or Metrics

For IT organizations that have adopted the Information Technology Infrastructure Library (ITIL) framework for best practices, there are ITIL-specific monitoring tools available. These tools are designed to take advantage of the device configuration databases and applications built to support the IT service management process. Beyond ITIL, however, there is not an industry standard approach to setting performance baselines. Support for monitoring tools and the breadth and depth of information made available can vary greatly among manufacturers, devices and operating systems, ultimately preventing a common set of metrics from being used in monitoring.

A good first place to start might be the networking vendors themselves. Every vendor has, at minimum, a list of the monitors a given device supports. Given the ubiquity of monitoring protocols such as SNMP, many vendors also have their own recommendation or best practices for monitoring and defining thresholds for their products. Armed with this information, administrators can initially focus on a narrow subset of available monitors and grow as needed. Cisco, for example, recommends not exceeding 60% of CPU utilization on its routers and has published an SNMP message to monitor that statistic.

Network Performance Monitoring: Taking Stock and Considering Virtualization

While building up your inventory of network devices to monitor, be sure to include both physical and virtual devices on your list. With the current trends in appliance and server virtualization, virtual switches (vSwitches) and virtualized application accelerators are important considerations when looking at network performance. Serving as network ports within the environment, vSwitches enable virtual machines to communicate with each other without having to traverse physical network adapters. While vSwitches speed inter-server communication, they don't enable a network monitoring tool to report these paths or receive application performance data. Fortunately, the networking industry has recognized the problem and is working to improve the situation, either with more intelligent vSwitches or through virtual server standards such as Virtual Ethernet Port Aggregator (VEPA), which would enable exposure of virtualized network traffic to traditional network monitoring tools.

Collecting Data to Set a Network Performance Baseline

After taking inventory of network devices, the next phase is analyzing the traffic running across the infrastructure. While an overall network utilization is a reasonable indicator of the overall health of the network, that single metric provides no context for what the users are actually doing on the network. In order to gain insight into how the network is being used, monitoring tools must collect and open actual packets of data.

There are two approaches to collecting network data for traffic analysis, each with its own pluses and minuses. Data capture or sniffing tools capture the entire stream of network data, giving administrators a full view of what is moving around the network at a given moment in time. Sniffing the network offers a complete view of what is going on. While this is vital for network forensic analysis and troubleshooting, it might be overkill for ongoing network monitoring and baseline analysis. For network performance monitoring, the metrics of application and network utilization are key, not necessarily the information within the individual packets. In these situations, network sniffing tools could provide the required information, but would do so with significant overhead.

Get Samples with Sflow/NetFlow Monitoring

Alternatively, protocols such as NetFlow or sFlow are designed to be less storage intensive by capturing traffic at assigned intervals. Built into many enterprise routers, NetFlow and variants can pass along sampled data to a monitor without the overhead of sniffers, providing a reasonable overview of which applications are running across the network. By performing packet analysis, administrators can see trends in application usage and assign a percentage of utilization for each application against total network usage.

Digging in deeper, most tools can also help parse out Internet traffic, separating, for example, use of cloud-based applications from general Web browsing. Knowing how much of the network each application consumes not only identifies the source of response time problems, but also enables administrators to see the impact of new applications and services as they are deployed on their networks.

Duration of Monitoring to Set a Network Performance Baseline

With all of the desired monitors in place, the next step is to let the monitors run and build up data points. Many experts cite seven days as an effective monitoring window to allow performance trends to appear.

It is important to consider the context of when the traffic was captured. Cyclical usage patterns exist in most organizations and any traffic analysis should be sensitive to those patterns. A large retailer, for example, would no doubt see network and application use spike during the holiday season. A manufacturer might actually see the opposite effect with plant shutdowns significantly lowering network utilization during the same holiday period. If the analyst does not account for these business cycles, network performance baseline results could vary widely in either direction.

Any significantly high or low spikes in the numbers must be identified and a determination must be made as to why they occurred and if they are indeed part of the network norm. If you see occasional spikes because of an identified problem, build the baseline on the remaining data points. If the spikes are identified as a common occurrence, include them in the average for the metric. It's also possible that the network experienced a significant problem during your monitoring cycle. In that case, it would be safer to toss those data points and rerun the metrics after the situation has been addressed.

When a reasonable amount of monitoring data has been collected and radical shifts have been accounted for, a baseline for each of the metrics can be assigned. The ultimate result is determining the typical range of values for each of your defined monitors. The combined set of ranges is the current network performance baseline.

The final point to consider is that the network performance baselines you set today are only good until something changes. Network equipment upgrades, new servers and new applications will have an impact on today's baselines and will require some care and feeding of the monitoring solution on an ongoing basis. The good news, however, is that in most cases, not everything changes at once, so a few tweaks can be made as applications, services or devices are added or removed.

Network Performance Management

Network performance management is vital to assuring mission-critical business service availability and performance. Any disruption can negatively impact productivity, customer satisfaction and ultimately revenue. IT teams are challenged to respond to triggers - often in the form of a user complaint that "the network is slow" then quickly identify the source of the problem in a complex service and network environment. Optimizing performance has become an imperative in the face of ongoing digital transformation, with initiatives that include data center consolidation, virtualization, migration to Cloud-based services, and evolution to sophisticated voice and collaboration services.

The performance management system includes the following features: consolidated monitoring, monitoring in real time, with the Accounting stream protocols Netflow/ sFlow, Measurement of service level protocols with ALS and AAS.

Consolidated Monitoring

Consolidated monitoring consists of measuring an indicator regularly and presenting its changes over time in a concise and accurate report in the form of a graph suitable to the indicator represented. SmartReport uses the SNMP to collect the value of the performance indicators of each equipment.

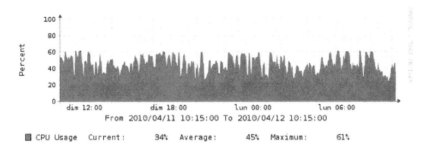

Equipment Models

SmartReport bases its operation on a system of equipment model. To each type of equipment, there is a monitoring model. A router is not supervised in the same way as a firewall. Similarly, a Cisco router is not supervised in the same way as a Juniper router.

The aim of the equipment model is to define what are the indicators to monitor and the reports to procude in order to provide immediatly a relevant and appropriate monitoring for each equipment, without any knowledge of the SNMP protocol, or of the MIB of the equipment to be supervised. Amongst the indicators available in the equipment model, we often find the most common indicators, published by almost all the manageable equipments (e.g. Bandwidth used on the network interface, CPU load) as well as the specific indicators typical of the role of each device (e.g. use of buffers on a router, packages dropper on a firewall, requests served on a Web server, et).

The equipment models also provide information about the SNMP Traps in order to be able to recognize and interpret traps emitted by equipment.

Real Time Monitoring

For some indicators (traffic, CPU, temperature, RMON) SmartReport can allow a re-al-time monitoring. It presents the same information as the consolidated monitoring, but with much closer measures, the measurement step can decrease by at least 5 sec-onds. It is an excellent complement to the consolidated monitoring when it comes to making a diagnosis on a current problem.

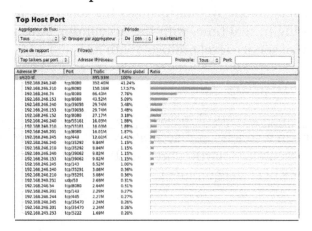

Unlike the consolidated monitoring, the measurements taken by real-time moni-toring are not recorded and consolidated in a database for exploration over a longer period.

The measures related to the real-time monitoring are carried out directly by the ad-ministrator's workstation, through a Java module loaded in the SmartReport interface. Note that a network access (SNMP) to the equipment is necessary from the supervisory position used for this feature and that all the indicators cannot be monitored in real time, including those requiring scripts on the appliance.

Flows Analysis and Netflow / Sflow Collector

SmartReport includes a Netflow and sFlow collector. Coupled with a powerful scanning and access-list engine, the xFlow collector provides vision on your network flows, with classification (TopTalkers, Top Protocols,) and graphs.

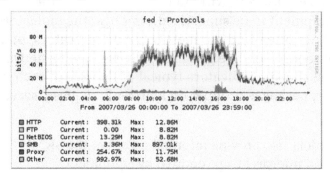

Regardless of how well the physical network is planned and managed, overall network performance will suffer if the applications that are hosted on the network, in the cloud, or in a hybrid of the two and transmit information are compromised. Examples of adverse application performance include erroneous execution, which can completely disable the application or cause the application to overwhelm servers or circuits, and inappropriate or unanticipated utilization, such as when personnel download large files or streaming video or when demand for access exceeds projections. Similarly, in a cloud or hybrid environment you can lose visibility and control of what's being transmitted and how - often resulting in a poor end-user experience.

Adverse conditions can arise due to planned or unanticipated events that drive change. For planned activities, IT can leverage the network performance baseline to simulate and test the effects of proposed modifications, such as the introduction of new users or applications, and determine if the current network architecture is adequate or requires reconfiguration or upgrade. When unexpected scenarios unfold, network performance monitoring tools can alert IT to deviations from the nominal baseline so corrective action can be initiated.

The goal of network performance monitoring tools is to provide a depiction of operations so potential problems can be proactively avoided, and anomalies that do occur can be detected, isolated, and resolved with a minimum mean-time-to-repair. Unfortunately, the network monitoring function is often siloed by geography, department, service, or network layer, which inhibits realizing the objective.

Key Considerations for a Network Performance Monitoring Tool

The ideal network performance monitoring tools are comprehensive. Network monitoring tools must have breadth, meaning that the network monitoring tools are scalable and robust enough to accommodate an end-to-end perspective across the enterprise, even for large organizations. Network performance monitoring tools also must possess depth, with the capability to span all seven layers of the network stack. Without both dimensions, IT is severely restricted in its efforts to identify the location of the problem, and to pinpoint if the root cause of the problem lies in an application, a system/server, or in a core network element such as a router or switch.

Perhaps more significantly, a comprehensive network performance monitoring tool promotes the resolution of more complex anomalies. Straightforward, linear degradations are often obvious, but intermittent issues are far more challenging to address. Likewise, while some problems may manifest themselves on the network, the source of the trouble may reside outside the enterprise's domain – with a service provider. These types of anomalies simply cannot be brought to closure quickly by point solutions.

Superior network performance can be attained thanks to network management and monitoring tools, but only if the tools account for the following key considerations:

- Horizontal breadth (the software has an end-to-end purview throughout the enterprise).

- Vertical depth (the software traverses all seven layers of the network to incorporate application, server, and network performance data).

- Real-time and back-in-time views (the software can display and assess current and historical information to find the root cause of problems that arise intermittently).

- Comprehensive interfaces (the software offers a centralized repository from all data sources so IT can leverage easy-to-understand charts, graphs, and reports to speed accurate problem resolution).

Network Capacity

In the context of networks, capacity is the complex measurement of the maximum amount of data that may be transferred between network locations over a link or network path. Because of the amount of intertwined measurement variables and scenarios, actual network capacity is rarely accurate.

Capacity is also known as throughput.

Capacity depends on the following variables, which are never constant:

- Network engineering

- Subscriber services

- Rate at which handsets enter and leave a covered cell site area.

Wireless carriers are pushed to increase network capacity to accommodate user demand for high-bandwidth services. Until recently, subscribers used wireless networks to make calls or send Short Message Service (SMS)/Multimedia Message Service (MMS) messages. Today, capacity is required to handle increased subscribers and additional services, including:

- Web browsing

- Facebook updates

- Digital file downloads, like e-books

- Streaming audio/video

- Online multiplayer games.

Because of marginal network capacity costs, providers focus on offering packaged and a la carte services, such as location-based add-ons and products, like ring tones, to create additional revenue with negligible operational expense effect.

When monitoring performance in modern businesses, network capacity now offers more important information than bandwidth, which used to be a primary network metric. Path-based metrics like capacity are more indicative of actual user experience. That's essential for organizations today in their near-universal quest to improve end-user experience.

Reasons for Measuring Bandwidth

Enterprise IT teams purchase bandwidth in either single or redundant connections from an ISP. Every business needs sufficient bandwidth to get internal network traffic to the myriad SaaS apps and cloud platforms available and in use today. Measuring bandwidth is relatively easy: Flood the network for a short burst of time to fill it with traffic, and identify the maximum allowed bandwidth between source and destination.

However, networks aren't static. Traffic traversing any meaningful distance will hit multiple routers and, more often than not, multiple ISPs. Flooding any of those networks won't give accurate results if the provider rate-limits the traffic due to the spike. Additionally, ISP networks are often load-balanced, so the observed bandwidth from flooding will be one particular route of many routes that will likely change over time. The bandwidth also depends on the physical infrastructure, the cross-traffic within the ISP and the ISP peering relationships as your data is being transmitted.

Ways to use Capacity Metrics Wisely

Capacity is an end-to-end metric, limited by the most congested hop along the application delivery path. There are two things to know about capacity: First, it's dynamic. It's affected by both what infrastructure the packets traverse and the other traffic in the pipe. Second, capacity is not going to be equal to bandwidth. With the increase in physical distance between employees and their apps (think Workday) there are more logical steps, and physical devices, in between the traffic source and traffic destination.

The bandwidth offered by ISPs is typically a theoretical maximum that you'll never physically achieve on the network. You can come close, but there will always be a certain amount of bandwidth that can't be used. Flooding techniques can tell you what that achievable maximum is, but only at a single point in time. However, capacity monitoring allows you to identify the achievable space on the network continuously.

Measuring capacity can reduce knee-jerk bandwidth purchases, since bandwidth sometimes gets blamed when it's actually a capacity problem. Improving capacity can result in a reduced MTTR when troubleshooting user issues. And, historical capacity data can help uncover network issues that bandwidth can't, and help IT identify future needs.

Network Capacity Planning

Today's network managers have to balance two conflicting demands: the desire for increased speed of response and optimal end user performance, and the need to reduce operational costs. Traffic – business or otherwise – tends to expand to fill the available network bandwidth capacity, degrading performance across the most congested links. Network managers cannot simply throw bandwidth at the network capacity problem, but have to demonstrate that a link is experiencing congestion for a significant amount of time due to legitimate business usage before they can add additional network capacity. Break away from the traditional approach to capacity planning by understanding the new principles for effective network capacity planning.

Reasons for Effective Network Capacity Planning is Becoming Critical

In any distributed organization, the cost of network connectivity is always difficult to quantify. Traffic on the network tends to expand to fill the available bandwidth, whether or not that traffic is crucial to the business. Usage of business-critical applications is also difficult to measure. It may be within expected parameters for 90% of the time, but no business wants to experience degraded performance for the remaining 10%.

Network performance requirements put constant pressure on IT to increase network capacity in order to provide an effective service to the business, while cost management requires that this is limited, or even reduced. So, how can an IT organization manage these conflicting pressures?

Technical challenges with network capacity planning:

- To identify a link that requires additional bandwidth capacity, you must demonstrate that it is experiencing congestion for a significant amount of time.

- It can be costly, time-consuming (sometimes, depending on the tools used, even impossible) to correctly represent congestion over long time periods.

- Congestion must be caused by legitimate business usage, not recreational or rogue usage ("other" traffic): bandwidth spending is the final resort, removing "other" traffic from the network comes as a much earlier option.

Common Approaches to Network Capacity Planning

- Long-range views of average utilization: this will show a long-term trend of utilization, but the long-term view will average out those spikes of high utilization, thus hiding the problem.

- Peak utilization, e.g. showing the busiest minute for each day in a month: This shows what days had a busy minute, but doesn't give insight into the amount of time during which time a link is congested.

- Traffic totals: easy to show all links on a single view, showing the links with most traffic and even periodic trends to show month-by-month usage. However, it does not give any indication of congestion except in extreme cases.

Network Delay

In general terms Network delay is the time needed for a signal to traverse a network. The extent of the delay caused by the network may be effectively constant, but in most cases it is variable. If the variable delay can be guaranteed not to exceed some predetermined value, then the network has a bounded delay. In other cases the delay is not bounded but can grow without limit, although with a decreasing probability of a longer delay.

In a circuit switching network the only significant delay arises from the finite speed with which the signals propagate along the transmission medium. For electrical signals on a conducting wire, electromagnetic waves in free space, or light signals in an optical fiber, this speed is of the same order as the speed of light, 300 000 km per second, and the network delay in a circuit-switched system is of the order of 3–5 microseconds per km. There may also be delays arising from the finite time needed by amplifiers or repeaters to pass a signal from their input to output; these delays are again in the order of microseconds. The delay in a signal crossing the Atlantic (5000 km) is of the order of 25 milliseconds, and for a signal routed via a geostationary satellite (total round trip of 80 000 km) it is of the order of 400 milliseconds.

In a packet switching network the situation is more complex. The time needed to traverse the network is normally measured as the period between the sender indicating that the transmission is to start, and the delivery of the last bit of the packet to the destination. This time is the sum of times needed to traverse each sector of the network, and contains a number of different contributions. If the data source is not capable of generating a network packet directly, it will need to be connected to a PAD that will assemble the data into packets; devices that can generate their own packets will not require a PAD. It may well be that although a PAD is not present as a separate component; it is still there conceptually, where for example a (human) user is using a PC or workstation to connect to a remote system. Once packets have been generated, each packet will move between successive pairs of network nodes until it reaches the destination. Each sector has contributions from:

a) The transit time along the medium connecting the two nodes;

b) The time needed to disassemble the outgoing packet into its component bits at the transmitting node (necessarily identical with the time needed to reassemble the incoming packet at the receiving node);

c) The time needed by the switching process within the receiving node to determine the route the outgoing packet is to follow, and carry out the switching.

The first of these is essentially similar to the transit time in a circuit-switched network, and has a similar value of say 3–5 microseconds per km. The second is essentially equal to the packet size multiplied by the inter-bit time on the transmission line. The third is a function of the organization of the switching nodes, of their processing speeds, and of the extent to which the switching must be delayed until the information needed to allow switching to start is determined by the internal structure of the packet. The use of cell relay systems, in which switching can start before the entire packet has been received, allows this time to be reduced.

A heavily loaded system will have queues (lines) of packets in each node, leading to a further complication. The queue may either be of outgoing packets awaiting the attention of the switching process to determine on which onward connection they should be transmitted, or of packets that have been rerouted to an onward connection that is already active, requiring the packet to wait until those ahead of it have been transmitted.

In networks using only terrestrial links, the total network delay is typically dominated by packet assembly times, (b) above. This is not the case where satellite links are used, especially where geostationary satellites are involved.

Network Quality of Service

Quality of Service (QoS) refers to the capability of a network to provide better service to selected network traffic over various technologies, including Frame Relay, Asynchronous Transfer Mode (ATM), Ethernet and 802.1 networks, SONET, and IP-routed networks that may use any or all of these underlying technologies. The primary goal of QoS is to provide priority including dedicated bandwidth, controlled jitter and latency (required by some real-time and interactive traffic), and improved loss characteristics. Also important is making sure that providing priority for one or more flows does not make other flows fail. QoS technologies provide the elemental building blocks that will be used for future business applications in campus, WAN, and service provider networks.

Important Flow Characteristics of the QoS

Reliability

If a packet gets lost or acknowledgement is not received (at sender), the re-transmission of data will be needed. This decreases the reliability.

The importance of the reliability can differ according to the application.

For Example:

E- mail and file transfer need to have a reliable transmission as compared to that of an audio conferencing.

Delay

Delay of a message from source to destination is a very important characteristic. However, delay can be tolerated differently by the different applications.

For Example:

The time delay cannot be tolerated in audio conferencing (needs a minimum time delay), while the time delay in the e-mail or file transfer has less importance.

Jitter

The jitter is the variation in the packet delay.

If the difference between delays is large, then it is called as high jitter. On the contrary, if the difference between delays is small, it is known as low jitter.

For Example:

Case 1: If 3 packets are sent at times 0, 1, 2 and received at 10, 11, 12. Here, the delay is same for all packets and it is acceptable for the telephonic conversation.

Case 2: If 3 packets 0, 1, 2 are sent and received at 31, 34, 39, so the delay is different for all packets. In this case, the time delay is not acceptable for the telephonic conversation.

Bandwidth

Different applications need the different bandwidth.

For Example:

Video conferencing needs more bandwidth in comparison to that of sending an e-mail.

Integrated Services and Differentiated Service

These two models are designed to provide quality of service (qos) in the network.

Integrated Services(IntServ)

Integrated service is flow-based QoS model and designed for IP.

In integrated services, user needs to create a flow in the network, from source to destination and needs to inform all routers (every router in the system implements IntServ) of the resource requirement.

Following are the steps to understand how integrated services works.

- Resource Reservation Protocol (RSVP)

  An IP is connectionless, datagram, packet-switching protocol. To implement a flow-based model, a signaling protocol is used to run over IP, which provides the signaling mechanism to make reservation (every applications need assurance to make reservation), this protocol is called as RSVP.

- Flow Specification

  While making reservation, resource needs to define the flow specification. The flow specification has two parts:

  ◦ Resource Specification

  It defines the resources that the flow needs to reserve. For example: Buffer, bandwidth, etc.

  ◦ Traffic Specification

  It defines the traffic categorization of the flow.

- Admit or Deny

  After receiving the flow specification from an application, the router decides to admit or deny the service and the decision can be taken based on the previous commitments of the router and current availability of the resource.

Classification of Services

The two classes of services to define integrated services are:

a) Guaranteed Service Class

This service guarantees that the packets arrive within a specific delivery time and not discarded, if the traffic flow maintains the traffic specification boundary.

This type of service is designed for real time traffic, which needs a guaranty of minimum end to end delay.

For example: Audio conferencing.

b) Controlled Load Service Class

This type of service is designed for the applications, which can accept some delays, but are sensitive to overload network and to the possibility to lose packets.

For example: E-mail or file transfer.

Problems with Integrated Services

The two problems with the Integrated services are:

i) Scalability

In Integrated Services, it is necessary for each router to keep information of each flow. But, this is not always possible due to growing network.

ii) Service-type Limitation

The integrated services model provides only two types of services, guaranteed and control-load.

Differentiated Services (DS or Diffserv)

DS is a computer networking model, which is designed to achieve the scalability by managing the network traffic.

DS is a class based QoS model specially designed for IP.

DS was designed by IETF (Internet Engineering Task Force) to handle the problems of Integrated Services.

The solutions to handle the problems of Integrated Services are explained below.

Scalability

The main processing unit can be moved from central place to the edge of the network to achieve the scalability. The router does not need to store the information about the flows and the applications (or the hosts) define the type of services they want every time while sending the packets.

Service Type Limitation

The routers, route the packets on the basis of class of services define in the packet and not by the flow. This method is applied by defining the classes based on the requirement of the applications.

References

- Network-performance-30022: techopedia.com, Retrieved 24 April 2018

- 7-factors-that-can-impact-your-network-performance: annese.com, Retrieved 19 June 2018

- Measuring-network-performance-latency-throughput-packet-loss: performancevision.com, Retrieved 26 May 2018

- How-to-set-a-network-performance-baseline-for-network-monitoring: searchnetworking.techtarget.com, Retrieved 19 July 2018

- Network-performance-management: netscout.com, Retrieved 10 June 2018

- Capacity-network-18179: techopedia.com, Retrieved 31 March 2018

- Network-capacity-vs-bandwidth-dont-waste-it-budget: appneta.com, Retrieved 12 April 2018

- Quality-of-service-qos-in-computer-network, computer-network: tutorialride.com, Retrieved 20 June 2018

4

Network Address

In a telecommunication network, a network address is the identifier for a host or a node. It is a unique identifier across the network. This chapter has been carefully written to provide an extensive understanding of network address through the elucidation of topics such as IP address, virtual IP address, private IP address, unicast address, etc.

A network address is any logical or physical address that uniquely distinguishes a network node or device over a computer or telecommunications network. It is a numeric/symbolic number or address that is assigned to any device that seeks access to or is part of a network.

A network address is a key networking technology component that facilitates identifying a network node/device and reaching a device over a network. It has several forms, including the Internet Protocol (IP) address, media access control (MAC) address and host address.

Computers on a network use a network address to identify, locate and address other computers. Besides individual devices, a network address is typically unique for each interface; for example, a computer's Wi-Fi and local area network (LAN) card has separate network addresses.

A network address is also known as the numerical network part of an IP address. This is used to distinguish a network that has its own hosts and addresses. For example, in the IP address 192.168.1.0, the network address is 192.168.1.

A network address always points to host / node / server or it can represent a whole network. Network address is always configured on network interface card and is generally mapped by system with the MAC address (hardware address or layer-2 address) of the machine for Layer-2 communication.

There are different kinds of network addresses in existence:

- IP
- IPX
- AppleTalk

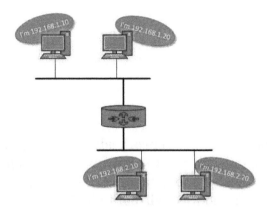

IP addressing provides mechanism to differentiate between hosts and network. Because IP addresses are assigned in hierarchical manner, a host always resides under a specific network.The host which needs to communicate outside its subnet, needs to know destination network address, where the packet/data is to be sent.

Hosts in different subnet need a mechanism to locate each other. This task can be done by DNS. DNS is a server which provides Layer-3 address of remote host mapped with its domain name or FQDN. When a host acquires the Layer-3 Address (IP Address) of the remote host, it forwards all its packet to its gateway. A gateway is a router equipped with all the information which leads to route packets to the destination host.

Routers take help of routing tables, which has the following information:

- Method to reach the network

Routers upon receiving a forwarding request, forwards packet to its next hop (adjacent router) towards the destination.

The next router on the path follows the same thing and eventually the data packet reaches its destination.

Network address can be of one of the following:

- Unicast (destined to one host)

- Multicast (destined to group)

- Broadcast (destined to all)

- Anycast (destined to nearest one)

A router never forwards broadcast traffic by default. Multicast traffic uses special treatment as it is most a video stream or audio with highest priority. Anycast is just similar to unicast, except that the packets are delivered to the nearest destination when multiple destinations are available.

IP Address

An IP address (internet protocol address) is a numerical representation that uniquely identifies a specific interface on the network.

Addresses in IPv4 are 32-bits long. This allows for a maximum of 4,294,967,296 (2^{32}) unique addresses. Addresses in IPv6 are 128-bits, which allows for 3.4 x 10^{38} (2^{128}) unique addresses.

The total usable address pool of both versions is reduced by various reserved addresses and other considerations.

IP addresses are binary numbers but are typically expressed in decimal form (IPv4) or hexadecimal form (IPv6) to make reading and using them easier for humans.

IP stands for Internet Protocol and describes a set of standards and requirements for creating and transmitting data packets, or datagrams, across networks. The Internet Protocol (IP) is part of the Internet layer of the Internet protocol suite. In the OSI model, IP would be considered part of the network layer. IP is traditionally used in conjunction with a higher-level protocol, most notably TCP. The IP standard is governed by RFC 791.

Working of IP

IP is designed to work over a dynamic network. This means that IP must work without a central directory or monitor, and that it cannot rely upon specific links or nodes existing. IP is a connectionless protocol that is datagram-oriented., so each packet must contain the source IP address , destination IP address, and other data in the header to be successfully delivered.

Combined, these factors make IP an unreliable, best effort delivery protocol. Error correction is handled by upper level protocols instead. These protocols include TCP, which is a connection-oriented protocol, and UDP, which is a connectionless protocol.

Most internet traffic is TCP/IP.

Checking your IP

Checking your IP address is easy to do.

- If you use Windows — Run a search on your computer for CMD. Once the command box is open, type "ipconfig" and hit enter.

- If you use a Mac — Go to Applications > Utilities > Terminal. Once you're in Terminal, type "ipconfig" and hit enter.

Subnet Masks

A single IP address identifies both a network, and a unique interface on that network. A subnet mask can also be written in dotted decimal notation and determines where the network part of an IP address ends, and the host portion of the address begins.

When expressed in binary, any bit set to one means the corresponding bit in the IP address is part of the network address. All the bits set to zero mark the corresponding bits in the IP address as part of the host address.

The bits marking the subnet mask must be consecutive on es. Most subnet masks start with 255. and continue on until the network mask ends. A Class C subnet mask would be 255.255.255.0.

IP Address Classes

Class	Lead-ing bits	Size of network numberbit field	Size of rest bit field	Number of networks	Addresses per network	Total addresses in class	Start address	End address
Class A	0	8	24	128 (2^7)	16,777,216 (2^{24})	2,147,483,648 (2^{31})	0.0.0.0	127.255.255.255
Class B	10	16	16	16,384 (2^{14})	65,536 (2^{16})	1,073,741,824 (2^{30})	128.0.0.0	191.255.255.255
Class C	110	24	8	2,097,152 (2^{21})	256 (2^8)	536,870,912 (2^{29})	192.0.0.0	223.255.255.255
Class D (multicast)	1110	not defined	not defined	not defined	not defined	268,435,456 (2^{28})	224.0.0.0	239.255.255.255
Class E (reserved)	1111	not defined	not defined	not defined	not defined	268,435,456 (2^{28})	240.0.0.0	255.255.255.255

Before variable length subnet masks allowed networks of any size to be configured, the IPv4 address space was broken into five classes.Before variable length subnet masks allowed networks of any size to be configured, the IPv4 address space was broken into five classes.

Class A

In a Class A network, the first eight bits, or the first dotted decimal, is the network part of the address, with the remaining part of the address being the host part of the address. There are 128 possible Class A networks.

0.0.0.0 to 127.0.0.0

However, any address that begins with 127. is considered a loopback address.

Example for a Class A IP address:

2.134.213.2

Class B

In a Class B network, the first 16 bits are the network part of the address. All Class B networks have their first bit set to 1 and the second bit set to 0. In dotted decimal notation, that makes 128.0.0.0 to 191.255.0.0 as Class B networks. There are 16,384 possible Class B networks.

Example for a Class B IP address:

135.58.24.17

Class C

In a Class C network, the first two bits are set to 1, and the third bit is set to 0. That makes the first 24 bits of the address the network address and the remainder as the host address. Class C network addresses range from 192.0.0.0 to 223.255.255.0. There are over 2 million possible Class C networks.

Example for a Class C IP address:

192.168.178.1

Class D

Class D addresses are used for multicasting applications. Unlike the previous classes, the Class D is not used for "normal" networking operations. Class D addresses have their first three bits set to "1" and their fourth bit set to "0". Class D addresses are 32-bit network addresses, meaning that all the values within the range of 224.0.0.0 – 239.255.255.255 are used to uniquely identify multicast groups. There are no host addresses within the Class D address space, since all the hosts within a group share the group's IP address for receiver purposes.

Example for a Class D IP address:

227.21.6.173

Class E

Class E networks are defined by having the first four network address bits as 1. That encompasses addresses from 240.0.0.0 to 255.255.255.255. While this class is reserved, its usage was never defined. As a result, most network implementations discard these addresses as illegal or undefined. The exception is 255.255.255.255, which is used as a broadcast address.

Example for a Class D IP address:

243.164.89.28

IP Address Classes and Bit-wise Representations

Class A

    0. 0. 0. 0 = 00000000.00000000.00000000.00000000

127.255.255.255 = 01111111.11111111.11111111.11111111

            0nnnnnnn.HHHHHHHH.HHHHHHHH.HHHHHHHH

Class B

128. 0. 0. 0 = 10000000.00000000.00000000.00000000

191.255.255.255 = 10111111.11111111.11111111.11111111

            10nnnnnn.nnnnnnnn.HHHHHHHH.HHHHHHHH

Class C

192. 0. 0. 0 = 11000000.00000000.00000000.00000000

223.255.255.255 = 11011111.11111111.11111111.11111111

            110nnnnn.nnnnnnnn.nnnnnnnn.HHHHHHHH

Class D

224. 0. 0. 0 = 11100000.00000000.00000000.00000000

239.255.255.255 = 11101111.11111111.11111111.11111111

            1110XXXX.XXXXXXXX.XXXXXXXX.XXXXXXXX

Class E

240. 0. 0. 0 = 11110000.00000000.00000000.00000000

255.255.255.255 = 11111111.11111111.11111111.11111111

            1111XXXX.XXXXXXXX.XXXXXXXX.XXXXXXXX

Private Addresses

Within the address space, certain networks are reserved for private networks. Packets from these networks are not routed across the public internet. This provides a way for private networks to use internal IP addresses without interfering with other networks. The private networks are,

10.0.0.1 - 10.255.255.255

172.16.0.0 - 172.32.255.255

192.168.0.0 - 192.168.255.255

Special Addresses

Certain IPv4 addresses are set aside for specific uses:

127.0.0.0   Loopback address (the host's own interface)

224.0.0.0   IP Multicast

255.255.255.255   Broadcast (sent to all interfaces on network)

There are two versions of IP in use today, IPv4 and IPv6.

IPv4 Address

IPv4 addresses are 32-bit numbers that are typically displayed in dotted decimal notation. A 32-bit address contains two primary parts: the network prefix and the host number.

All hosts within a single network share the same network address. Each host also has an address that uniquely identifies it. Depending on the scope of the network and the type of device, the address is either globally or locally unique. Devices that are visible to users outside the network (webservers, for example) must have a globally unique IP address. Devices that are visible only within the network must have locally unique IP addresses.

IP addresses are assigned by a central numbering authority called the Internet Assigned Numbers Authority (IANA). IANA ensures that addresses are globally unique where needed and has a large address space reserved for use by devices not visible outside their own networks.

IPv4 Classful Addressing

To provide flexibility in the number of addresses distributed to networks of different sizes, 4-octet (32-bit) IP addresses were originally divided into three different categories or classes: class A, class B, and class C. Each address class specifies a different number of bits for its network prefix and host number:

- Class A addresses use only the first byte (octet) to specify the network prefix, leaving 3 bytes to define individual host numbers.

- Class B addresses use the first 2 bytes to specify the network prefix, leaving 2 bytes to define host addresses.

- Class C addresses use the first 3 bytes to specify the network prefix, leaving only the last byte to identify hosts.

In binary format, with an x representing each bit in the host number, the three address classes can be represented as follows:

00000000 xxxxxxxx xxxxxxxx xxxxxxxx (Class A)

00000000 00000000 xxxxxxxx xxxxxxxx (Class B)

00000000 00000000 00000000 xxxxxxxx (Class C)

Because each bit (x) in a host number can have a 0 or 1 value, each represents a power of 2. For example, if only 3 bits are available for specifying the host number, only the following host numbers are possible:

111 110 101 100 011 010 001 000

In each IP address class, the number of host-number bits raised to the power of 2 indicates how many host numbers can be created for a particular network prefix. Class A addresses have 2^{24} (or 16,777,216) possible host numbers, class B addresses have 2^{16} (or 65,536) host numbers, and class C addresses have 2^{8} (or 256) possible host numbers.

IPv4 Dotted Decimal Notation

The 32-bit IPv4 addresses are most often expressed in dotted decimal notation, in which each octet (or byte) is treated as a separate number. Within an octet, the rightmost bit represents 2^{0} (or 1), increasing to the left until the first bit in the octet is 2^{7} (or 128). Following are IP addresses in binary format and their dotted decimal equivalents:

11010000 01100010 11000000 10101010 = 208.98.192.170

01110110 00001111 11110000 01010101 = 118.15.240.85

00110011 11001100 00111100 00111011 = 51.204.60.59

IPv4 Subnetting

Because of the physical and architectural limitations on the size of networks, you often must break large networks into smaller subnetworks. Within a network, each wire or ring requires its own network number and identifying subnet address.

Figure shows two subnets in a network.

Figure: shows three devices connected to one subnet and three more devices connected to a second subnet. Collectively, the six devices and two subnets make up the larger network. In this example, the network is assigned the network prefix 192.14.0.0, a class B address. Each device has an IP address that falls within this network prefix

In addition to sharing a network prefix (the first two octets), the devices on each subnet share a third octet. The third octet identifies the subnet. All devices on a subnet must have the same subnet address. In this case, the alpha subnet has the IP address 192.14.126.0 and the beta subnet has the IP address 192.14.17.0.

The subnet address 192.14.17.0 can be represented as follows in binary notation:

11000000 . 00001110 . 00010001 . xxxxxxxx

Because the first 24 bits in the 32-bit address identify the subnet, the last 8 bits are not significant. To indicate the subnet, the address is written as 192.14.17.0/24 (or just 192.14.17/24). The /24 is the subnet mask (sometimes shown as 255.255.255.0).

IPv4 Variable-length Subnet Masks

Traditionally, subnets were divided by address class. Subnets had either 8, 16, or 24 significant bits, corresponding to 2^{24}, 2^{16}, or 2^{8} possible hosts. As a result, an entire /16 subnet had to be allocated for a network that required only 400 addresses, wasting 65,136 ($2^{16} - 400 = 65,136$) addresses.

To help allocate address spaces more efficiently, variable-length subnet masks (VLSMs) were introduced. Using VLSM, network architects can allocate more precisely the number of addresses required for a particular subnet.

For example, suppose a network with the prefix 192.14.17/24 is divided into two smaller subnets, one consisting of 18 devices and the other of 46 devices.

To accommodate 18 devices, the first subnet must have 2^{5} (32) host numbers. Having 5 bits assigned to the host number leaves 27 bits of the 32-bit address for the subnet. The IP address of the first subnet is therefore 192.14.17.128/27, or the following in binary notation:

11000000 . 00001110 . 00010001 . 100xxxxx

The subnet mask includes 27 significant digits.

To create the second subnet of 46 devices, the network must accommodate 26 (64) host numbers. The IP address of the second subnet is 192.14.17.64/26, or

11000000 . 00001110 . 00010001 . 01xxxxxx

By assigning address bits within the larger/24 subnet mask, you create two smaller subnets that use the allocated address space more efficiently.

IPv6 Address

An IPv6 address is made of 128 bits divided into eight 16-bits blocks. Each block is then converted into 4-digit Hexadecimal numbers separated by colon symbols.

For example, given below is a 128 bit IPv6 address represented in binary format and divided into eight 16-bits blocks:

0010000000000001 0000000000000000 0011001000111000 1101111111100001 0000000001100011 0000000000000000 0000000000000000 1111111011111011

Each block is then converted into Hexadecimal and separated by ':' symbol:

2001:0000:3238:DFE1:0063:0000:0000:FEFB

Even after converting into Hexadecimal format, IPv6 address remains long. IPv6 provides some rules to shorten the address. The rules are as follows:

- Rule.1: Discard leading Zero(es):

  In Block 5, 0063, the leading two 0s can be omitted, such as (5th block):

  2001:0000:3238:DFE1:63:0000:0000:FEFB

- Rule.2: If two of more blocks contain consecutive zeroes, omit them all and replace with double colon sign ::, such as (6th and 7th block):

  2001:0000:3238:DFE1:63::FEFB

  Consecutive blocks of zeroes can be replaced only once by :: so if there are still blocks of zeroes in the address, they can be shrunk down to a single zero, such as (2nd block):

  2001:0:3238:DFE1:63::FEFB

Interface ID

IPv6 has three different types of Unicast Address scheme. The second half of the address (last 64 bits) is always used for Interface ID. The MAC address of a system is composed of 48-bits and represented in Hexadecimal. MAC addresses are considered to be uniquely assigned worldwide. Interface ID takes advantage of this uniqueness of MAC addresses. A host can auto-configure its Interface ID by using IEEE's Extended Unique Identifier (EUI-64) format. First, a host divides its own MAC address into two 24-bits halves. Then 16-bit Hex value 0xFFFE is sandwiched into those two halves of MAC address, resulting in EUI-64 Interface ID.

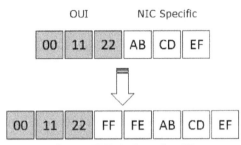

Figure: EUI-64 Interface ID

Conversion of EUI-64 ID into IPv6 Interface Identifier

To convert EUI-64 ID into IPv6 Interface Identifier, the most significant 7th bit of EUI-64 ID is complemented. For example:

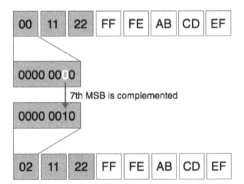

Global Unicast Address

This address type is equivalent to IPv4's public address. Global Unicast addresses in IPv6 are globally identifiable and uniquely addressable.

This address type is equivalent to IPv4's public address. Global Unicast addresses in IPv6 are globally identifiable and uniquely addressable.

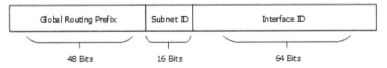

Figure: Global Unicast Address

Global Routing Prefix: The most significant 48-bits are designated as Global Routing Prefix which is assigned to specific autonomous system. The three most significant bits of Global Routing Prefix is always set to 001.

Link-local Address

Auto-configured IPv6 address is known as Link-Local address. This address always starts with FE80. The first 16 bits of link-local address is always set to 1111 1110 1000 0000 (FE80). The next 48-bits are set to 0, thus:

1111 1110 1000 0000 0000 0000 0000 0000 0000 0000 0000 0000 0000 0000 0000 0000	Interface ID

Figure: Link-local address

Link-local addresses are used for communication among IPv6 hosts on a link (broadcast segment) only. These addresses are not routable, so a Router never forwards these addresses outside the link.

Unique-local Address

This type of IPv6 address is globally unique, but it should be used in local communication. The second half of this address contain Interface ID and the first half is divided among Prefix, Local Bit, Global ID and Subnet ID.

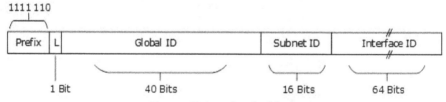

Figure: Unique-local address

Prefix is always set to 1111 110. L bit, is set to 1 if the address is locally assigned. So far, the meaning of L bit to 0 is not defined. Therefore, Unique Local IPv6 address always starts with 'FD'.

Scope of IPv6 Unicast Addresses

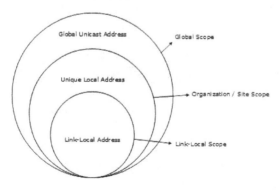

The scope of Link-local address is limited to the segment. Unique Local Address are locally global, but are not routed over the Internet, limiting their scope to an organization's boundary. Global Unicast addresses are globally unique and recognizable. They shall make the essence of Internet v2 addressing.

Special Addresses in IPV6

- ::/96 The zero prefix denotes addresses that are compatible with the previously used IPv4 protocol.

- ::/128 An IPv6 address with all zeroes in it is referred to as an unspecified address and is used for addressing purposes within a software.

- ::1/128 This is called the loop back address and is used to refer to the local host. An application sending a packet to this address will get the packet back after it is looped back by the IPv6 stack. The local host address in the IPv4 was 127.0.0.1.2001:db8::/32 This is a documentation prefix allowed in the IPv6. All the examples of IPv6 addresses should ideally use this prefix to indicate that it is an example.

- fec0::/10 This is a site-local prefix offered by IPv6. This address prefix signifies that the address is valid only within the local organization. Subsequently, the usage of this prefix has been discouraged by the RFC.

- fc00::/7 This is called the Unique Local Address (ULA). These addresses are routed only within a set of cooperating sites. These were introduced in the IPv6 to replace the site-local addresses. These addresses also provide a 40-bit pseudorandom number that reduces the risk of address conflicts.

- ff00::/8 This prefix is offered by IPv6 to denote the multicast addresses. Any address carrying this prefix is automatically understood to be a multicast address.

- fe80::/10 This is a link-local prefix offered by IPv6. This address prefix signifies that the address is valid only in the local physical link.

Examples of IPv6 Addresses

Example of Full and Collapsed IPv6 Address

Here is an example of a full IPv6 address:

FE80:0000:0000:0000:0202:B3FF:FE1E:8329

It shows a 128-bit address in eight 16-bit blocks in the format global:subnet:interface.

Here is an example of a collapsed IPv6 address:

FE80::0202:B3FF:FE1E:8329

The :: (consecutive colons) notation can be used to represent four successive 16-bit blocks that contain zeros. When SAS software encounters a collapsed IP address, it reconstitutes the address to the required 128-bit address in eight 16-bit blocks.

Example of an IPv6 Address that Includes a Port Number

Here is an example of an IP address that contains a port number:

[2001:db8:0:1]:80

The brackets are necessary only if also specifying a port number. Brackets are used to separate the address from the port number. If no port number is used, the brackets can be omitted.

As an alternative, the block that contains a zero can be collapsed. Here is an example:

[2001:db8::1]:80

Example of an IPv6 Address that Includes a URL

Here is an example of an IP address that contains a URL:

http://[2001:db8:0:1]:80

The http:// prefix specifies a URL. The brackets are necessary only if also specifying a port number. Brackets are used to separate the address from the port number. If no port number is used, the brackets can be omitted.

Transition From IPv4 to IPv6

Transition Requirements

The transition does not require any global coordination. Your sites and Internet service provider (ISP) can transition at their own pace. Furthermore, an effort has been made to minimize the number of dependencies during the transition. For instance, the transition does not require that routers be upgraded to IPv6 prior to upgrading hosts.

Different sites have different constraints during the transition process. Also, early adopters of IPv6 are likely to have different concerns than production users of IPv6. RFC 1933 defines the transition tools currently available. The rationale for transition is either the lack of IPv4 address space or the required use of new features in IPv6, or both. The IPv6 specification requires 100 per cent compatibility for the existing protocols. Compatibility is also required for existing applications during the transition.

- IPv4-only node – A host or router that implements only IPv4. An IPv4-only node does not understand IPv6. The installed base of IPv4 hosts and routers that exist before the transition begins are IPv4-only nodes.

- IPv6/IPv4 node – A host or router that implements both IPv4 and IPv6, which is also known as dual-stack.

- IPv6-only node – A host or router that implements IPv6, and does not implement IPv4.

- IPv6 node – Any host or router that implements IPv6. IPv6/IPv4 and IPv6-only nodes are both IPv6 nodes.

- IPv4 node – Any host or router that implements IPv4. IPv6/IPv4 and IPv4-only nodes are both IPv4 nodes.

- 6to4 router – Any boundary router that is configured with a 6to4 pseudo-interface on its IPv4 network connection. A 6to4 router serves as an endpoint of a 6to4 tunnel, over which the router forwards packets to another IPv6 site.

- 6to4 host – Any IPv6 host with an interface that is configured with a 6to4–derived address.

- Site – Piece of the private topology of the Internet that does not carry transit traffic for anybody and everybody. The site can span a large geographic area. For instance, the private network on a multinational corporation is one site.

Standardized Transition Tools

RFC 1933 defines the following transition mechanisms:

- When you upgrade your hosts and routers to IPv6, the hosts and routers retain their IPv4 capability. Consequently, IPv6 provides compatibility for all IPv4 protocols and applications. These hosts and routers are known as dual-stack.

- These hosts and routers use the name service, for example, DNS, to carry information about which nodes are IPv6 capable.

- IPv6 address formats can contain IPv4 addresses.

- You can tunnel IPv6 packets in IPv4 packets as a method of crossing routers that have not been upgraded to IPv6.

Implementing Dual-stack

The term dual-stack normally refers to a complete duplication of all levels in the protocol stack from applications to the network layer. An example of complete duplication is the OSI and TCP/IP protocols that run on the same system. However, in the context of IPv6 transition, dual-stack means a protocol stack that contains both IPv4 and IPv6.

The remainder of the stack is identical. Consequently, the same transport protocols, TCP, UDP, and so on, can run over both IPv4 and IPv6. Also, the same applications can run over both IPv4 and IPv6.

The following figure illustrates dual-stack protocols through the OSI layers.

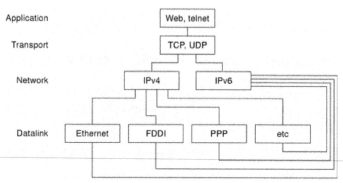

Figure: Dual-Stack Protocols

In the dual-stack method, subsets of both hosts and routers are upgraded to support IPv6, in addition to IPv4. The dual-stack approach ensures that the upgraded nodes can always interoperate with IPv4-only nodes by using IPv4.

Configuring Name Services

A dual node must determine if the peer can support IPv6 or IPv4 in order to check which IP version to use when transmitting. The control of the information that goes in the name service enables a dual node to determine which IP version to use. You define an IPv4 node's IP address and the IPv6 node's IP address in the name service. Thus, a dual node has both addresses in the name service.

The presence of an IPv6 address in the name service also signifies that the node is reachable by using IPv6. However, the node is only reachable by nodes that obtain information from that name service. For example, placing an IPv6 address in NIS implies that the IPv6 host is reachable by using IPv6. However, the IPv6 host is only reachable by IPv6 and dual nodes that belong to that NIS domain. The placement of an IPv6 address in global DNS requires that the node is reachable from the Internet IPv6 backbone. This situation is no different than in IPv4. For example, the mail delivery operation requires that IPv4 addresses exist for nodes that can be reached by using IPv4. The same situation is true for the HTTP proxy operation. When no reachability exists in IPv4, for instance, because of firewalls, the name service must be partitioned into an inside firewall and outside firewall database. Consequently, the IPv4 addresses are visible only where the IPv4 addresses are reachable.

The protocol that is used to access the name service is independent of the type of address that can be retrieved from the name service. This name service support, and dual-stacks, enables a dual node to use IPv4 when the dual node communicates with IPv4-only nodes. Also, this name service support enables a dual node to use IPv6 when the dual node communicates with IPv6 nodes. However, the destination must be reachable through an IPv6 route.

Using IPv4-compatible Address Formats

In many instances, you can represent a 32-bit IPv4 address as a 128-bit IPv6 address. The transition mechanism defines the following two formats.

- Pv4–compatible address

000 ... 000	IPv4 Address

- IPv4–mapped address

000 ... 000	0xffff	IPv4 Address

The compatible format is used to represent an IPv6 node. This format enables you to configure an IPv6 node to use IPv6 without having a real IPv6 address. This address format enables you to experiment with different IPv6 deployments because you can use automatic tunneling to cross IPv4–only routers. However, you cannot configure these addresses by using the IPv6 stateless address autoconfiguration mechanism. This mechanism requires existing IPv4 mechanisms such as DHCPv4 or static configuration files.

The mapped address format is used to represent an IPv4 node. The only currently defined use of this address format is part of the socket API. An application can have a common address format for both IPv6 addresses and IPv4 addresses. The common address format can represent an IPv4 address as a 128-bit mapped address. However, IPv4–to-IPv6 protocol translators also allow these addresses to be used.

Tunneling Mechanism

To minimize any dependencies during the transition, all the routers in the path between two IPv6 nodes do not need to support IPv6. This mechanism is called tunneling. Basically, IPv6 packets are placed inside IPv4 packets, which are routed through the IPv4 routers. The following figure illustrates the tunneling mechanism through IPv4 routers (R).

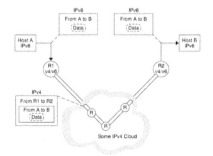

Figure: Tunneling Mechanism

The different uses of tunneling in the transition follow:

- Configured tunnels between two routers, as in the previous figure

- Automatic tunnels that terminate at the dual hosts.

A configured tunnel is currently used in the Internet for other purposes, for example, the MBONE, the IPv4 multicast backbone. Operationally, the tunnel consists of two routers that are configured to have a virtual point-to-point link between the two routers over the IPv4 network. This kind of tunnel is likely to be used on some parts of the Internet for the foreseeable future.

Automatic Tunnels

Automatic tunnels require IPv4–compatible addresses. Automatic tunnels can be used to connect IPv6 nodes when IPv6 routers are not available. These tunnels can originate either on a dual host or on a dual router by configuring an automatic tunneling network interface. The tunnels always terminate on the dual host. These tunnels work by dynamically determining the destination IPv4 address, the endpoint of the tunnel, by extracting the address from the IPv4–compatible destination address.

Interaction with Applications

Even on a node that has been upgraded to IPv6, the use of IPv6 is dependent on the applications. An application might not use a networking API that asks the name service for IPv6 addresses. The application might use an API, such as sockets, which requires changes in the application. Also, the provider of the API, such as an implementation of the java.net class might not support IPv6 addresses. In either situation, the node only sends and receives IPv4 packets like an IPv4 node would.

The following names have become standard terminology within the Internet community:

- IPv6–unaware—This application cannot handle IPv6 addresses. This application cannot communicate with nodes that do not have an IPv4 address.

- IPv6–aware—This application can communicate with nodes that do not have an IPv4 address, that is, the application can handle the larger IPv6 addresses. In some situations, the address might be transparent to the application, for example, when the API hides the content and format of the actual address.

- IPv6–enabled—This application can, in addition to being IPv6–aware, can use some IPv6–specific feature such as flow labels. The enabled applications can still operate over IPv4, though in a degraded mode.

- IPv6–required—This application requires some IPv6–specific feature. This application cannot operate over IPv4.

IPv4 and IPv6 Interoperability

During the gradual transition phase from IPv4 to IPv6, existing IPv4 applications must continue to work with newer IPv6–enabled applications. Initially, vendors provide host and router platforms that are running a dual-stack. A dual-stack is both an IPv4 protocol stack and an IPv6 protocol stack. IPv4 applications continue to run on a dual– stack that is also IPv6 enabled with at least one IPv6 interface. No changes need to be made to these applications, no porting required.

IPv6 applications that run on a dual-stack can also use the IPv4 protocol. IPv6 applications use an IPv4-mapped IPv6 address. Because of the design of IPv6, separate applications, IPv4 and IPv6, are not needed. For example, you do not need an IPv4 client on a dual host to "talk" with a server on an IPv4-only host. Also, you do not need a separate IPv6 client to talk with an IPv6 server. You need only to port their IPv4 client application to the new IPv6 API. The client can communicate with IPv4–only servers. The client can also communicate with IPv6 servers that run on either a dual host or an IPv6–only host.

The address that the client receives from the name server determines if IPv6 or IPv4 is used. For example, if the name server has an IPv6 address for a server, then the server runs IPv6.

The following table summarizes the interoperability between IPv4 and IPv6 clients and servers. The table assumes that the dual-stack host has both an IPv4 and IPv6 address in the respective name service database.

Table: Client-Server Applications: IPv4 and IPv6 Interoperability

Type of Application (Type of Node)	IPv6-Unaware Server (IPv4-Only Node)	IPv6-Unaware Server (IPv6-Enabled Node)	IPv6-Aware Server (IPv6-Only Node)	IPv6-Aware Server (IPv6-Enabled Node)
IPv6-unaware client (IPv4-only node)	IPv4	IPv4	X	IPv4
IPv6-unaware client (IPv6-enabled node)	IPv4	IPv4	X	IPv4
IPv6-aware client (IPv6-only node)	X	X	IPv6	IPv6
IPv6-aware client (IPv6-enabled node)	IPv4	(IPv4)	IPv6	IPv6

X means that the server cannot communicate with the client.

(IPv4) denotes that the interoperability depends on the address that is chosen by the client. If the client chooses an IPv6 address, the client fails. However, an IPv4 address that is returned to the client as an IPv4–mapped IPv6 address causes an IPv4 datagram to be sent successfully.

In the first phase of IPv6 deployment, most implementations of IPv6 are on dual-stack nodes. Initially, most vendors do not release IPv6–only implementations.

Site Transition Scenarios

Each site and each ISP requires different steps during the transition phase. This part provides some examples of site transition scenarios.

The first step to transition a site to IPv6 is to upgrade the name services to support IPv6 addresses. For DNS, upgrade to a DNS server that supports the new AAAA (quad-A), such as BIND 4.9.4 and later. Two new NIS maps and a new NIS+ table have been introduced for storing IPv6 addresses. The new NIS maps and new NIS+ table can be created and administered on any Solaris system. .

After the name service is able to distribute IPv6 addresses, you can start transitioning hosts. You can transition hosts in the following ways:

- Upgrade one host at a time. Use IPv4–compatible addresses and automatic tunneling. No routers need to be upgraded. Use this method for initial experimental transition. This method offers only a subset of the IPv6 benefits. This method does not offer stateless address autoconfiguration or IP multicast. You can use this scenario to verify that applications work over IPv6. This scenario also verifies that the application can use IPv6 IP-layer security.

- Upgrade one subnet at a time. Use configured tunnels between the routers. In this scenario, at least one router per subnet is upgraded to dual. The dual routers in the site are tied together by using configured tunnels. Then, hosts on those subnets can use all the IPv6 features. As more routers become upgraded in this incremental scheme, you can remove the configured tunnels.

- Upgrade all the routers to dual before any host is upgraded. Though this method appears orderly, the method does not provide any IPv6 benefits until all the routers have been upgraded. This scenario constrains the incremental deployment approach.

6to4 as a Transition Mechanism

The Solaris operating system includes 6to4 as a preferred interim method for making the transition from IPv4 to IPv6 addressing. 6to4 enables isolated IPv6 sites to communicate across an automatic tunnel over an IPv4 network that does not support IPv6. To use 6to4 tunnels, you must configure a boundary router on your IPv6 network as one endpoint of the 6to4 automatic tunnel. Thereafter, the 6to4 router can participate in a tunnel to another 6to4 site, or, if required, to a native IPv6, non-6to4 site.

This part is concerned with the following 6to4 subjects:

- Topology of the 6to4 tunnel

- 6to4 addressing, including the format of the advertisement

- Description of packet flow across a 6to4 tunnel

- Topology of a tunnel between a 6to4 router and 6to4 relay router

- Points to consider before you configure 6to4 relay router support.

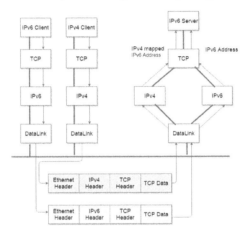

Participants in a 6to4 Tunnel

The following figure shows a 6to4 tunnel between two 6to4 sites.

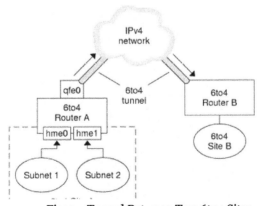

Figure: Tunnel Between Two 6to4 Sites

The figure depicts two isolated 6to4 networks, Site A and Site B. Each site has configured a router with an external connection to an IPv4 network. In the figure, a 6to4 tunnel across the IPv4 network connects the 6to4 sites.

Before an IPv6 site can become a 6to4 site, you must configure at least one router inter-face for 6to4 support. This interface must provide the external connection to the IPv4 network. The address that you configure on qfe0 must be globally unique. In the previ-ous figure, boundary Router A's interface qfe0 connects Site A to the IPv4 network. In-terface qfe0 must already be configured with an IPv4 address before you can configure qfe0 as a 6to4 pseudo-interface.

In the figure, 6to4 Site A is composed of two subnets, which are connected to interfaces hme0 and hme1 on Router A. All IPv6 hosts on either subnet of Site A automatically re-configure with 6to4–derived addresses on receipt of the advertisement from Router A.

Site B is the opposite endpoint of the tunnel from Site A. To correctly receive traffic from Site A, a boundary router on Site B must be configured for 6to4 support. Other-wise, packets that the router receives from Site A are not recognized and dropped.

6to4-Derived Addressing

As with native IPv6 routers, you must advertise the subnet prefixes derived from the site 6to4 prefix in /etc/inet/ndpd.conf. The next figure shows the parts of a prefix for a 6to4 site.

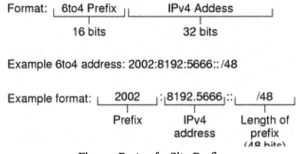

Figure: Parts of a Site Prefix

The next figure shows the parts of a subnet prefix for a 6to4 site, such as you would include in the ndpd.conf file.

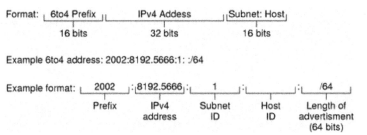

Figure: Parts of a Subnet Prefix

6to4 Prefix Format

The format line in the previous figure contains the following parts.

Part	Length	Definition
Prefix	16 bits	6to4 prefix 2002 (0x2002).
IPv4 ad-dress	32 bits	Unique IPv4 address that is already configured on the 6to4 interface. For the advertisement, you specify the hexadecimal representation of the IPv4 address, rather than the IPv4 dotted–decimal representation.
Subnet ID	16 bits	Subnet ID, which must be a value that is unique for the link at your 6to4 site.

6to4 Advertisement Example

The example in the previous figure has the following values.

Advertisement Part	Corresponding Value
6to4 prefix	2002
IPv4 address	8192:56bb, which corresponds to IPv4 address 129.146.87.188
Subnet ID	1
/64	Length of prefix

6to4-Derived Addressing on a Host

When an IPv6 host receives the 6to4–derived prefix by way of a router advertisement, the host automatically reconfigures a 6to4–derived address on an interface. The address has the following form.

prefix:IPv4 address:subnet ID:host ID/64

The results of ifconfig –a on a host with a 6to4 interface might resemble the following:

qfe1:3: flags=2180841<UP,RUNNING,MULTICAST,ADDRCONF,ROUTER,IPv6>

 mtu 1500 index 7

net6 2002:8192:56bb:9258:a00:20ff:fea9:4521/64

The 6to4–derived address follows inet6 in the output from ifconfig.

Address Part	Corresponding Value
Prefix	2002, which is the 6to4 prefix
IPv4 value	8192:56bb, which is the IPv4 address, in hexadecimal notation, for the 6to4 pseudo-interface that is configured on the 6to4 router

Address Part	Corresponding Value
subnet ID	9258, which is the address of the subnet of which this host is a member
MAC address	a00:20ff:fea9:4521, which is the link layer address of the host interface that is now configured for 6to4

Packet Flow through the 6to4 Tunnel

This part describes the path of packets from a host at one 6to4 site to a host in a remote 6to4 site. The next scenario uses the topology that is shown in figures below as its example. Moreover, the scenario assumes that the 6to4 routers and 6to4 hosts are already configured.

1. A host on Subnet 1 of 6to4 Site A sends a transmission, with a host at 6to4 Site B as the destination. Each packet header in the flow has a source 6to4–derived address and destination 6to4– derived address.

2. 6to4 Router A receives the outgoing packets and creates a tunnel over an IPv4 network to 6to4 Site B.

3. Site A's router encapsulates each 6to4 packet into an IPv4 header. Then the router uses standard IPv4 routing procedures to forward the packet over the IPv4 network.

4. Any IPv4 routers that the packets encounter use the packets' destination IPv4 address for forwarding. This address is the globally unique IPv4 address of the interface on Router B, which also serves as the 6to4 pseudo-interface.

5. Packets from Site A arrive at Router B, which decapsulates the IPv6 packets from the IPv4 header.

6. Router B then uses the destination address in the IPv6 packet to forward the packets to the recipient host at Site B.

Considerations for Tunnels to a 6to4 Relay Router

6to4 relay routers function as endpoints for tunnels from 6to4 routers that need to communicate with native IPv6, non-6to4 networks. Relay routers are essentially bridges between the 6to4 site and native IPv6 sites. Because this solution is very insecure, by default the Solaris operating system does not enable 6to4 relay router support. However, if your site requires such a tunnel, you use the 6to4relay command to enable the following tunneling scenario.

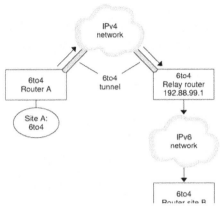

Figure: Tunnel From a 6to4 Site to a 6to4 Relay Router

In the above figures, 6to4 Site A needs to communicate with a node at native IPv6 Site B. The figure shows the path of traffic from Site A onto a 6to4 tunnel over an IPv4 network. The tunnel has 6to4 Router A and a 6to4 relay router as its endpoints. Beyond the 6to4 relay router is the IPv6 network, to which IPv6 Site B is connected.

Packet flow between a 6to4 Site and Native IPv6 Site

This part describes the flow of packets from a 6to4 site to a native IPv6 site. The text uses the scenario that is shown in figures below 4–6 as an example.

1. A host on 6to4 Site A sends a transmission that specifies as the destination a host at native IPv6 Site B. Each packet header in the flow has a 6to4–derived address as its source address. The destination address is a standard IPv6 address.

2. 6to4 Router A receives the outgoing packets and creates a tunnel over an IPv4 network to a 6to4 relay router. 6to4 relay routers that are part of the 6to4 relay router anycast group have the address 192.88.99.1. This anycast address is the default address for 6to4 relay routers. If you need to use a specific 6to4 relay router, you can override the default and specify that router's IPv4 address.

3. Site A's 6to4 router encapsulates each packet into a IPv4 header, which has the IPv4 address of the 6to4 relay router as its destination. The 6to4 router uses standard IPv4 routing procedures to forward the packet over the IPv4 network. Any IPv4 routers that the packets encounter forward the packets to the 6to4 relay router.

4. The physically closest anycast 6to4 relay router to Site A retrieves the packets that are destined for the 192.88.99.1 anycast group.

5. The relay router decapsulates the IPv4 header from the 6to4 packets, revealing the native IPv6 destination address.

6. The relay router then sends the now IPv6–only packets onto the IPv6 network, where the packets are ultimately retrieved by a router at Site B. The router then forwards the packets to the destination IPv6 node.

Security Issues for 6to4 Relay Router Support

By nature, a tunnel between a 6to4 router and 6to4 relay router is insecure. Security problems, such as the following, are inherent in such a tunnel.

- Though 6to4 relay routers do encapsulate and decapsulate packets, these routers do not check the data that is contained within the packets.

- Address spoofing is a major issue on tunnels to a 6to4 relay router. For incoming traffic, the 6to4 router is unable to match the IPv4 address of the relay router with the IPv6 address of the source. Therefore, the address of the IPv6 host can easily be spoofed. The address of the 6to4 relay router can also be spoofed.

- By default, no trust mechanism exists between 6to4 routers and 6to4 relay routers. Thus, a 6to4 router cannot identify whether the 6to4 relay router is to be trusted, or even a legitimate 6to4 relay router. A trust relationship between the 6to4 site and the IPv6 destination must exist, or the both sites leave themselves open to possible attacks.

These problems and other security issues that are inherent with 6to4 relay routers are explained in Internet Draft Security Considerations for 6to4. Generally, you should consider enabling support for 6to4 relay routers only for the following reasons:

- Your 6to4 site intends to communicate with a private, trusted IPv6 network. For example, you might enable 6to4 relay router support on a campus network that consists of isolated 6to4 sites and native IPv6 sites.

- Your 6to4 site has a compelling business reason to communicate with certain native IPv6 hosts.

- You have implemented the checks and trust models that are suggested in Internet Draft, Security Considerations for 6to4.

Known Issues with 6to4 Router

The following known bugs affect 6to4 configuration:

- 4709338 – Need a RIPng implementation which recognizes static routes

- 4152864 – Configuring two tunnels with the same tsrc/tdst pair works.

Implementing Static Routes at the 6to4 Site (BugID 4709338)

The following issue occurs on 6to4 sites with routers that are internal to the 6to4 boundary router. When you configure the 6to4 pseudo-interface, the static route 2002::/16 is automatically added to the routing table on the 6to4 router. Bug 4709338 describes a limitation in the Solaris RIPng routing protocol that prevents this static route from being advertised to the 6to4 site.

Either of the following work arounds are available for Bug 4709338.

- Add the 2002::/16 static route to the routing tables of all intra-site routers within the 6to4 site.

- Use a routing protocol other than RIPng on the 6to4 site's internal router.

Configuring Tunnels with the Same Source Address (BugID 4152864)

Bug ID 4152864 describes problems that occur when two tunnels are configured with the same tunnel source address, which is a serious issue for 6to4 tunnels.

Caution – Do not configure a 6to4 tunnel and an automatic tunnel with the same tunnel source address.

Other Transition Mechanisms

The mechanisms that were specified previously handle interoperability between dual nodes and IPv4 nodes, if the dual nodes have an IPv4 address. The mechanisms do not handle interoperability between IPv6-only nodes and IPv4-only nodes. Also, the mechanisms do not handle interoperability between dual nodes that have no IPv4 address and IPv4-only nodes. Most implementations can be made dual. However, a dual implementation requires enough IPv4 address space to assign one address for every node that needs to interoperate with IPv4-only nodes.

Several possibilities enable you to accomplish this interoperability without requiring any new transition mechanisms.

- Use application layer gateways (ALG) that sit at the boundary between the IPv6-only nodes and the remainder of the Internet. Examples of ALGs in use today are HTTP proxies and mail relays.

- Companies are already selling network address translators (NAT) boxes for IPv4. The NAT boxes translate between the private IP addresses, for example, network 10—see RFC 1918, on the inside and other IP addresses on the outside. These companies will likely upgrade their NAT boxes to also support IPv6–to–IPv4 address translation.

Unfortunately, both ALG and NAT solutions create single points of failure. By using these solutions, the Internet becomes less effective. The IETF is working on a better solution for IPv6-only interoperability with IPv4-only nodes. One proposal is to use header translators with a way to allocate IPv4–compatible addresses on demand. Another proposal is to allocate IPv4–compatible addresses on demand and use IPv4 in IPv6 tunneling to bridge the IPv6-only routers.

The stateless header translator translates between IPv4 and IPv6 header formats if the IPv6 addresses in use can be represented as IPv4 addresses. The addresses must be IPv4-compatible. Or, the addresses must be IPv4-mapped addresses. The support for these translators has been built into the IPv6 protocol. The translation can occur without any information loss, except for encrypted packets. Rarely used features such as source routing can produce information loss.

Virtual IP Address

A virtual IP address (VIPA) is an IP address assigned to multiple domain names or servers that share an IP address based on a single network interface card (NIC). VIPAs are allocated to virtual private servers, websites or any other application residing on a single server. The host server for these applications has a network IP address assigned by a network administrator, whereas the different server applications have VIPAs. VIPAs enhance network load balancing and redundancy.

VIPAs are primarily implemented for the following reasons:

- To consolidate resources through the allocation of one network interface per hosted application

- To improve redundancy by providing alternative failover options on one machine.

A server IP address depends on the Media Access Control (MAC) address of the attached NIC, and only one logical IP address may be assigned per card. However, VIP addressing enables hosting for several different applications and virtual appliances on a server with only one logical IP address. The VIPA is used for communication by all hosted applications - even though data packets are routed through actual network interfaces.

Several different application instances may be hosted with different VIPAs on the same server and easily switched for improved load balancing/performance and reduced latency.

VIPAs have several variations and implementation scenarios, including Common Address Redundancy Protocol (CARP) and Proxy Address Resolution Protocol (Proxy ARP).

Creating and Deleting Virtual IPs from a Batch/Shell Script

To create virtual IPs from a batch/shell script:

- Run CreateVIP.bat/sh file from <SimulatorHome>/bin/cmdline directory.

- Specify the starting IP address and the number of devices for which the virtual IPs must be created and click OK. The specified number of virtual ips will be created.

Syntax: CreateVIP.bat <Starting IP Address> <No. of IP Addresses to be created>

Example: CreateVIP.bat 192.168.1.1 100

To delete virtual IPs from a batch/shell script:

- Run DeleteVIP.bat/sh file from <SimulatorHome>/bin/cmdline directory.

- Specify the starting IP address and the number of virtual IPs to be deleted and click OK. The specified number of virtual ips will be deleted from the system.

Syntax: DeleteVIP.bat <Starting IP Address> <No. of IP Addresses to be deleted>

Example:DeleteVIP.bat 192.168.1.1 100.

Manual Configuration of Virtual IP address

Create the Virtual ip address for Windows 7:

The procedure to configure multiple virtual IP addresses in Windows 7 is given below. This procedure can be performed only by an user with admin privilege.

1. Start ---> ControlPanel --->Network and Internet -->Network Connections --> Local Area Connection

2. Right click the "Local Area Connection" and select the Properties Menu.

3. Select "Internet Protocol Version 4 (TCP/IPv4)" and click the "Properties".

4. Select the "Use the following IP address" radio button.

5. Enter the IpAddress and Subnet mask and click "OK" button.

6. Re-start the system for the changes to take effect.

Configuring Virtual IP Address in Windows NT

The procedure to configure multiple virtual IP addresses in Windows NT is given below. This procedure can be performed only by an user with admin privilege.

1. Click on the Start Menu on the Taskbar and choose Control Panel.

2. Double-click Network among the components displayed in the Control Panel. This opens up a Network dialog with 5 tabs.

3. Choose the Protocols tab and click on TCP / IP Protocol from listed protocols.

4. Click on Properties button when TCP / IP Protocol is selected.

5. This brings up the Microsoft TCP / IP properties dialog ; choose IP Address tab.

6. Click the Advanced button ; this will bring the Advanced IP addressing with the Adapter Name shown above the configured IP addresses in your system.

7. Click Add to display the TCP/ IP Address dialog. Specify IP Address and the corresponding Subnet Mask.

8. Re-start the system for the changes to take effect.

Configuring Virtual IP Address in Windows XP/2000/ ME/2003

The procedure to configure virtual IP addresses in bulk under Windows XP/2000/ME is given below. This procedure can be performed only by an user with admin privilege.

1. Click on the Start Menu and choose Settings.

2. Among the listed items select Network and Dial-up connections.

3. Select Local area connection from the items under Network and Dial-up connections ; this opens with the general information on Local area connection status.

4. Click on the Properties button. The Local area connection properties dialog opens listing all the protocols.

5. Choose Internet Protocol (TCP / IP) and click on the Properties button.

6. The Internet Protocol TCP / IP Properties dialog is invoked. Click on the Advanced button at the bottom of the dialog. The Advanced TCP / IP settings dialog displays all the configured IP addresses in your system.

7. Click Add button next to the displayed IP addresses to add an IP address with a corresponding sub-net mask.

8. You will have to re-start the system for the changes to take effect.

Configuring Virtual IP Address in Bulk under Windows 2000

The procedure to configure virtual IP addresses in bulk under Windows 2000 is given below. This procedure can be performed only by an user with admin privilege.

1. Select Start ->Run and type regedt32 in the run dialog (or you can type it on the DOS prompt) .

2. This will bring up the Registry Editor - HKEY_LOCAL_MACHINE on Local Machine screen.

3. Choose the HKEY_LOCAL_MACHINE on the tree displayed on the left hand side.

4. Choose the path : HKEY_LOCAL_MACHINE -> System -> CurrentControl-Set -> Services > NetBT -> Parameters -> Interfaces. Here, you will find a series of Tcpip_{labels} under Interfaces, an example is Tcpip_{2B34C0C3_FCA8_486C_8559_989429901786}

5. Select all the Tcpip_{labels} listed to check if the right hand side data content which has Netbios Options:REG_DWORD :0x1 and make a note of this Tcpip_{ label } .

6. Search for this label under HKEY_LOCAL_MACHINE ->System -> Current-ControlSet -> Services -> Tcpip -> Parameters -> Interfaces. Here, you will find the same Tcpip_{label} (that you had noted down in point 5). When you select this, the right side data content will display IP address and properties.

7. Double click on the IP address field . This opens a Multi-String editor where the virtual IP addresses you want have to be keyed in. You can cut and paste to minimise the time for large number of IPs .

8. When you have finished entering the IP addresses, select the subnetmask field (255.255.255.0) in the right hand side. This opens a Multi-String editor where the subnetmask you want have to be keyed in. Enter the same number of sub-netmasks(255.255.255.0) as the number of IPs.

9. You will have to re-start the system for the changes to take effect.

10. Now you should be able to ping these virtual IP addresses. Also, make sure that there are no conflicts in the network (i.e the virtual IP you have configured is not already being used by some other user).

Configuring Virtual IP Address in Windows in DHCP Mode

The procedure to configure virtual IP addresses in windows with DHCP mode is the same as Configuring Virtual IP Address in bulk under Windows 2000

Configuring Virtual IP Address in Linux

1. Invoke the linuxconf tool. (type linuxconf in the shell prompt and press Enter). For starting this tool you have to be logged in as Super user.

2. In the displayed menu, select the menu item : IP Aliases for virtual hosts and

press Enter. This will display the two interfaces eth0 and lo. (Ethernet interfaces in Linux are called by such names as eth0 and eth1)

3. Select eth0 and press Enter. This will show all the IP aliases configured for the selected interface.

4. In the field IP alias or range, enter the desired IP address or the range with a corresponding Netmask.

Example:

IP alias or range : 177.177.177.1-25

Netmask : 255.255.255.0

Note:

1. These commands have to be executed with the super user privilege.

2. You will have to re-start the system for the changes to take effect.

3. When you are configuring a large number of IP address, it might take a long time to boot up.

Using the following command, we can configure Virtual IPs in the Linux box at run-time without re-booting the machine or re-starting the network.

/sbin/ip addr add 172.19.1.2/32 dev eth0

/sbin/ip addr add 172.19.1.3/32 dev eth0

The same interfaces can be made down by using the following command.

/sbin/ip addr del 172.19.1.2/32 dev eth0

/sbin/ip addr del 172.19.1.3/32 dev eth0

Note:

1. These commands have to be executed with the super user privilege.

2. It can be used in versions up to 7.2

3. The configurations will not be available when you re-start your system.

Virtual IP Address Benefits

In spite of their simplicity, virtual IP addresses offer the following advantages over their physical counterparts:

- Improves availability. The virtual IP addresses are bound to virtual adapters instead of physical adapters. The host mask for the virtual adapter allows each cluster resource to have its own entry in the routing tables. The virtual IP addresses are resilient to physical interface failures because we know if a resource destination is reachable.

- Improves mobility. The virtual IP addresses are not tied to any IP address range of a physical network segment. A service can be moved between physical segments without the need to change the resource IP address.

- Simplifies name resolution. The association of cluster resource names to IP addresses can be maintained independently of the location of the cluster resource in the business continuity cluster.

These advantages exist because virtual IP addresses are purely virtual and are not bound to a physical network component.

High Availability

Each cluster node is running a routing protocol and is advertising its internal virtual IP network—which only it knows about and can reach—to other network nodes. The virtual IP addresses of the cluster resources are highly available because each resource has its own entry in the routing tables of the LAN routers. This allows you to know whether a destination is reachable. However, with secondary IP addresses, you know only whether there is a route to a segment.

The virtual IP address feature circumvents this problem by creating a virtual IP network different from any of the existing physical IP networks. As a result, any packet that is destined for the virtual IP address is forced to use a virtual link as its last hop link. Because it is purely virtual, this last hop link is always up. Also, because all other real links are forcibly made to act as intermediate links, their failures are easily worked around by the dynamic routing protocols.

Generally speaking, if a connection between two machines is established by using a virtual IP address as the end-point address at either end, the connection is resilient to physical adapter failures if the server has multiple adapters.

There are two important benefits that follow from the highly reachable nature of virtual IP addresses:

- A multi-homed server with a virtual IP address no longer needs to carry multiple DNS entries for its name in the naming system.

- If one of the subnets that a server interfaces to fails completely or is taken out of service for maintenance, the routing protocols can reroute the packets addressed to the virtual IP address through one of the other active subnets.

Unlimited Mobility

Unlike physical IP addresses which are limited in their mobility, virtual IP addresses are highly mobile. The degree of mobility is determined by the number of servers that an IP address on a specific server could be moved to. In other words, if
you choose a physical IP address as an IP address of a network resource, you are
limiting the set of potential servers to which this resource could be transparently
failed-over.

If you choose a virtual IP address, the set of servers that the resource could be transparently moved to is potentially unlimited. This is because of the nature of virtual IP
addresses; they are not bound to a physical wire and, as a result, carry their virtual
network to wherever they are moved. There is an implicit assumption here that the
location of a virtual IP address is advertised to the owning server through some routing
protocol. The ability to move an IP address across different machines becomes particularly important when it is required to transparently move (or fail over) a network
resource that is identified by an IP address (which could be a shared volume or a mission-critical service) to another server.

This unlimited mobility of virtual IP addresses is an advantage to network administrators, offering them more ease of manageability and greatly minimizing network
reorganization overhead. For network administrators, shuffling services between
different IP networks is the rule rather than the exception. The need often arises to
move a machine hosting a particular service to some other IP network, or to move a
service hosted on a particular machine to be rehosted on some other machine connected to a different IP network. If the service is hosted on a physical IP address,
accommodating these changes involves rehosting the service on a different IP address pulled out from the new network and appropriately changing the DNS entry
for the service to point to the new IP address. However, unless everyone accesses a
service via its DNS name instead of its IP address, an IP address change can break
the service for the IP address users. In contrast, if the service is hosted on a virtual
IP address, the necessity of changing the DNS entries for the service is eliminated,
and the service is not broken even for those who use the IP address instead of the
DNS name.

Automatic Name Resolution

In any network environment, one of the first obstacles is how clients locate and connect
to the services. A business continuity cluster can exacerbate this problem because services can migrate to nodes on a completely different network segment. Although there
are many potential solutions to this problem, such as DNS and SLP, none of them offers
the simplicity and elegance of virtual IP addresses. With virtual IP addresses, the IP address of the service can follow the service from node to node in a single cluster, as well
as from node to node in separate, distinct clusters. This makes the client reconnection

problem trivial; the client just waits for the new route information to be propagated to the routers on the network. No manual steps are required, such as modifying a DNS server.

Private IP Addresses

A private IP address is an IP address that's reserved for internal use behind a router or other Network Address Translation (NAT) device, apart from the public.

Private IP addresses are in contrast to public IP addresses, which are public and can not be used within a home or business network.

Sometimes a private IP address is also referred to as a local IP address.

Private IP Addresses

The Internet Assigned Numbers Authority (IANA) reserves the following IP address blocks for use as private IP addresses:

- 10.0.0.0 to 10.255.255.255

- 172.16.0.0 to 172.31.255.255

- 192.168.0.0 to 192.168.255.255

The first set of IP addresses from above allow for over 16 million addresses, the second for over 1 million, and over 65,000 for the last range.

Another range of private IP addresses is 169.254.0.0 to 169.254.255.255, but those addresses are for Automatic Private IP Addressing (APIPA) use only.

In 2012, the IANA allocated 4 million addresses of 100.64.0.0/10 for use in carrier-grade NAT environments.

Reasons for using Private IP Addresses

Instead of having devices inside a home or business network each use a public IP address, of which there's a limited supply, private IP addresses provide an entirely separate set of addresses that still allow access on a network but without taking up a public IP address space.

example, let's consider a standard router on a home network. Most routers in homes and businesses across the globe, probably yours and your next door neighbor's, all have the IP address of 192.168.1.1, and assign 192.168.1.2, 192.168.1.3, ... to the various devices that connect to it (via something called DHCP).

It doesn't matter how many routers use the 192.168.1.1 address, or how many dozens or hundreds of devices inside that network share IP addresses with users of other networks, because they aren't communicating with each other directly.

Instead, the devices in a network use the router to translate their requests through the public IP address, which can communicate with other public IP addresses and eventually to other local networks.

The hardware within a specific network that are using a private IP address can communicate with all the other hardware within the confines of that network, but will require a router to communicate with devices outside the network, after which the public IP address will be used for the communication.

For example, before landing on this page, your device (be it a computer, phone, or whatever), which uses a private IP address, requested this page through a router, which has a public IP address. Once the request was made and Lifewire responded to deliver the page, it was downloaded to your device through a public IP address before reaching your router, after which it got handed off to your private/local address to reach your device.

All the devices (laptops, desktops, phones, tablets, etc.) that are contained within private networks around the world can use a private IP address with virtually no limitation, which can't be said for public IP addresses.

Private IP addresses also provide a way for devices that don't need contact with the internet, like file servers, printers, etc., to still communicate with the other devices on a network without being directly exposed to the public.

Reserved IP Addresses

Another set of IP addresses that are restricted even further are called reserved IP addresses. These are similar to private IP addresses in the sense that they can't be used for communicating on the greater internet, but they're even more restrictive than that.

The most famous reserved IP is 127.0.0.1. This address is called the loopback address and is used to test the network adapter or integrated chip. No traffic addressed to 127.0.0.1 is sent over the local network or public internet.

Technically, the entire range from 127.0.0.0 to 127.255.255.255 is reserved for loopback purposes but you'll almost never see anything but 127.0.0.1 used in the real world.

Addresses in the range from 0.0.0.0 to 0.255.255.255 are also reserved but don't do anything at all. If you're even able to assign a device an IP address in this range, it will not function properly no matter where on the network it's installed.

Process to Find your Private IP Address

Knowing your private IP address is only helpful in specific, and for most people rare, situations.

If you want to connect one computer to another on your network, like with a mapped network drive, you can do so through its local IP address. You can also use a local IP address with remote desktop software to control a computer from afar. A private IP address is also needed when directing a specific network port from a router to a particular computer on the same network, a process called port forwarding.

Figure: Finding a Private IP Address With the 'ipconfig' Command (Windows 10)

The easiest way to find your private IP address in Windows is via Command Prompt with the ipconfig command.

When a device like a router is plugged in, it receives a public IP address from an ISP. It's the devices that are then connected to the router that are given private IP addresses.

As we mentioned above, private IP addresses can't communicate directly with a public IP address. This means if a device that has a private IP address is connected directly into the internet, and therefore becomes non-routable, the device will have no network connection until the address is translated into a working address through a NAT, or until the requests it's sending are sent through a device that does have a valid public IP address.

All traffic from the internet can interact with a router. This is true for everything from regular HTTP traffic to things like FTP and RDP. However, because private IP addresses are hidden behind a router, the router must know which IP address it should forward information to if you're wanting something like an FTP server to be set up on a home network.

For this to work properly for private IP addresses, you must set up port forwarding.

Forwarding one or more ports to a specific private IP address involves logging into the router to access its settings, and then choosing which port(s) to forward, and to where it should go.

Unicast Address

A unicast address is an address that identifies a unique node on a network. Unicast addressing is available in IPv4 and IPv6 and typically refers to a single sender or a single receiver, although it can be used in both sending and receiving.

A unicast address packet is transferred to a network node, which includes an interface address. The unicast address is then inserted into the destination's packet header, which is sent to the network device destination.

Unicast is the most common form of IP addressing.

A unicast address identifies a network device, such as a workstation or a server. A unicast address on a local area network (LAN) contains a subnet prefix and an interface ID.

A unicast address is used in the following instances:

- Unspecified Interface Address: A unicast address with a value of 0:0:0:0:0:0:0:0 is used in the absence of an unspecified interface address.

- Loopback Address: A unicast address with a value of 0:0:0:0:0:0:0:1 is used to specify a loopback address used to redirect the packets to their source.

IPv6 includes two different unicast address assignments:

- Global unicast address

- Link-local address

The type of unicast address is determined by the leftmost (high order) contiguous bits in the address, which contain the prefix.

The unicast address format is organized in the following hierarchy:

- Public topology

- Site (private) topology

- Interface ID

Global Unicast Address

The global unicast address is globally unique in the Internet. The example IPv6 address that is shown in Prefixes in IPv6 is a global unicast address. The next figure shows the scope of the global unicast address, as compared to the parts of the IPv6 address.

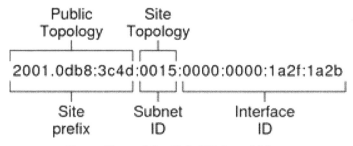

Figure: Parts of the Global Unicast Address

Public Topology

The site prefix defines the public topology of your network to a router. You obtain the site prefix for your enterprise from an ISP or Regional Internet Registry (RIR).

Site Topology and IPv6 Subnets

IN IPv6, the subnet ID defines an administrative subnet of the network and is up to 16 bits in length. You assign a subnet ID as part of IPv6 network configuration. The subnet prefix defines the site topology to a router by specifying the specific link to which the subnet has been assigned.

IPv6 subnets are conceptually the same as IPv4 subnets, in that each subnet is usually associated with a single hardware link. However, IPv6 subnet IDs are expressed in hexadecimal notation, rather than in dotted decimal notation.

Interface ID

The interface ID identifies an interface of a particular node. An interface ID must be unique within the subnet. IPv6 hosts can use the Neighbor Discovery protocol to automatically generate their own interface IDs. Neighbor Discovery automatically generates the interface ID, based on the MAC or EUI-64 address of the host's interface. You can also manually assign interface IDs, which is recommended for IPv6 routers and IPv6-enabled servers. For instructions on how to create a manual EUI-64 address, refer to RFC 3513 Internet Protocol Version 6 (IPv6) Addressing Architecture.

Transitional Global Unicast Addresses

For transition purposes, the IPv6 protocol includes the ability to embed an IPv4 address within an IPv6 address. This type of IPv4 address facilitates the tunneling of IPv6 packets over existing IPv4 networks. One example of a transitional global unicast address is the 6to4 address. For more information on 6to4 addressing, refer to 6to4 Automatic Tunnels.

Link-local Unicast Address

The link-local unicast address can be used only on the local network link. Link-local addresses are not valid nor recognized outside the enterprise. The following example shows the format of the link-local address.

Example: Parts of the Link-Local Unicast Address

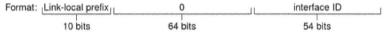

Example: fe80::123e:456d

A link-local prefix has the following format:

        fe80::interface-ID/10

The following is an example of a link-local address:

        fe80::23a1:b152

        fe80

Hexadecimal representation of the 10-bit binary prefix 1111111010. This prefix identifies the type of IPv6 address as link local.

Interface-ID

Hexadecimal address of the interface, which is usually derived from the 48-bit MAC address.

When you enable IPv6 during Solaris installation, the lowest numbered interface on the local machine is configured with a link-local address. Each interface requires at least one link-local address to identify the node to other nodes on the local link. Therefore, you need to manually configure link-local addresses for additional interfaces of a node. After configuration, the node uses its link-local addresses for automatic address configuration and neighbor discovery.

Multicast Address

The multicast address range is 224.0.0.0 to 239.255.255.255 and forms the Class D range which is made up of the high order bits 1110 followed by the 28 bit multicast group ID. There is no subnetting with these Class D addresses. A multicast group can have a permanently-assigned address or the group may be Transient. Well-known Class D addresses are assigned by the Internet Assigned Numbers Authority (IANA) and some of these are detailed in the following table:

Address	Purpose
224.0.0.1	All hosts on a subnet
224.0.0.2	All routers on a subnet
224.0.0.4	All DVMRP routers
224.0.0.5	All OSPF routers (DR Others)
224.0.0.6	All OSPF Designated Routers
224.0.0.7	ST Routers
224.0.0.8	ST Hosts
224.0.0.9	All RIPv2 routers
224.0.0.10	All EIGRP routers
224.0.0.11	Mobile-Agents
224.0.0.12	DHCP Server/Relay Agent
224.0.0.13	All PIM routers
224.0.0.14	RSVP Encapsulation
224.0.0.15	All CBT routers
224.0.0.18	VRRP
224.0.0.22	IGMPv3 Membership Reports
224.0.1.1	NTP
224.0.1.8	SUN NIS+
224.0.1.39	Cisco RP Announce
224.0.1.40	Cisco RP Discovery

The range 224.0.0.0 to 224.0.0.255 are reserved for local purposes meaning that routers should not forward these datagrams since the applications that use these addresses do not need the datagrams to go further than one hop. The range 239.0.0.0 to 239.255.255.255 is reserved for administrative scoping. This is where groups of routers agree an address range to and from which multicast traffic is prevented from entering or leaving a defined zone.

In order to do away with the need for ARP when resolving Ethernet MAC addresses to IP multicast addresses the IANA have reserved a block of Ethernet addresses that map on to the Class D multicast addresses. The reserved address 0x0100.5e00.0000 is used by Ethernet to determine a unique multicast MAC. The following figure illustrates the mapping:

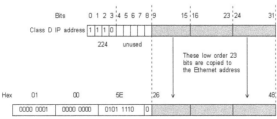

The low order 23 bits of the MAC address give a range of 0x0000.5e00.0000 to 0x0000.5eff. ffff. Half of these are used for multicast addresses and since the least significant bit of the first byte of a MAC address is the I/G bit (Individual/Group) this is set to 1 giving the hex value of 01 for the first octet of the multicast address. The range of MAC addresses used for multicast is therefore 0x0100.5e00.0000 to 0x0100.5e7f.ffff. The E comes from the fact that the LSB of the third octet is always 0.

The problem with this address mapping is that we have only got 23 bits in the MAC address and the IP multicast addresses have 28 bits. Only the least significant 23 bits of the IP multicast address are placed into the MAC address and the other 5 bits are ignored. This results in 25 = 32 different multicast groups overlapping. An example is the Class D address 224.26.10.5 (binary = 11100000.00011010.00001010.00000101 which in hex is E0.1A.0A.05) and the Class D address 236.154.10.5 (binary = 1110110 0.10011010.00001010.00000101 which in hex is EC.9A.0A.05). Although the Class D multicast addresses are different you will see that they differ only in the 5 most significant bits, the 23 least significant bits remain the same so both these addresses map to the same MAC address of 0x0100.5E1A.0A05. Although mathematically there are 32 possibilities for overlap of addresses it is very unlikely to happen in real life and if it does, the impact is that another set of stations receives the multicast traffic. This is still far preferable to ALL stations receiving the traffic. Notice how that the second most significant octet in 224.26.10.5 differs from that in 236.154.10.5 by 128. This is always the case where two IP multicast addresses share the same MAC address.

Token Ring use one of the functional addresses for multicast addresses and have both the locally administered bit and the I/G bit set as well as the functional address bit set the address format is as follows:

Octet	1	2	3	4	5	6
Bits	11000000	00000000	0XXXXXXX	XXXXXXXX	XXXXXXXX	XXXXXXXX

The first two bits are the I/G and U/L bits and are set to 1 in this instance and therefore indicate that the address is a multicast/broadcast (Group) address and it is Locally administered. The first bit in the third octet is the Functional Address Indicator Bit and when it is set to 0, it indicates that the remaining bits form the functional address (used by the various Token Ring functions as detailed below). This results in a functional address such as 0xC000.0004.0000 (non-canonical) which happens to be the one used for multicasting in Token Ring. Be aware that the address 0xc000.0004.0000 is not used exclusively for multicasting! Some Token Ring NICs cannot deal with interrupting the CPU when multicast MACs are received so sometimes the only choice is to use the broadcast address 0xFFFF.FFFF.FFFF.

FDDI frame format corresponds to Ethernet other than they are transmitted 'little-endian' or non-canonical so that a Sniffer analysing the FDDI frames would not see the addresses 0x0100.5Exx.xxxx but 0x8000.7axx.xxxx.

The source of the multicast does not need to know to whom it is sending the traffic, nor does it have to be a member of the multicast group.

Once the client has determined the multicast group that it wishes to join (via means such as Session Description Protocol (SDP), Session Advertisement Protocol (SAP) etc.), the client then makes a join request. In a simple network, the multicast server (Source) converts the multicast address to the Ethernet group address and the clients (Receivers) participating in the multicast communication are configured to receive datagrams from the specified multicast address.

When more devices are involved across a more complex network then routers become involved and they need to be selective as to where they forward this traffic. A distribution tree is set up to manage the traffic flow through the switches and the routers. This tree aids in establishing a path.

Rather than entirely leave the task to routers, to look for hosts that want to join a particular group, the hosts can actively request to join or leave multicast groups. This aids in creating an efficiently 'pruned' distribution tree that enhances the efficiency of the network. In addition, where a number of routers take part in multicast routing, one router is elected as the 'Querier' i.e. the one that forwards the multicast stream.

Internet Group Management Protocol (IGMP)

IGMPv1

IGMP is a mechanism within IPv4 to let multicast routers know of hosts that members of multicast groups. IGMP operates on local network switches where the hosts connect. There are three versions of IGMP.

IGMPv1 controls the flow of multicast traffic. Devices such as routers are called Queriers and belong to the same multicast group as the hosts receiving the data. These Queriers send messages to find out which devices are members of a particular multicast group. These devices respond to inform the Querier of its membership status.

IGMP uses IP protocol 2 and the router always sets the TTL to 1 so that it remains purely within the local network. The IGMPv1 packet is described below:

Bits	5	3	8	16	32
	Ver	Type	Unused	Checksum	Group Address

- Type - Type 1 is a Host membership query and Type 2 is Host Membership report.

- Checksum - this is the 16-bit one's complement of the one's complement sum of the 8-bit IGMP message.

- Group Address - this is only in the Host Membership Report and contains the address of the group being reported.

  IGMPv1 operation:

1. When a host wants to join a multicast group it sends an unsolicited Host Membership Report to the All-hosts Group Address 224.0.0.1. Normally a couple are sent at intervals of 10 seconds just to ensure that the router receives them and the other hosts.

2. Every 60 seconds the Querier (there could be a number of them with IGMPv1) sends Host Membership Queries (or General Query) to the All-hosts address 224.0.0.1 to discover which hosts belong to which multicast group. When a host receives a query it starts a countdown timer for each multicast group being asked about and for which it is a member. This countdown timer has a random value between 1 and 10 seconds and is not configurable.

3. When the timer reaches zero the host sends a membership report to all in the group including the Querier (using 224.0.0.1 again, unless the host receives a membership report from another host, in which case it cancels the timer. This is called Report Suppression and saves bandwidth since only one host per group sends a membership report.

4. If a router does not receive any reports after a number of queries it turns off the multicast stream since the group has timed out on a particular interface.

IGMPv2

The IGMPv2 packet is described below:

Bits	5	3	8	16	32
	Ver	Type	Unused	Checksum	Group Address

- Type - 0x11 is a Membership Query, 0x12 is a Version 1 Membership Report, 0x16 is a Version 2 Membership Report and 0x17 is a Leave Report.

- Maximum Response Time - The default is 10 seconds and this can be changed in increments of 0.1 seconds.

- Group Address - 0 is a General Query whereas a multicast address in here means that it is a group-specific query.

IGMPv2 operation:

1. When routers first come on line they perform a Querier Election to determine the Querier for each network. When a multicast router first connects it sends a General Query. It keeps sending the General Query every 60 seconds whilst

listening for other routers' General Queries. If it sees another router's General Query, it examines the IP address of the source router and if that address is lower than its own the router stops sending General Queries. Eventually, the last remaining router sending General Queries is the one with the lowest IP address and becomes the Querier for the network. The other Non-querier routers listen for queries all the time so that if they do not hear any for 120 seconds, the election process starts again. The Query-Interval Response Time controls the burstiness of reports.

2. Joining a multicast group in version 2 is the same process as version 1 by sending a host membership report to 224.0.0.1.

3. Using queries and reports the multicast router builds a table of the hosts in each multicast group on each interface. This table is called the Group Database and details the up time and the time left before expiry depending on Host Membership Reports.

4. As well as there being the General Query, the Group Specific Query has been introduced so that the router queries membership of specific groups using the group's multicast address rather than use the General Query to the all hosts address 224.0.0.1.

5. The group is maintained as in IGMPv1 with Membership Queries to the all hosts address 224.0.0.1 and the timers on the hosts randomly set.

6. When a host receives a Group-Specific Query for which it is a member then it sets the timer according to the randomly generated number provided that this number is less than the time left on an existing countdown if there is one from another query. The Maximum Response Time is a new field that can be set.

7. On expiry of the timer the host sends a Version 2 Membership Report.

8. If a host wants to leave a group it can now send a Leave Group Message to the All Routers Group address 224.0.0.2 (only the routers need to see this). This reduces the leave latency when the last host in a particular group leaves. The router can therefore cut short the multicast stream sooner than it would have happened with version 1 i.e. in version 1 the datastream would continue for a maximum of 60 seconds. The router does this by immediately sending a Group-Specific Query to check if there are any hosts left in that group before shutting down the multicast stream.

IGMPv3

IGMP version 3 is a major revision of the IGMP protocol. RFC 3376 allows receiver hosts to determine specifically which groups they will receive multicast data from and from which sources. This is called source filtering. The receiver has a filter list which it can use in one of two filter modes:

- Include Mode - The receiver announces membership to a group and sends an Include list of IP addresses from which it will receive the multicast stream.

- Exclude Mode - The receiver announces membership to a group and sends an Exclude list of IP addresses from which it does not want to receive the multicast stream.

The benefits of IGMPv3 are that less multicast traffic will occur as the Include and Exclude lists limit the memberships. Related to that is that Denial of service attacks from unknown sources is less likely. Also IGMPv3 can be used with Source Specific Multicast (SSM). IGMPv3 has to be available in the routers, the switches and the hosts, otherwise it will not operate correctly and will revert to IGMPv2 or IGMPv1 operation as it is backwardly compatible.

The Membership Query message (0x11) has become more complex:

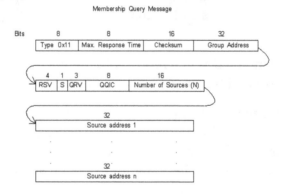

- Type - 0x11 is a Membership Query, 0x12 is a Version 1 Membership Report, 0x16 is a Version 2 Membership Report, 0x17 is a Leave Report and 0x22 is a Version 3 Membership Report. In this case we are looking at 0x11, a Membership Query.

- Maximum Response Time - The default is 10 seconds and this can be changed in increments of 0.1 seconds.

- Checksum - this is the 16-bit one's complement of the one's complement sum of the 8-bit IGMP message.

- Group Address - a value of '0' is a General Query whereas a multicast address in here means that it is a group-specific query.

- Reserved - set to '0'.

- Suppress Router-side processing (S) - if set to one, the 'S' Flag tells the receiving multicast router that is to to suppress the normal timer updates it performs when hearing a Query.

- Querier Robustness Variable (QRV) - multicast routers take on the value sent by the previous querier up to a value of '7'.

- Querier's query Interval Code (QQIC) - is a code value for the query interval used by the querier. If the interval is less than 128 seconds then the 8 bit field represents the number of seconds directly. If the interval is equal to or greater than 128 seconds then this code is made up of binary '1' in the first bit, the exponent in the next three bits and the mantissa in the final four bits.

- Number of sources (N) - the number of source addesses in the query.

- Source addresses - a list of 'N' source addresses.

The query message sent by the multicast routers can be one of three forms:

- General Query - group address and source address fields are zero.

- Group-Specific Query - group address field contains the group address, whereas the address fields are zero.

- Group-and_Source-Specific Query - group address field contains the group address, and the source address fields contain the sources that are emanating the multicast streams.

The Membership Report message (0x22) is new:

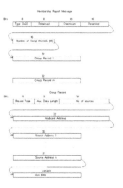

- Type - 0x11 is a Membership Query, 0x12 is a Version 1 Membership Report, 0x16 is a Version 2 Membership Report, 0x17 is a Leave Report and 0x22 is a Version 3 Membership Report. In this case we are looking at 0x22, a Membership Report.

- Reserved - set to '0'.

- Checksum - this is the 16-bit one's complement of the one's complement sum of the 8-bit IGMP message.

- Reserved - set to 'o'.

- Number of Group Records (M) - the number of group records in this query.

- Group Record.

- Record Type.

- Aux Data Length - in units of 32-bit words, this must be zero at the moment because this is only for future use!

- Number of sources (N) - the number of source addresses.

- Multicast address of this group record.

- Source addresses - the source of the multicast streams.

There are a number of Group record types:

- Current-state-record - which could be MODE_IS_INCLUDE or MODE_IS_ EXCLUDE representing the filter state of the interface when filtering the source addresses to include or exclude when joining this group records group address.

- Filter-mode-change-record - indicating a filter mode change, either CHANGE_ TO_INCLUDE_MODE or CHANGE_TO_EXCLUDE_MODE.

- Source-list-change-record - either ALLOW_NEW_SOURCES or BLOCK_ OLD_SOURCES.

IGMPv3 membership reports are sent to the address 224.0.0.22, all IGMPv3 capable routers listen on this address.

Cisco Group Multicast Protocol (CGMP)

Layer 2 switches on seeing the multicast MAC address will naturally forward this un-known address out of ALL its ports. This loads the switch up and results in multicast traffic being unnecessarily sent to hosts that have not requested it.

IGMP Snooping

One method is IGMP Snooping where the switch has the intelligence to examine all the multicast queries and reports to determine the port mappings of the group members. Using this information it then rewrites its own forwarding tables. This is processor in-tensive for the switch and the router has all this information already.

Manual Configuration

Another method is to manually configure multicast MAC addresses within the switch forwarding table, however this can be tedious, prone to error and inflexible.

GMRP

As part of 802.1p and therefore an open standard, GARP Multicast Registration Protocol (GMRP) allows dynamic learning of multicast MAC addresses within a switch.

CGMP

Cisco's proprietary Cisco Group Management Protocol (CGMP) takes the multicast information, such as which hosts are members of which groups, and allows the routers/layer 3 switches to directly write the information to the layer 2 forwarding tables of the switches so that the switches can dynamically switch the IP multicasts at switch speed. If non-Cisco routers are using multicast, say with Distance Vector Multicast Routing Protocol (DVMRP), then although Cisco does not fully support DVMRP, the router will 'proxy' for these other routers and feed this information into the switches configured for CGMP.

In CGMP, the multicast router is considered to be the server since it has done all the work and the layer 2 switch is the CGMP client that uses the router's information to construct its forwarding tables (CAM) i.e. the router produces the CGMP packet and the switch reads it.

A CGMP router starts by sending a Join packet with the Group Destination MAC Address set to all zeros (meaning all multicast groups) and the source address as its own MAC address. This packet is sent every 60 seconds so that connected switches know that a CGMP router is online.

The CGMP packet looks as follows:

Bits 4	4	16	8	48	48
Version	Type	Reserved	Count	GDA	USA

- Version - Always set to 0x1.

- Type - Either Join (0x0), or Leave (0x1).

- Reserved - Always set to 0x0000.

- Count - How many GDA/USA pairs are in the packet.

- Group Destination Address (GDA) - MAC address of multicast group.

- Unicast Source Address (USA) - MAC address of group member.

When a multicast router sees a client's IGMP packet it creates a CGMP packet. It maps the client's MAC address to the multicast MAC address within the CGMP packet. The CGMP packet contains a type field (Join or Leave a multicast group), the MAC address of the IGMP client and the multicast address of the group. The router is considered a CGMP server and the switch is the CGMP client. CGMP multicast packets are sent to the switches using the well-known multicast address 0x0100.0cdd.dddd. The switches take the CGMP mapping information and the forwarding table is programmed accordingly because the switch knows which client MAC address needs to see data from the multicast MAC address and adds the port to its list of forwarding ports for that particular mulicast group. Similarly, when a client wishes to leave a multicast group, a CGMP Leave message is created by the router and this results in the switch removing the client port from the forwarding table, thereby minimising the traffic throughput.

Broadcast Address

A broadcast address is a special Internet Protocol (IP) address used to transmit messages and data packets to network systems. Network administrators (NA) verify successful data packet transmission via broadcast addresses.

Dynamic Host Configuration Protocol (DHCP) and Bootstrap Protocol (BOOTP) clients use broadcast IP addresses to locate and transmit respective server requests.

When IP classes were designed, certain IP addresses were reserved for specific tasks. Broadcast addressing was designed to facilitate message broadcasting for all network devices.

The following is a broadcast addressing analogy:

A teacher is preparing to announce the winner of a student competition and can use either of the following approaches:

1. The teacher could stop by each student's desk and discreetly reveal the winner's name, or

2. The teacher could announce the winner's name to the class and then ask the winner to stand for recognition. The second option, which is more efficient, is broadcast addressing in the real world.

In computing, a broadcast addressing example is Internet Protocol Version 6 (IPv6), which does not support IPv4's zero network broadcast address (255.255.255.255). As a workaround, IPv6 sends a multicast message to each host group member.

Anycast Addressing

Anycast is a network addressing and routing method in which incoming requests can be routed to a variety of different locations or "nodes." In the context of a CDN, Anycast typically routes incoming traffic to the nearest data center with the capacity to process the request efficiently. Selective routing allows an Anycast network to be resilient in the face of high traffic volume, network congestion, and DDoS attacks.

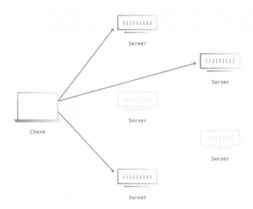

Working of Anycast

Anycast network routing is able to route incoming connection requests across multiple data centers. When requests come into a single IP address associated with the Anycast network, the network distributes the data based on some prioritization methodology. The selection process behind choosing a particular data center will typically be optimized to reduce latency by selecting the data center with the shortest distance from the requester. Anycast is characterized by a 1-to-1 of many association, and is one of the 5 main network protocol methods used in the Internet protocol.

Reasons to use an Anycast Network

If many requests are made simultaneously to the same origin server, the server may become overwhelmed with traffic and be unable to respond efficiently to additional incoming requests. With an Anycast network, instead of one origin server taking the brunt of the traffic, the load can also be spread across other available data centers, each of which will have servers capable of processing and responding to the incoming request. This routing method can prevent an origin server from extending capacity and avoids service interruptions to clients requesting content from the origin server.

Difference between Anycast and Unicast

Most of the Internet works via a routing scheme called Unicast. Under Unicast, every node on the network gets a unique IP address. Home and office networks use Unicast; when a computer is connected to a wireless network and gets a message saying the IP address is already in use, an IP address conflict has occurred because another computer on the same Unicast network is already using the same IP. In most cases, that isn't allowed.

When a CDN is using a unicast address, traffic is routed directly to the specific node. This creates a vulnerability when the network experiences extraordinary traffic such as during a DDoS attack. Because the traffic is routed directly to a particular data center, the location or its surrounding infrastructure may become overwhelmed with traffic, potentially resulting in denial-of-service to legitimate requests.

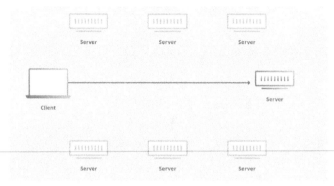

Using Anycast means the network can be extremely resilient. Because traffic will find the best path, an entire data center can be taken offline and traffic will automatically flow to a proximal data center.

Ways by which an Anycast Network Mitigate a DDoS Attack

After other DDoS mitigation tools filter out some of the attack traffic, Anycast distributes the remaining attack traffic across multiple data centers, preventing any one location from becoming overwhelmed with requests. If the capacity of the Anycast network is greater than the attack traffic, the attack is effectively mitigated. In most DDoS attacks, many compromised "zombie" or "bot" computers are used to form what is known as a botnet. These machines can be scattered around the web and generate so much traffic that they can overwhelm a typical Unicast-connected machine.

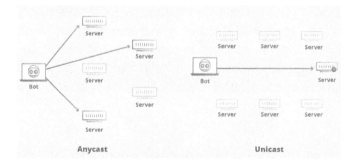

A properly Anycasted CDN increases the surface area of the receiving network so that the unfiltered denial-of-service traffic from a distributed botnet will be absorbed by each of the CDN's data centers. As a result, as a network continues to grow in size and capacity it becomes harder and harder to launch an effective DDoS against anyone using the CDN.

It is not easy to setup a true Anycasted network. Proper implementation requires that a CDN provider maintains their own network hardware, builds direct relationships with their upstream carriers, and tunes their networking routes to ensure traffic doesn't "flap" between multiple locations.

MAC Address

MAC Addresses are unique 48-bits hardware number of a computer, which is embedded into network card (known as Network Interface Card) during the time of manufacturing. MAC Address is also known as Physical Address of a network device. In IEEE 802 standard, Data Link Layer is divided into two sublayers:

1. Logical Link Control(LLC) Sublayer

2. Media Access Control(MAC) Sublayer

MAC address is used by Media Access Control (MAC) sublayer of Data-Link Layer. MAC Address is word wide unique, since millions of network devices exists and we need to uniquely identify each.

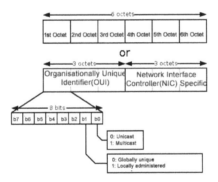

Format of MAC Address

MAC Address is a 12-digit hexadecimal number (6-Byte binary number), which is mostly represented by Colon-Hexadecimal notation. First 6-digits (say 00:40:96) of MAC Address identifies the manufacturer, called as OUI (Organizational Unique Identifier). IEEE Registration Authority Committee assign these MAC prefixes to its registered vendors.

Here are some OUI of well known manufacturers :

      CC:46:D6 - Cisco

      3C:5A:B4 - Google, Inc.

3C:D9:2B - Hewlett Packard

00:9A:CD - HUAWEI TECHNOLOGIES CO.,LTD

The rightmost six digits represents Network Interface Controller, which is assigned by manufacturer.

MAC address is represented by Colon-Hexadecimal notation. But this is just a conversion, not mandatory. MAC address can be represented using any of the following formats.

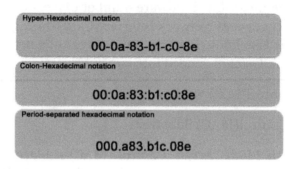

Finding MAC Address

Command for UNIX/Linux - ifconfig -a

ip link list

ip address show

Command forWindows OS - ipconfig /all

MacOS -   TCP/IP Control Panel

Types of MAC Address

1. Unicast – A Unicast addressed frame is only sent out to the interface leading to specific NIC. If the LSB (least significant bit) of first octet of an address is set to zero, the frame is meant to reach only one receiving NIC. MAC Address of source machine is always Unicast.

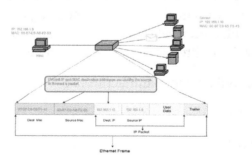

2. Multicast – Multicast address allow the source to send a frame to group of devices. In Layer-2 (Ethernet) Multicast address, LSB (least significant bit) of first octet of an address is set to one. IEEE has allocated the address block 01-80-C2-xx-xx-xx (01-80-C2-00-00-00 to 01-80-C2-FF-FF-FF) for group addresses for use by standard protocols.

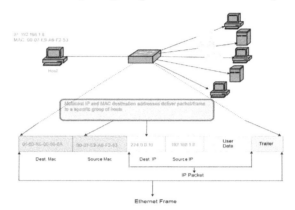

3. Broadcast – Similar to Network Layer, Broadcast is also possible on underlying layer(Data Link Layer). Ethernet frames with ones in all bits of the destination address (FF-FF-FF-FF-FF-FF) are referred as broadcast address. Frames which are destined with MAC address FF-FF-FF-FF-FF-FF will reach to every computer belong to that LAN segment.

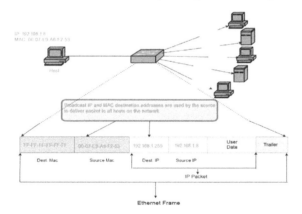

MAC Cloning

Some ISPs use MAC address inorder to assign IP address to gateway device. When device connects to the ISP, DHCP server records the MAC address and then assign IP address. Now the system will be identified through MAC address. When the device get disconnected, it looses the IP address. If user wants to reconnect, DHCP server checks if the device is connected before. If so, then server tries to assign same IP address (in case lease period not expired). In case user changed the router, user has to inform the ISP about new MAC address because new MAC address is unknown to ISP, so connection cannot be established.

Or the other option is Cloning, user can simply clone the registered MAC address with ISP. Now router keeps reporting old MAC address to ISP and there will be no connection issue.

Applications

The following network technologies use the MAC-48 identifier format:

- Ethernet,

- 802.11 wireless networks,

- Bluetooth,

- IEEE 802.5 token ring,

- most other IEEE 802 networks,

- Fiber Distributed Data Interface (FDDI),

- Asynchronous Transfer Mode (ATM), switched virtual connections only, as part of an NSAP address,

- Fibre Channel and Serial Attached SCSI (as part of a World Wide Name),

- The ITU-T G.hn standard, which provides a way to create a high-speed (up to 1 gigabit/s) local area network using existing home wiring (power lines, phone lines and coaxial cables). The G.hn Application Protocol Convergence (APC) layer accepts Ethernet frames that use the MAC-48 format and encapsulates them into G.hn Medium Access Control Service Data Units (MSDUs).

Every device that connects to an IEEE 802 network (such as Ethernet and WiFi) has a MAC-48 address. Common networked consumer devices such as PCs, smartphones and tablet computers use MAC-48 addresses.

EUI-64 identifiers are used in:

- IEEE 1394 (FireWire)

- IPv6 (Modified EUI-64 as the least-significant 64 bits of a unicast network address or link-local address when stateless autoconfiguration is used)

- ZigBee / 802.15.4 / 6LoWPAN wireless personal-area networks.

Usage in Hosts

On broadcast networks, such as Ethernet, the MAC address is expected to uniquely identify each node on that segment and allows frames to be marked for specific hosts. It thus forms the basis of most of the link layer (OSI Layer 2) networking upon which upper layer protocols rely to produce complex, functioning networks.

Although intended to be a permanent and globally unique identification, it is possible to change the MAC address on most modern hardware. Changing MAC addresses is necessary in network virtualization. It can also be used in the process of exploiting security vulnerabilities. This is called MAC spoofing.

In IP networks, the MAC address of an interface can be queried given the IP address using the Address Resolution Protocol (ARP) for Internet Protocol Version 4 (IPv4) or the Neighbor Discovery Protocol (NDP) for IPv6. In this way, ARP or NDP is used to relate IP addresses (OSI layer 3) to Ethernet MAC addresses (OSI layer 2).

A MAC address is like a social security number which remains unchanged for a person's life time (here, the device), while an IP address is like a postal code which can be changed.

Spying

According to Edward Snowden, the US National Security Agency has a system that tracks the movements of everyone in a city by monitoring the MAC addresses of their electronic devices. As a result of users being trackable by their devices' MAC addresses, Apple has started using random MAC addresses in their iOS line of devices while scanning for networks. Other vendors quickly followed: MAC address randomization during scanning was added in Android starting from version 6.0, Windows 10, and Linux kernel 3.18. The actual implementations of the MAC address randomization technique vary largely in different devices. Moreover, various flaws and shortcomings in these implementations may allow an attacker to track a device even if its MAC address is changed, for instance its probe requests' other elements, or their timing. If random MAC addresses are not used, researchers have confirmed that it is possible to link a real identity to a particular wireless MAC address.

Many network interfaces (including wireless ones) support changing their MAC address. The configuration is specific to the operating system. On most Unix-like systems, the ifconfig command may be used to add and remove "link" (Ethernet MAC family) address aliases. For instance, the "active" ifconfig directive may then be used on NetBSD to specify which of the attached addresses to activate. Hence, various configuration scripts and utilities allow to randomize the MAC address at boot or network connection time.

Using wireless access points in SSID-hidden mode, a mobile wireless device may not only disclose its own MAC address when traveling, but even the MAC addresses associated to SSIDs the device has already connected to, if they are configured to send these as part of probe request packets. Alternative modes to prevent this include configuring access points to be either in beacon-broadcasting mode, or probe-response with SSID mode. In these modes, probe requests may be unnecessary, or sent in broadcast mode without disclosing the identity of previously-known networks.

Notational Conventions

The standard (IEEE 802) format for printing MAC-48 addresses in human-friendly form is six groups of two hexadecimal digits, separated by hyphens (-) in transmission order (e.g. *01-23-45-67-89-AB*). This form is also commonly used for EUI-64 (e.g. *01-23-45-67-89-AB-CD-EF*). Other conventions include six groups of two hexadecimal digits separated by colons (:) (e.g. *01:23:45:67:89:AB*), and three groups of four hexadecimal digits separated by dots (.) (e.g. *0123.4567.89AB*); again in transmission order.

Bit-reversed Notation

The standard notation, also called canonical format, for MAC addresses is written in transmission order with the least significant bit of each byte transmitted first, and is used in the output of the ifconfig, iproute2, and ipconfig commands, for example.

However, since IEEE 802.3 (Ethernet) and IEEE 802.4 (Token Bus) send the bytes (octets) over the wire, left-to-right, with least significant bit in each byte first, while IEEE 802.5 (Token Ring) and IEEE 802.6 (FDDI) send the bytes over the wire with the most significant bit first, confusion may arise when an address in the latter scenario is represented with bits reversed from the canonical representation. For example, an address in canonical form *12-34-56-78-9A-BC* would be transmitted over the wire as bits 01001000 00101100 01101010 00011110 01011001 00111101 in the standard transmission order (least significant bit first). But for Token Ring networks, it would be transmitted as bits 00010010 00110100 01010110 01111000 10011010 10111100 in most-significant-bit first order. The latter might be incorrectly displayed as *48-2C-6A-1E-59-3D*. This is referred to as *bit-reversed order, non-canonical form, MSB format, IBM format*, or *Token Ring format*, as explained in RFC 2469.

MAC Filtering

MAC Address filtering is a technique that is implemented on many wireless networks to filter which devices are able to connect to the wireless network. MAC Address filtering allows an administrator to allow specific devices to connect to the network while blocking all other devices. MAC Address filtering is a free service provided by most routers and/or access points and prevents unauthorized users from downloading illegal content, accessing network resources, and using additional bandwidth.

Working of MAC Address Filtering

MAC Address filtering is accessible through most routers and can be activated by entering the URL of the router's control panel, which is printed on the back of the router, into any web browser and navigating to the Security menu. From here, the user should see something along the lines of "MAC Address Filtering", "MAC Filter", or "Source MAC Filtering". This menu will allow the user to enter a device's MAC address into the Allowed or Blocked list, which will allow or block that device from accessing the network.

A device's MAC Address can be found by opening the Start menu, selecting "Run", entering "getmac", and clicking OK. Alternatively, the user can enter "cmd", click OK, and then enter "ipconfig /all". The user can look for the "Physical Address", which is the MAC Address, and enter it into the appropriate field on the router's MAC Address filter.

Applications

MAC Address filtering can be implemented for a number of reasons, but is designed to permit specific devices to access a network while blocking all other devices. When MAC Address filtering is enabled, only devices that are specifically listed in an administrator's MAC Address filtering list will be allowed to connect to his/her network. However, MAC Address filtering can be confusing to novice users or users who have forgotten that it is enabled, which may not be able to add a new device to his/her own network.

Security Issues

The main reason why it doesn't make your network more secure is because it's really easy to spoof a MAC address. A network hacker, which can literally be anyone since the tools are so easy to use, can easily figure out the MAC addresses on your network and then spoof that address onto their computer.

So, you may ask, how can they get your MAC address if they can't connect to your network? Well, that's an inherent weakness with WiFi. Even with a WPA2 encrypted network, the MAC addresses on those packets are not encrypted. This means that anyone with network sniffing software installed and a wireless card in range of your network, can easily grab all the MAC addresses that are communicating with your router.

They can't see the data or anything like that, but they don't really have to break the encryption to access your network. Why? Because now that they have your MAC address, they can spoof it and then send out special packets to your router called disassociation packets, which will disconnect your device from the wireless network.

Then, the hackers' device will try to connect to the router and will be accepted because it is now using your valid MAC address. This is why this feature can make your network less secure because now the hacker doesn't have to bother trying to crack your WPA2 encrypted password at all! They simply have to pretend to be a trusted computer.

Again, this can be done by someone who little to no knowledge of computers. If you just Google crack WiFi using Kali Linux, you'll get tons of tutorials on how to hack into your neighbor's WiFi within a few minutes. So do those tools always work?

Best Way to Stay Secure

Those tools will work, but not if you are using WPA2 encryption along with a fairly long WiFi password. It's really important that you don't use a simple and short WiFi password because all a hacker does when using these tools is a brute force attack.

```
Region Selection
Region:
North America          ▼

Wireless Network (2.4GHz b/g/n)
☑ Enable SSID Broadcast
Name (SSID):                    FIOS-ZOPPY
Channel:                        01     ▼
Mode:                           Up to 450 Mbps ▼
Transmit Power Control          100% ▼

Security Options
○ None
◉ WPA2-PSK [AES]
○ WPA-PSK [TKIP] + WPA2-PSK [AES]
○ WPA/WPA2 Enterprise
```

With a brute force attack, they will capture the encrypted password and try to crack it using the fastest machine and the biggest dictionary of passwords they can find. If your password is secure, it can take years for the password to be cracked. Always try to use WPA2 with AES only. You should avoid the WPA [TKIP] + WPA2 [AES] option as it's much less secure.

However, if you have MAC address filtering enabled, the hacker can bypass all that trouble and simply grab your MAC address, spoof it, disconnect you or another device on your network from the router and connect freely. Once they are in, they can do all kinds of damage and access everything on your network.

References

- Network-address-20969: techopedia.com, Retrieved 16 June 2018

- Network-addressing, data-communication-computer-network: tutorialspoint.com, Retrieved 16 May 2018

- Virtual-ip-address-vipa-2467: techopedia.com, Retrieved 21 April 2018

- What-is-a-private-ip-address-2625970: lifewire.com, Retrieved 17 May 2018

- Unicast-address-2464: techopedia.com, Retrieved 11 March 2018

- Computer-network-introduction-mac-address: geeksforgeeks.org, Retrieved 10 July 2018

- Mac-address-filtering: tech-faq.com, Retrieved 28 April 2018

- Mac-address-filtering, networking: helpdeskgeek.com, Retrieved 14 May 2018

5

Routing

The selection of a path for traffic in a single network or multiple networks is possible through the process of routing. It works on the assumption that network addresses are structured in a way that similarity in addresses implies proximity within that network. This chapter explores the fundamentals of routing and elucidates its central concepts like routing table, IP routing, routing algorithms, route selection, etc.

Routing is the act of moving information across an inter-network from a source to a destination. Along the way, at least one intermediate node typically is encountered. It's also referred to as the process of choosing a path over which to send the packets. Routing is often contrasted with bridging, which might seem to accomplish precisely the same thing to the casual observer. The primary difference between the two is that bridging occurs at Layer 2 (the data link layer) of the OSI reference model, whereas routing occurs at Layer 3 (the network layer). This distinction provides routing and bridging with different information to use in the process of moving information from source to destination, so the two functions accomplish their tasks in different ways. The routing algorithm is the part of the network layer software responsible for deciding which output line an incoming packet should be transmitted on, i.e. what should be the next intermediate node for the packet.

Routing protocols use metrics to evaluate what path will be the best for a packet to travel. A metric is a standard of measurement; such as path bandwidth, reliability, delay, current load on that path etc.; that is used by routing algorithms to determine the optimal path to a destination. To aid the process of path determination, routing algorithms initialize and maintain routing tables, which contain route information. Route information varies depending on the routing algorithm used.

Routing algorithms fill routing tables with a variety of information. Mainly Destination/Next hop associations tell a router that a particular destination can be reached optimally by sending the packet to a particular node representing the "next hop" on the way to the final destination. When a router receives an incoming packet, it checks the destination address and attempts to associate this address with a next hop. Some of the routing algorithm allows a router to have multiple "next hop" for a single destination depending upon best with regard to different metrics. For example, let's say router R2 is be best next hop for destination "D", if path length is considered as the metric; while Router R3 is the best for the same destination if delay is considered as the metric for making the routing decision.

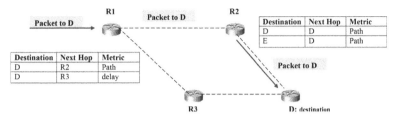

Figure: Typical routing in a small network

The above figure shows a small part of a network where packet destined for node "D", arrives at router R1, and based on the path metric i.e. the shortest path to destination is forwarded to router R2 which forward it to the final destination. Routing tables also can contain other information, such as data about the desirability of a path. Routers compare metrics to determine optimal routes, and these metrics differ depending on the design of the routing algorithm used. Routers communicate with one another and maintain their routing tables through the transmission of a variety of messages. The routing update message is one such message that generally consists of all or a portion of a routing table. By analyzing routing updates from all other routers, a router can build a detailed picture of network topology. A link-state advertisement, another example of a message sent between routers, informs other routers of the state of the sender's links. Link information also can be used to build a complete picture of network topology to enable routers to determine optimal routes to network destinations.

Desirable properties of a router are as follows:

- Correctness and simplicity: The packets are to be correctly delivered. Simpler the routing algorithm, it is better.

- Robustness: Ability of the network to deliver packets via some route even in the face of failures.

- Stability: The algorithm should converge to equilibrium fast in the face of changing conditions in the network.

- Fairness and optimality: obvious requirements, but conflicting.

- Efficiency: Minimum overhead.

While designing a routing protocol it is necessary to take into account the following design parameters:

- Performance Criteria: Number of hops, Cost, Delay, Throughput, etc.

- Decision Time: Per packet basis (Datagram) or per session (Virtual-circuit) basis.

- Decision Place: Each node (distributed), Central node (centralized), Originated node (source).

- Network Information Source: None, Local, Adjacent node, Nodes along route, All nodes.

- Network Information Update Timing: Continuous, Periodic, Major load change, Topology change.

Classification of Routers

Routing algorithms can be classified based on the following criteria:

- Static versus Adaptive

- Single-path versus multi-path

- Intra-domain versus inter-domain

- Flat versus hierarchical

- Link-state versus distance vector

- Host-intelligent versus router-intelligent.

Static versus Adaptive

This category is based on how and when the routing tables are set-up and how they can be modified, if at all. Adaptive routing is also referred as dynamic routing and Non- adaptive is also known as static routing algorithms. Static routing algorithms are hardly algorithms at all; the table mappings are established by the network administrator before the beginning of routing. These mappings do not change unless the network administrator alters them. Algorithms that use static routes are simple to design and work well in environments where network traffic is relatively predictable and where network design is relatively simple. Routing decisions in these algorithms are in no way based on current topology or traffic.

Because static routing systems cannot react to network changes, they generally are considered unsuitable for today's large, constantly changing networks. Most of the dominant routing algorithms today are dynamic routing algorithms, which adjust to changing network circumstances by analyzing incoming routing update messages. If the message indicates that a network change has occurred, the routing software recalculates routes and sends out new routing update messages. These messages permeate the network, stimulating routers to rerun their algorithms and change their routing tables accordingly. Dynamic routing algorithms can be supplemented with static routes where appropriate.

Single-path versus Multi-path

This division is based upon the number of paths a router stores for a single destination.

Single path algorithms are where only a single path (or rather single next hop) is stored in the routing table. Some sophisticated routing protocols support multiple paths to the same destination; these are known as multi-path algorithms. Unlike single-path algorithms, these multipath algorithms permit traffic multiplexing over multiple lines. The advantages of multipath algorithms are obvious: They can provide substantially better throughput and reliability. This is generally called load sharing.

Intradomain versus Interdomain

Some routing algorithms work only within domains; others work within and between domains. The nature of these two algorithm types is different. It stands to reason, therefore, that an optimal intra-domain-routing algorithm would not necessarily be an optimal inter-domain-routing algorithm

Flat versus Hierarchical

Some routing algorithms operate in a flat space, while others use routing hierarchies. In a flat routing system, the routers are peers of all others. In a hierarchical routing system, some routers form what amounts to a routing backbone. Packets from non-backbone routers travel to the backbone routers, where they are sent through the backbone until they reach the general area of the destination. At this point, they travel from the last backbone router through one or more non-backbone routers to the final destination.

Routing systems often designate logical groups of nodes, called domains, autonomous systems, or areas. In hierarchical systems, some routers in a domain can communicate with routers in other domains, while others can communicate only with routers within their domain. In very large networks, additional hierarchical levels may exist, with routers at the highest hierarchical level forming the routing backbone.

The primary advantage of hierarchical routing is that it mimics the organization of most companies and therefore supports their traffic patterns well. Most network communication occurs within small company groups (domains). Because intradomain routers need to know only about other routers within their domain, their routing algorithms can be simplified, and, depending on the routing algorithm being used, routing update traffic can be reduced accordingly.

Link-state versus Distance Vector

This category is based on the way the routing tables are updated.

Distance vector algorithms (also known as Bellman-Ford algorithms): Key features of the distance vector routing are as follows:

- The routers share the knowledge of the entire autonomous system
- Sharing of information takes place only with the neighbors

- Sharing of information takes place at fixed regular intervals, say every 30 seconds.

Link-state algorithms (also known as shortest path first algorithms) have the following key feature:

- The routers share the knowledge only about their neighbors compared to all the routers in the autonomous system

- Sharing of information takes place only with all the routers in the internet, by sending small updates using flooding compared to sending larger updates to their neighbors

- Sharing of information takes place only when there is a change, which leads to lesser internet traffic compared to distance vector routing.

Because convergence takes place more quickly in link-state algorithms, these are somewhat less prone to routing loops than distance vector algorithms. On the other hand, link-state algorithms require more processing power and memory than distance vector algorithms. Link-state algorithms, therefore, can be more expensive to implement and support. Link-state protocols are generally more scalable than distance vector protocols.

Host-intelligent versus Router-intelligent

This division is on the basis of whether the source knows about the entire route or just about the next-hop where to forward the packet. Some routing algorithms assume that the source end node will determine the entire route. This is usually referred to as source routing. In source-routing systems, routers merely act as store-and-forward devices, mindlessly sending the packet to the next stop. These algorithms are also referred to as Host-Intelligent Routing, as entire route is specified by the source node.

Other algorithms assume that hosts know nothing about routes. In these algorithms, routers determine the path through the Internet based on their own strategy. In the first system, the hosts have the routing intelligence. In the latter system, routers have the routing intelligence.

Routing Table

A routing table is a set of rules, often viewed in table format that is used to determine where data packets traveling over an Internet Protocol (IP) network will be directed. All IP-enabled devices, including routers and switches, use routing tables.

A routing table contains the information necessary to forward a packet along the best path toward its destination. Each packet contains information about its origin and destination. When a packet is received, a network device examines the packet and matches it to the routing table entry providing the best match for its destination. The table then provides the device with instructions for sending the packet to the next hop on its route across the network.

A basic routing table includes the following information:

- Destination: The IP address of the packet's final destination
- Next hop: The IP address to which the packet is forwarded
- Interface: The outgoing network interface the device should use when forwarding the packet to the next hop or final destination
- Metric: Assigns a cost to each available route so that the most cost-effective path can be chosen
- Routes: Includes directly-attached subnets, indirect subnets that are not attached to the device but can be accessed through one or more hops, and default routes to use for certain types of traffic or when information is lacking.

Routing tables can be maintained manually or dynamically. Tables for static network devices do not change unless a network administrator manually changes them. In dynamic routing, devices build and maintain their routing tables automatically by using routing protocols to exchange information about the surrounding network topology. Dynamic routing tables allow devices to "listen" to the network and respond to occurrences like device failures and network congestion.

Source of Route Lookup

Where to route to **192.168.1.20** ???

192.168.1.20/32 *via* 10.254.2.1

192.168.1.0/24 *via* *10.254.3.1*

192.168.1.30/32 *via* *10.254.3.1*

via 10.254.4.1, check interface and send out!

Having the destination IP of packet, routers always choose best matching ROUTING ENTRY. That means LONGEST PREFIX MATCH. This means that in our case entry: 192.168.1.20/32 is more accurate that 192.168.1.0/24 in the search for 192.168.1.20.

Why this one is more accurate? Because 192.168.1.20/32 entry matches exactly 32 bits of our destination IP whereas 192.168.1.0/24 matches only 24 bits of our address.

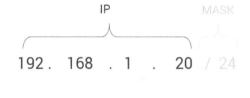

Learning of the Correct Destinations by Routers

There are two options :

We can tell the router explicitly how to route to destination: for example: if want to go to C, go via Router 2. This is so called STATIC ROUTING where the destinations are written to router's configuration statically (by hand of network admin). On picture below, orange entries need to be provided to router by hand.

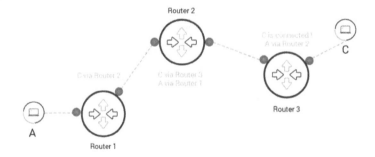

Now, imagine that you need to configure all Internet destinations, over 600 000 routes! Would we need to provide over 600K entries by hand? No way. There is smarter idea and is called.

DYNAMIC ROUTING. With dynamic routing we can configure the routers to learn the IP destinations from other routers, which participate also in the same routing process.

Example: Router 3 has Laptop C connected to it, so it advertises the C network address to it's neighboring routers. Neighboring router, Router 2 receives an advertisement and injects C prefix into its routing table and in turn sends the C network information to its respective neighbors (Router 1). In this way without human intervention whole network is able to learn the destinations and create routing topology.

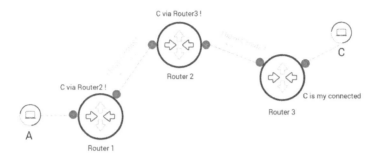

IP Routing

IP Routing is an umbrella term for the set of protocols that determine the path that data follows in order to travel across multiple networks from its source to its destination. Data is routed from its source to its destination through a series of routers, and across multiple networks. The IP Routing protocols enable routers to build up a forwarding table that correlates final destinations with next hop addresses.

These protocols include:

- BGP (Border Gateway Protocol)
- IS-IS (Intermediate System - Intermediate System)
- OSPF (Open Shortest Path First)
- RIP (Routing Information Protocol)

When an IP packet is to be forwarded, a router uses its forwarding table to determine the next hop for the packet's destination (based on the destination IP address in the IP packet header), and forwards the packet appropriately. The next router then repeats this process using its own forwarding table, and so on until the packet reaches its destination. At each stage, the IP address in the packet header is sufficient information to determine the next hop; no additional protocol headers are required.

The Internet, for the purpose of routing, is divided into Autonomous Systems (ASs). An AS is a group of routers that are under the control of a single administration and exchange routing information using a common routing protocol. For example, a corporate intranet or an ISP network can usually be regarded as an individual AS. The Internet can be visualized as a partial mesh of ASs. An AS can be classified as one of the following three types.

A Stub AS has a single connection to one other AS. Any data sent to, or received from, a destination outside the AS must travel over that connection. A small campus network is an example of a stub AS.

A Transit AS has multiple connections to one or more ASs, which permits data that is not destined for a node within that AS to travel through it. An ISP network is an example of a transit AS.

A Multihomed AS also has multiple connections to one or more ASs, but it does not permit data received over one of these connections to be forwarded out of the AS again. In other words, it does not provide a transit service to other ASs. A Multihomed AS is similar to a Stub AS, except that the ingress and egress points for data traveling to or from the AS can be chosen from one of a number of connections, depending on which connection offers the shortest route to the eventual destination. A large enterprise network would normally be a multihomed AS.

An Interior Gateway Protocol (IGP) calculates routes within a single AS. The IGP enables nodes on different networks within an AS to send data to one another. The IGP also enables data to be forwarded across an AS from ingress to egress, when the AS is providing transit services.

Routes are distributed between ASs by an Exterior Gateway Protocol (EGP). The EGP enables routers within an AS to choose the best point of egress from the AS for the data they are trying to route.

The EGP and the IGPs running within each AS cooperate to route data across the Internet. The EGP determines the ASs that data must cross in order to reach its destination, and the IGP determines the path within each AS that data must follow to get from the point of ingress (or the point of origin) to the point of egress (or the final destination).

Example

We will use the following topology to Describe Steps: Below we have two host computers and two routers. H1 is going to send an IP packet to H2, which has to be routed by R1 andR2.

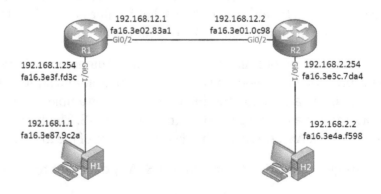

IP Routing Process

Let's look at this step-by-step, device-by-device.

H1

Let's start with H1. This host creates an IP packet with its own IP address (192.168.1.1) as the source and H2 (192.168.2.2) as the destination. The first question that H1 will ask itself is:

Is the destination local or remote?

It answers this question by looking at its own IP address, its subnet mask and the destination IP address:

```
C:\Users\H1>ipconfig

Windows IP Configuration

Ethernet adapter Ethernet 1:

   Connection-specific DNS Suffix. : nwl.local

   Link-local IPv6 Address . . . . . : fe80::88fd:962a:44d6:3a1f%4

   IPv4 Address. . . . . . . . . . . : 192.168.1.1

   Subnet Mask . . . . . . . . . . . : 255.255.255.0

   Default Gateway . . . . . . . . . : 192.168.1.254
```

H1 is in network 192.168.1.0/24 so all IP addresses in the 192.168.1.1 – 254 ranges are local. Our destination (192.168.2.2) is outside of the local subnet so that means we have to use the default gateway.

H1 will now build an Ethernet frame, enters its own source MAC address and asks itself the second question; do we know the destination MAC address of the default gateway?

It checks its ARP table to find the answer:

```
C:\Users\H1>arp -a

Interface: 192.168.1.1 --- 0x4

   Internet Address        Physical Address        Type

   192.168.1.254           fa-16-3e-3f-fd-3c       dynamic

   192.168.1.255           ff-ff-ff-ff-ff-ff                static

   224.0.0.22              01-00-5e-00-00-16       static
```

```
224.0.0.251              01-00-5e-00-00-fb        static

224.0.0.252              01-00-5e-00-00-fc        static

239.255.255.250          01-00-5e-7f-ff-fa        static
```

H1 has an ARP entry for 192.168.1.254. If not, it would have sent an ARP request. We now have an Ethernet frame that carries an IP packet with the following addresses:

Source: fa16.3e87.9c2a	Destination: fa16.3e3f.fd3c	Source: 192.168.1.1	Destination: 192.168.2.2

The frame will be on its way to R1.

R1

This Ethernet frame makes it to R1, which has more work to do than our host. The first thing it does is check if the FCS (Frame Check Sequence) of the Ethernet frame is correct or not:

Preamble	SFD	Destination	Source	Type	IP Packet	FCS

If the FCS is incorrect, the frame is dropped right away. There is no error recovery for Ethernet; this is something that is done by protocols on upper layers, like TCP on the transport layer.

If the FCS is correct, we will process the frame if:

The destination MAC address is the address of the interface of the router.

The destination MAC address is a broadcast address of the subnet that the router interface is connected to.

The destination MAC address is a multicast address that the router listens to.

In this case, the destination MAC address matches the MAC address of R1's Gigabit Ethernet 0/1 interface so we will process it. We de-encapsulate (extract) the IP packet out of the Ethernet frame, which is then discarded:

Preamble	SFD	Destination	Source	Type	IP Packet	FCS

The router will now look at the IP packet, and the first thing it does is check if the header checksum is OK:

If the header checksum is not correct, the IP packet is dropped right away. There is also no error recovery on the network layer; we rely on upper layers for this. If the header checksum is correct, we continue by looking at the destination IP address:

R1 now checks its routing table to see if there is a match:

```
R1#show ip route

Codes: L - local, C - connected, S - static, R - RIP, M - mo-
bile, B - BGP

        D - EIGRP, EX - EIGRP external, O - OSPF, IA - OSPF in-
ter area

        N1 - OSPF NSSA external type 1, N2 - OSPF NSSA external
type 2

        E1 - OSPF external type 1, E2 - OSPF external type 2

        i - IS-IS, su - IS-IS summary, L1 - IS-IS level-1, L2 -
IS-IS level-2

        ia - IS-IS inter area, * - candidate default, U -
per-user static route

        o - ODR, P - periodic downloaded static route, H - NHRP,
l - LISP
```

```
    a - application route

    + - replicated route, % - next hop override, p - over-
rides from PfR
```

Gateway of last resort is not set

```
    192.168.1.0/24 is variably subnetted, 2 subnets, 2 masks

C       192.168.1.0/24 is directly connected, GigabitEther-
net0/1

L       192.168.1.254/32 is directly connected, GigabitEther-
net0/1

S     192.168.2.0/24 [1/0] via 192.168.12.2

    192.168.12.0/24 is variably subnetted, 2 subnets, 2 masks

C       192.168.12.0/24 is directly connected, GigabitEther-
net0/2

L       192.168.12.1/32 is directly connected, GigabitEther-
net0/2
```

Above you can see that R1 knows how to reach the 192.168.2.0/24 network, the next hop IP address is 192.168.12.2. It will now do a second routing table lookup to see if it knows how to reach 192.168.12.2, we call this recursive routing. As you can see, there is an entry for 192.168.12.0/24 with GigabitEthernet 0/2 as the interface to use.

There is one thing left to do with the IP packet before we can forward it. Since we are routing it, we have to decrease the TTL (Time to Live) field by one. R1 will do this and since this changes the IP header, we have to calculate a new header checksum.

Version	Header Length	Type of Service	Total Length	
Identification			IP Flags	Fragment Offset
Time to Live 254		Protocol	Header Checksum	
Source: 192.168.1.1				
Destination: 192.168.2.2				
IP Option				

Once this is done, R1 checks its ARP table to see if there is an entry for 192.168.12.2:

```
R1#show ip arp
```

```
Protocol  Address          Age (min)   Hardware Addr   Type
Interface

Internet  192.168.1.1            58    fa16.3e87.9c2a  ARPA
GigabitEthernet0/1

Internet  192.168.1.254          -     fa16.3e3f.fd3c  ARPA
GigabitEthernet0/1

Internet  192.168.12.1           -     fa16.3e02.83a1  ARPA
GigabitEthernet0/2

Internet  192.168.12.2           95    fa16.3e01.0c98  ARPA
GigabitEthernet0/2
```

No problem there, we have an entry in the ARP table. If not, R1 will send an ARP request to find the MAC address of 192.168.12.2. R1 builds a new Ethernet frame with its own MAC address of the GigabitEthernet 0/2 interface and R2 as the destination. The IP packet is then encapsulated in this new Ethernet frame.

Source:	Destination:	Source:	Destination:
fa16.3e02.83a1	fa16.3e01.0c98	192.168.1.1	192.168.2.2

And the frame will be on its way towards R2.

R2

This Ethernet frame makes it to R2. Like R1 it will first do this:

- Check the FCS of the Ethernet frame.
- De-encapsulates the IP packet, discard the frame.
- Check the IP header checksum.
- Check the destination IP address.

In the routing table, we find this:

```
R2#show ip route

Codes: L - local, C - connected, S - static, R - RIP, M - mo-
bile, B - BGP

       D - EIGRP, EX - EIGRP external, O - OSPF, IA - OSPF in-
ter area

       N1 - OSPF NSSA external type 1, N2 - OSPF NSSA external
type 2
```

```
        E1 - OSPF external type 1, E2 - OSPF external type 2

        i - IS-IS, su - IS-IS summary, L1 - IS-IS level-1, L2 -
IS-IS level-2

        ia - IS-IS inter area, * - candidate default, U -
per-user static route

        o - ODR, P - periodic downloaded static route, H - NHRP,
l - LISP

        a - application route

        + - replicated route, % - next hop override, p - over-
rides from PfR


Gateway of last resort is not set


S     192.168.1.0/24 [1/0] via 192.168.12.1

      192.168.2.0/24 is variably subnetted, 2 subnets, 2 masks

C        192.168.2.0/24 is directly connected, GigabitEther-
net0/1

L        192.168.2.254/32 is directly connected, GigabitEther-
net0/1

      192.168.12.0/24 is variably subnetted, 2 subnets, 2 masks

C        192.168.12.0/24 is directly connected, GigabitEther-
net0/2

L        192.168.12.2/32 is directly connected, GigabitEther-
net0/2
```

Network 192.168.2.0/24 is directly connected to R2 on its GigabitEthernet 0/1 interface. R2 will now reduce the TTL of the IP packet from 254 to 253, recalculate the IP header checksum and checks its ARP table to see if it knows how to reach 192.168.2.2:

```
R2#show ip arp

Protocol  Address            Age (min)  Hardware Addr    Type
Interface
```

```
Internet   192.168.2.2              121    fa16.3e4a.f598   ARPA
GigabitEthernet0/1

Internet   192.168.2.254             -     fa16.3e3c.7da4   ARPA
GigabitEthernet0/1

Internet   192.168.12.1             111    fa16.3e02.83a1   ARPA
GigabitEthernet0/2

Internet   192.168.12.2              -     fa16.3e01.0c98   ARPA
GigabitEthernet0/2
```

There is an ARP entry there. The new Ethernet frame is created, the IP packet encapsulated and it has the following addresses:

Source:	Destination:	Source:	Destination:
fa16.3e3c.7da4	fa16.3e4a.f598	192.168.1.1	192.168.2.2

The frame is then forwarded to H2.

H2

H2 receives the Ethernet frame and will:

- Check the FCS.
- Find its own MAC address as the destination MAC address.
- De-encapsulates the IP packet from the frame.
- Finds its own IP address as the destination in the IP packet.

H2 then looks for the protocol field to figure out what transport layer protocol we are dealing with, what happens next depends on the transport layer protocol that is used. That's a story for another time.

In conclusion, you have now learned how an IP packet is forwarded from one router to another, also known as IP routing.

Let's summarize this process.

The host has a simple decision to make:

- Is the destination on the local subnet?
  - Check ARP table for destination IP address, if empty, send an ARP request.
- Is the destination on a remote subnet?
  - Check ARP table for default gateway IP address, if empty, send an ARP request.

- The router has to perform a number of tasks:

- When it receives an Ethernet frame, check if the FCS (Frame Check Sequence) is correct. If not, drop the frame.

- Check if the destination address of the frame is:

- destined to our MAC address

- destined to a broadcast address of the subnet our interface is in.

- destined to a multicast address that we listen to.

- De-encapsulate the IP packet from the frame, discard the Ethernet frame.

- Look for a match in the routing table for the destination IP address, figure out what the outgoing interface and optionally, the next hop IP address is.

- Decrease the TTL (Time to Live) field in the IP header, recalculate the header checksum.

- Encapsulate the IP packet in a new Ethernet frame.

- Check the ARP table for the destination IP address or next hop IP address.

- Transmit the frame.

Routing Algorithms

A Routing Algorithm is a method for determining the routing of packets in a node. For each node of a network, the algorithm determines a routing table, which in each destination matches an output line. The algorithm should lead to a consistent routing, that is to say without loop. This means that you should not route a packet a node to another node that could send back the package.

There are three main types of routing algorithms:

- Distance Vector (distance-vector routing);

- To link state (link state routing);

- Path to vector (path-vector routing).

Distance vector routing algorithms require that each node exchange information between neighbors, that is to say between nodes directly connected. Therefore, each node can keep updated a table by adding information on all its neighbors. This table shows the distance is each node and each network to be reached. First to be implemented in the Arpanet, this technique quickly becomes cumbersome when the number of nodes increases since we must carry a lot of information node to node. RIP (Routing Information Protocol) is the best example of a protocol using distance vector.

In this type of algorithm, each router broadcasts to its neighbors a vector that lists each network it can reach the metric associated with, that is to say the number of hops. Each router can therefore build a routing table with information received from its neighbors but has no idea of the identity of routers that are on the selected route. Therefore, the use of this solution poses numerous problems for external routing protocols. Indeed, it is assumed that all routers use the same metric, which may not be the case between autonomous systems. Furthermore, an autonomous system can have special reasons to behave differently from another autonomous system. In particular, if an autonomous system needs to determine how else autonomous system will pass its messages, e.g. for security reasons, he can not know.

The algorithms link state had initially intended to overcome the shortcomings of distance vector routing. When a router is initialized, it must define the cost of each of its links connected to another node. The node then broadcasts the information to all nodes in the autonomous system, and therefore not only to its neighbors. From all this information, the nodes can perform their calculation for obtaining a routing table indicating the cost of achieving each destination. When a router receives information that alters its routing table, it notifies all intervening routers in its configuration. As each node has the network topology and costs of each link, routing can be seen as central in each node. OSPF (Open Shortest Path First) implements this technique, which is the second generation of Internet protocols.

The algorithms link state solves the problems mentioned above for external routing but raise other. The various autonomous systems may have different metrics and specific restrictions, so it is not possible to achieve a coherent route. The dissemination of all information necessary for all the autonomous systems can also quickly become unmanageable.

The purpose of the path-vector algorithms is to overcome the shortcomings of the first two categories by providing metrics and seeking to know which network can be reached by any node and autonomous systems which must be crossed for it. This approach is very different from that distance-vector because the paths vectors do not take into account the distances or costs. In addition, the fact that each list routing information all autonomous systems that must be traversed to reach the destination router, the path vector approach is much more directed towards the external routing systems. BGP (Border Gateway Protocol) belongs to this category.

RIP (Routing Information Protocol)

RIP is the most widely used protocol in the TCP/IP environment to route packets between the gateways of the Internet. It is a protocol IGP (Interior Gateway Protocol), which uses an algorithm to find the shortest path.

By the way, refers to the number of nodes crossed, which must be between 1 and 15. The value 16 indicates impossibility. In other words, if the path to get from one point to another of the Internet is above 15, the connection cannot be established. RIP messages to establish the routing tables are sent approximately every 30 seconds. If a RIP message does not reach its neighbor after three minutes, the latter considers that the link is no longer valid; the number of links is greater than 15. RIP is based on a periodic distribution of states network from a router to its neighbors. The release includes a RIP2 routing subnet, message authentication, multipoint transmission, etc.

OSPF (Open Shortest Path First)

OSPF is part of the second generation of routing protocols. Much more complex than RIP, but at higher performance rates, it uses a distributed database that keeps track of the link state. This information forms a description of the network topology and the status of nodes, which defines the routing algorithm by calculating the shortest paths.

The algorithm allows OSPF, from a node, to calculate the shortest path, with the constraints specified in the content associated with each link. OSPF routers communicate with each other via the OSPF protocol, placed on top of IP. Now look at this protocol a bit more detail.

The assumption for link state protocols is that each node can detect link status with its neighbors (on or off) and the cost of this link. We must give to each node enough information to enable him to find the cheapest route to any destination. Each node must have knowledge of its neighbors. If each node to the knowledge of other nodes, a complete map of the network can be established. An algorithm based on the state of the neighboring requires two mechanisms: the dissemination of reliable information on the state of the links and the calculation of routes by summing the accumulated knowledge of the link state.

One solution is to provide a reliable flood of information, to ensure that each node receives his copy of the information from all other nodes. In fact, each node floods its neighbors, which, in turn, flood their own neighbors. Specifically, each node creates its own update packets, called LSP (Link-State Packet), containing the following information:

- Identity of the node that creates the LSP.
- List of neighboring nodes with the cost of the associated link.
- Sequence Number.
- Timer (Time to Live) for this message.

The first two information is needed to calculate routes. The last two aim to make reliable flooding. The sequence number allows to put in order the information that would have been received out of order. The protocol has error detection and retransmission elements.

The route calculation is performed after receiving all the information on the links. From the complete map of the network and costs of links, it is possible to calculate the best route. The calculation is performed using Dijkstra's algorithm on the shortest path.

In the acronym OSPF (Open Shortest Path First) Open the word indicates that the algorithm is open and supported by the IETF. Using the mechanisms outlined above, the OSPF protocol adds the following additional properties:

- Authentication of routing messages. Malfunction can lead to disasters. For example, a node that, following the receipt of wrong messages, intentionally or not, or a striker messages modifying its routing table, calculates a routing table in which all nodes can be achieved at a cost zero automatically receives all network packets. These problems can be avoided by authenticating issuer's messages. Early versions had a OSPF authentication password of 8 bytes. The latest versions have much stronger authentication.

- New hierarchy. This hierarchy allows for better scalability. OSPF introduces another level of hierarchy by partitioning the areas into eras (area). This means that a router within a domain does not need to know how to reach all the networks in the field. Just that he knows how to reach the right age. This results in a reduction of information to be transmitted and stored.

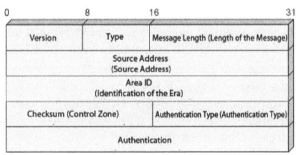

Header Format OSPF

The current version is 2. Five types were defined with values from 1 to 5. The source address indicates the sender of the message. The identification of the era indicates the era in which lies the sending node. The authentication type has the value 0 if there is no authentication, 1 if the authentication password and 2 if an authentication technique is implemented and described in the following 4 bytes.

The five types of messages have the Hello message as Type 1. This message is sent by a node to its neighbors to tell them that it is always present and not broken. The four other types are used to send information such as queries, shipments or acquittals LSP messages. These messages mainly carrying LSA (Link-State Advertisement), that is to say, information about link state. A message can contain several OSPF LSA.

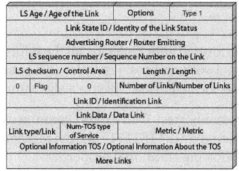

LS Age / Age of the Link		Options	Type 1
Link State ID / Identity of the Link Status			
Advertising Router / Router Emitting			
LS sequence number / Sequence Number on the Link			
LS checksum / Control Area		Length / Length	
0	Flag	0	Number of Links/Number of Links
Link ID / Identification Link			
Link Data / Data Link			
Link type/Link	Num-TOS type of Service	Metric / Metric	
Optional Information TOS / Optional Information About the TOS			
More Links			

OSPF message with an LSA

IS-IS

The IS-IS algorithm was primarily developed by ISO (ISO 10589). It discloses a hierarchical routing based on the decomposition of communication networks into domains. In one area, the nodes indicate their state to IS-IS routers related. The cross-domain communications are performed by a routing to a domain access point determined by the routers responsible for external communications field.

IGRP (Interior Gateway Routing Protocol)

Improved version of RIP, IGRP was designed by Cisco Systems for its own routers. It integrates multipath routing, management of default routes, dissemination of information every 90 seconds instead of every 30 seconds, detection of closures, that is to say, returns to a point whereby the packet has already passed, etc. The protocol itself has been extended for better protection against the loops by EIGRP (Extended IGRP).

EGP (Exterior Gateway Protocol)

EGP is the first routing algorithms have been developed in the early 1980 for routing a packet of an autonomous system to another.

It has three essential procedures that allow the exchange of information. The first procedure concerns the definition of a nearby bridge. The latter is known, a second procedure determines the link that allows the two neighbors to communicate. The third procedure for the exchange of packets between two neighbors connected by a link. The weaknesses of EGP have emerged with the exponential growth of the Internet and the need to avoid some politically sensitive areas.

BGP (Border Gateway Protocol)

To address the weaknesses of EGP, a new algorithm has been initiated by the IETF under the name of BGP. A first version, BGP-1, was implemented in 1990, followed closely by BGP-2 and BGP-3. After a few years was deployed BGP-4, which can handle a lot more effectively large routing tables by bringing together in a single line multiple subnets.

BGP provides new properties compared to EGP, especially to manage loops, which became common in EGP protocol since it deals only couples neighbors, without taking into account possible loop backs by a third autonomous network.

The messages exchanged via BGP-4 are:

- OPEN: to open a relationship with a neighboring node.

- UPDATE: to convey information about a single route or request the destruction of roads that is no longer available.

- KEEPALIVE: to pay the OPEN messages and confirm that the neighbor relationship is still alive.

- NOTICE: To send an error message.

The following three functional procedures are defined in BGP:

- Acquisition of the neighboring nodes;

- Ability to reach the neighbor;

- Ability to reach networks.

Two routers are considered neighbors if they are in the same network. If the two routers are in separate autonomous areas, they may need to exchange routing information. For this, we must first carry out an acquisition of the neighbors, that is to say, allow two nodes that are not in the same autonomous system to share routing information. The acquisition must be made by a formal procedure since the two nodes may not want to exchange routing information. To complete the acquisition, a node transmits the message OPEN. If the remote router accepts the connection, it sends a KEEPALIVE. Once the relationship, to maintain active relationship nodes are exchanged KEEPALIVE. Each node maintains a database of networks it can reach and the route for arriving at these different networks. When a change occurs, the router broadcasts an update message to other routers, which allows them to be updated.

The figure illustrates the format of BGP update packet.

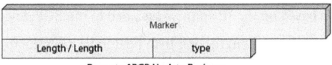

Format of BGP Update Package

The Marker field is reserved for authentication. The transmitter can put a cipher text that can be decrypted by the receiver with the encryption key. Length gives the message length in bytes. The message types are OPEN, UPDATE, KEEPALIVE, and NOTIFICA-TION.

To set up a neighborhood relationship, the starting router initiates a TCP connection and sends an OPEN message. This message indicates the autonomous system in which the transmitter is located and the IP address of the router. It also includes a HOLD TIME PARAMETER, which indicates the number of seconds available for the Hold Timer to determine the maximum time between two messages from the transmitter (KEEPALIVE, UPDATE). If the remote accepts the connection, it calculates the minimum of its own Hold Timer and that of the transmitter and sends it to the transmitter.

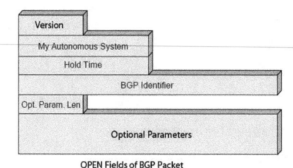

OPEN Fields of BGP Packet

The fields of the OPEN package are shown in Figure. These fields are:

- Version: one-byte value indicating the BGP protocol version used (4 for BGP-4).

- My Autonomous System (my autonomous system): 2-byte value indicating the Autonomous System number of the sender.

- Hold Time (retention time): 2-byte field indicating the number of seconds that the sender proposes for the chosen counter. This avoids the endless closures in the autonomous systems. Once a device receives a BGP OPEN message, it must calculate the value of the hold-down timer that will be used. For this, he chose the smaller of the retaining counter he just received his OPEN message and the value that was set for himself. The selected value is actually the number of seconds between receipt of KEEPALIVE and UPDATE messages sent by the transmitter.

- Identify BGP (BGP identifier): 4-byte field indicating the BGP identifier. This identifier is based on the IP address assigned to the BGP device.

- Optional Parameters Length: one-byte field indicating the total size of the Optional Parameters field in byte. If the value is 0, there are no optional parameters.

- Optional Parameters: field containing the list of optional parameters that are represented by triplets Parameter Type, Length and Parameter Value. The Parameter Type field uniquely identifies each optional parameter. The Parameter Length field indicates the size in bytes of the Parameter Value field. The Parameter Value field is

- A variable size field (which is why its size is shown in the Parameter Length field) containing the optional parameter itself.

- The KEEPALIVE message takes into account the BGP message header. It must be issued often enough to the Hold Timer does not fire. UPDATE messages are used to route two types of messages:

  ◦ Information about a single road, which are recorded in databases of information routers.

  ◦ Information about a list of routes that will be destroyed. The NOTIFICATION messages are sent when an error has been detected. The following errors may be issued:

  ◦ MESSAGE HEADER ERROR: an error in the header of the message was detected as an authentication failure or a syntax error.

  ◦ OPEN MESSAGE ERROR: an error in the syntax of the OPEN message or a rejection of the value of the Hold Timer has been detected.

  ◦ UPDATE ERROR MESSAGE: An error in the UPDATE message was detected as a syntax error.

  ◦ HOLD TIMER EXPIRED: the Hold Timer has expired, and neighborhood session is closed.

  ◦ FINITE STATE MACHINE ERROR: a procedural error occurred.

  ◦ CEASE: to close a connection to another router in a circumstance not taken care of by the previous messages.

IDRP (Inter Domain Routing Protocol)

Estimates planned departure Internet would consist of dozens of networks and hundreds of machines. These figures have been multiplied by 10, 100 and 1000 for networks and by 1000, 10 000 and 100 000 for the machines. These gear ratios are not the only developers of Internet success. The measurements show that the flow passing over the network goes far beyond that represented by all telephone words exchanged worldwide.

Such an explosion is the question of the capacity of the routing mechanisms to bear the load. To reduce the risk of saturation and extend the current arrangements, the immediate solution is to generalize the subnetting. The subnetting is to give a special joint address, subnet mask, to all stations participating in the same logical network, even if the IP address of the logical network stations are from different subnets. This allows routing tables to grow more slowly.

In the IPv6 environment, a new protocol, IDRP, the result of studies on the routing between routing domains (routing domain) by ISO, was adapted to the internet world to achieve routing between autonomous systems. The role of IDRP is slightly different from that of protocols operating within a domain, as it defines a policy routing between autonomous systems and not only a routing algorithm. The policy defined in this proposal leads routers in an autonomous system to agree to, for example, do not go through a particular area or not allow other autonomous systems to send IP packets to a standalone system determined. In other words, there must be consultation between routers to provide only the information corresponding to the defined policy.

The OSPF or RIP routing algorithms kind applied by routers that have the same goal: finding the best possible route, minimizing the number of jump, the time of crossing the network, or by optimizing the transport capacity. These algorithms are based on notions of weight if the links have weight or the path taken is the one for which the sum of the weights of links traversed is lowest. The IDRP routing also aims to find the right paths, but with restrictions for each autonomous system. The algorithm based on distance vectors (Path Vector Routing), taking into account the end-to-end path in addition to the weight to go to neighboring nodes.

As the number of autonomous systems can grow rapidly with increasing routers processing capabilities, it was decided to group the autonomous systems in confederations. The IDRP protocol works on the routing between these confederations. To convey routing information, IDRP uses specific packets carried in IP packets. In the IP area, the Next header field has the number 45 indicates the IDRP protocol.

Route Selection

Crucial to the proper ability of hosts to exchange IP packets is the correct selection of a route to the destination. The rules for the selection of route path are traditionally made on a hop-by-hop basis based solely upon the destination address of the packet. Linux behaves as a conventional routing device in this way, but can also provide a more flexible capability. Routes can be chosen and prioritized based on other packet characteristics.

The route selection algorithm under Linux has been generalized to enable the powerful latter scenario without complicating the overwhelmingly common case of the former scenario.

The Common Case

Local network and the default gateway expose the importance of destination address for route selection. In this simplified model, the kernel need only know the destination address of the packet, which it compares against the routing tables to determine the route by which to send the packet.

The kernel searches for a matching entry for the destination first in the routing cache and then the main routing table. In the case that the machine has recently transmitted a packet to the destination address, the routing cache will contain an entry for the destination. The kernel will select the same route, and transmit the packet accordingly.

If the Linux machine has not recently transmitted a packet to this destination address, it will look up the destination in its routing table using a technique known longest prefix match . In practical terms, the concept of longest prefix match means that the most specific route to the destination will be chosen.

The use of the longest prefix match allows routes for large networks to be overridden by more specific host or network routes, Conversely, it is this same property of longest prefix match, which allows routes to individual destinations to be aggregated into larger network addresses. Instead of entering individual routes for each host, large numbers of contiguous network addresses can be aggregated. This is the realized promise of CIDR networking

In the common case, route selection is based completely on the destination address. Conventional (as opposed to policy-based) IP networking relies on only the destination address to select a route for a packet.

Because the majority of Linux systems have no need of policy based routing features, they use the conventional routing technique of longest prefix match. While this meets the needs of a large subset of Linux networking needs, there are unrealized policy routing features in a machine operating in this fashion.

The Whole Story

With the prevalence of low cost bandwidth, easily configured VPN tunnels, and increasing reliance on networks, the technique of selecting a route based solely on the destination IP address range no longer suffices for all situations. The discussion of the common case of route selection under Linux neglects one of the most powerful features in the Linux IP stack. Since kernel 2.2, Linux has supported policy based routing through the use of multiple routing tables and the routing policy database (RPDB). Together, they allow a network administrator to configure a machine select different routing tables and routes based on a number of criteria.

Selectors available for use in policy-based routing are attributes of a packet passing through the Linux routing code. The source address of a packet, the ToS flags, an fw-mark (a mark carried through the kernel in the data structure representing the packet), and the interface name on which the packet was received are attributes, which can be used as selectors. By selecting a routing table based on packet attributes, an administrator can have granular control over the network path of any packet.

With this knowledge of the RPDB and multiple routing tables, let's revisit in detail the method by which the kernel selects the proper route for a packet. Understanding the series of steps the kernel takes for route selection should demystify advanced routing. In fact, advanced routing could more accurately be called policy-based networking.

When determining the route by which to send a packet, the kernel always consults the routing cache first. The routing cache is a hash table used for quick access to recently used routes. If the kernel finds an entry in the routing cache, the corresponding entry will be used. If there is no entry in the routing cache, the kernel begins the process of route selection. For details on the method of matching a route in the routing cache,

The kernel begins iterating by priority through the routing policy database. For each matching entry in the RPDB, the kernel will try to find a matching route to the destination IP address in the specified routing table using the aforementioned longest prefix match selection algorithm. When a matching destination is found, the kernel will select the matching route, and forward the packet. If no matching entry is found in the specified routing table, the kernel will pass to the next rule in the RPDB, until it finds a match or falls through the end of the RPDB and all consulted routing tables.

Here is a snippet of python-esque pseudocode to illustrate the kernel's route selection process again. Each of the lookups below occurs in kernel hash tables, which are accessible to the user through the use of various iproute2 tools.

Routing Selection Algorithm in Pseudo-code

```
if packet.routeCacheLookupKey in routeCache :

    route = routeCache[ packet.routeCacheLookupKey ]

else

    for rule in rpdb :

        if packet.rpdbLookupKey in rule :

            routeTable = rule[ lookupTable ]

            if packet.routeLookupKey in routeTable :

                route = route_table[ packet.routeLookup_key ]
```

This pseudocode provides some explanation of the decisions required to find a route. The final piece of information required to understand the decision making process is the lookup process for each of the three hash table lookups. In the Table given below, "Keys used for hash table lookups during route selection", each key is listed in order of importance. Optional keys are listed in italics and represent keys that will be matched if they are present.

Table: Keys used for Hash Table Lookups During Route Selection.

route cache	RPDB	route table
destination	source	destination
source	destination	ToS
ToS	ToS	scope
fwmark	fwmark	oif
iif	iif	

The route cache (also the forwarding information base) can be displayed using ip route show cache. The routing policy database (RPDB) can be manipulated with the ip rule utility. Individual route tables can be manipulated and displayed with the ip route command line tool.

Listing The Routing Policy Database (RPDB)

[root@isolde]# ip rule show

0:     from all lookup local

32766: from all lookup main

32767: from all lookup 253

Observation of the output of ip rule show above "Listing the Routing Policy Database (RPDB)" on a box whose RPDB has not been changed should reveal a high priority rule, rule 0. This rule, created at RPDB initialization, instructs the kernel to try to find a match for the destination in the local routing table. If there is no match for the packet in the local routing table, then, per rule 32766, the kernel will perform a route lookup in the main routing table. Normally, the main routing table will contain a default route if not a more specific route. Failing a route lookup in the main routing table the final rule (32767) instructs the kernel to perform a route lookup in table 253.

A common mistake when working with multiple routing tables involves forgetting about the statelessness of IP routing. This manifests when the user configuring the policy routing machine accounts for outbound packets (via fwmark, or ip rule selectors), but forgets to account for the return packets.

Path Selection

Determination of the Best Path

In the process of constructing the routing database, the router may face the issue of selection when multiple paths are proposed to it by several fellow routers. In that case, the router asks two important questions: What's the most trusted source? And what's the lowest distance? Obviously, and based on what we discussed earlier on how routing protocols calculate path distance, the router uses this trust preference order:

- ITSELF (connected routes)

- The Administrator (Static routes)

- EIGRP

- OSPF

- RIP routes (there are more than three dynamic routing protocols and so the preference list is much longer).

This trust preference order is called Administrative Distance.

What if the router has several possible paths to the same destination from the same routing source? Here the second question, what's the lowest distance route, acts as a tie breaker, and a distance preference order is used based on a Metric value.

Now the final case is what if the packet received by the router matches several entries in the same database? Here a third question has to be asked: What's the most specific entry? This is determined by the using the entry with longest prefix or matching bits.

But what if the packet matches multiple entries with the same matching bits? The router load balances the packets to the possible forwarders. Meaning that if the routers receives, let's say, twenty packets and has four different matching paths, it will divide the load (the packets) to make the routing process faster and more efficient which results in a better network performance.

BGP Attributes

Path Attributes as the name suggests are the characteristics of an advertised BGP Route. BGP routing policy is set and communicated using the path attributes.

Path Attributes fall into one of the two categories:

1. Well-known Path Attributes

2. Optional Path Attributes.

Well-known: Meaning these attributes must be recognized by all the BGP implementations.

Well- Known BGP Path Attributes fall into two sub-categories known as:

1. Mandatory (Called as Well-known Mandatory)

2. Discretionary (Called as Well-Known Discretionary).

Mandatory: This means the attribute must be always included and carried in all BGP update messages to peers. The BGP implementation has to recognize the attribute, accept it and also advertise it to its peers.

Discretionary: Meaning these are recognized by the BGP implementation but may or may not be sent in a specific Update message. Its up to the discretion of BGP Implementation to send or not to send these attributes in the update messages to the peers.

Optional: Meaning these attributes may or may not be supported by the BGP implementations.

Optional BGP Path attributes also fall into two sub-categories:

1. Transitive (Called as Optional Transitive)

2. Non-transitive (Called as Optional Non-transitive)

Transitive: BGP process has to accept the path in which it is included and should pass it on to other peers even if these attributes are not supported. Meaning if any optional attribute is not recognized by a BGP implementation, then BGP looks to check if the transitive flag is set. If the transitive flag is set then BGP implementation should accept the attribute and advertise it to its other BGP Peers.

Non-transitive: If the BGP process does not recognize the attribute then it can ignore the update and not advertise the path to its peers. If the transitive flag is not set then BGP implementation can quietly ignore the attribute, it does not have to accept and advertise this attribute to its other peers.

To summarize the BGP Path Attribute Categories:

1. Well-known Mandatory: Recognized and Included in all BGP Update messages.

2. Well-known Discretionary: Recognized and May or May not include in BGP Update messages

3. Optional Transitive: Even if Not Supported it Still need to accept and Send in Update Message.

4. Optional Non-transitive: Can be ignored and not advertise to peers.

List of bgp path attributes	
Attribute Name	Category / Class
ORIGIN	Well-Known Mandatory
AS_PATH	Well-Known Mandatory
NEXT_HOP	Well-Known Mandatory
LOCAL_PREF	Well-Known Discretionary
ATOMIC_AGGREGATE	Well-Known Discretionary
AGGREGATOR	Optional Transitive
COMMUNITY	Optional Transitive
MULTI_EXIT_DISC (MED)	Optional Non-Transitive
ORIGINATOR_ID	Optional Non-Transitive
CLUSTER LIST	Optional Non-Transitive
MULTIPROTOCOL Reachable NLRI	Optional Non-Transitive
MULTIPROTOCOL Unreachable NLRI	Optional Non-Transitive

ORIGIN Attribute

As the name suggests the ORIGIN attribute specifies the origin of the routing update. This is a Well-known Mandatory BGP Attribute and hence has to be recognized and sent to peers by all BGP implementations. The ORIGIN attribute can contain one of these three values:

1. IGP

2. EGP

3. Incomplete

If BGP has multiple routes then ORIGIN is one of the factors in determining the preferred route. IGP is the highest preferred ORIGIN value followed by EGP and Incomplete ORIGIN Attribute is the lowest preferred ORIGIN value of the three.

IGP: It means that the NLRI was learnt from an internal routing protocol of the originating AS.

EGP: This ORIGIN code specifies that the NLRI be learnt from EGP.

Incomplete: Usually misunderstood, this value means that the NLRI was learnt from some other means, it does not mean that the route is faulty, it only specifies that the information to determine the ORIGIN is not complete. All redistributed routes into BGP have an Incomplete ORIGIN attribute, since the origin of these routes cannot be determined.

AS_PATH Attribute

AS_Path describes the inter-AS path taken to reach a destination. It gives a list of AS

Numbers traversed when reaching to a destination. Every BGP speaker when advertising a route to a peer will include its own AS number in the NLRI. The subsequent BGP speakers who advertise this route will add their own AS number to the AS_Path, the subsequent AS numbers get prepended to the list. The end result is the AS_Path attribute is able to describe all the autonomous systems it has traversed, beginning with the most recent AS and ending with the originating AS.

AS_Path is a well-known attribute, so if a BGP speaker advertises the route to a destination then it has to include its AS number in the advertisement if its originating the NLRI or if its advertising a received NLRI to other peers then it has to prepend its AS number to the existing list of autonomous systems in the AS_path attribute.

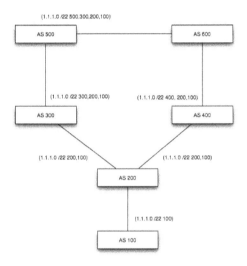

Lets assume AS-100 is advertising 1.1.1.0/22 to AS-200 Since AS-100 is originating the NLRI the advertisement will be [1.1.1.0/22 100]

AS-200 will receive this NLRI and advertise it to its peers AS-300 and AS-400, the NLRI advertisement will look like [1.1.1.0/22 200,100] – specifying that to reach the network 1.1.1.0/22 you have a path where you can to traverse AS-200 then AS-100.

The subsequent autonomous systems AS-300, AS-400 and others do the same. In the end AS-600 receives two routes to reach the network 1.1.1.0/22. To reach any host in network 1.1.1.0/22 it can either reach through AS-500 or from AS-400, since BGP is a path vector protocol by default AS-600 will choose the path from AS-400 since its shorter (less number of Autonomous Systems to traverse). Also note by default EBGP will not load balance across the two paths and will select only one best path, but it can be configured to load balance.

Also, BGP Speaker will add its AS number to the AS_Path only when an Update message is being sent to the neighbor which means only when BGP is advertising the route to the peer it will prepend its AS number to the AS_Path attribute.

AS_Path Prepend to Prefer one Route to Another

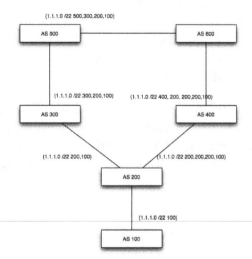

In BGP the outgoing route advertisements directly influence the incoming traffic. In the example lets assume the link between AS-200 and AS-400 is a T1 and AS-200 does not want to prefer this route. Since the outgoing advertisements directly influence the incoming traffic in BGP, and AS-200 wants to prefer AS-300 assuming this is a high speed Gig link, AS-200 will prepend its AS number is the advertisements to AS-400 so that it makes it less preferable, the new BGP path ratio is reflected in the example diagram. AS-600 will now prefer the path from AS-500 and will follow the path 500-300-200-100 to reach 1.1.1.0/22 since this one becomes the shorter path.

AS_Path prepending is one of the ways to influence how the BGP advertisements and the incoming traffic is handled.

AS_Path Attribute also makes sure that there is no routing loop, if an NLRI advertisement is received from a BGP peer and the receiving AS sees its own AS number in the AS_Path list of the destination route which is received, then the receiving BGP speaker knows that there is a loop and will not accept the advertisement.

AS_Path can be shown by issuing the command "sh ip bgp" on a cisco router.

NEXT_HOP Attribute

NEXT_HOP Attribute specifies the next hop IP address to reach the destination advertised in the NLRI. NEXT_HOP is a well-known mandatory attribute and it has some set of rules to be followed for different BGP scenarios.

1. If the BGP Peers are in different Autonomous Systems then the NEXT_HOP IP address that will be sent in the update message will be the IP address of the advertising router.

2. If the BGP peers are in the same AS (IBGP Peers), and the destination network being advertised in the update message is also in the same AS, then the NEXT_ HOP IP address that will be sent in the update message will be the IP address of the advertising router.

3. If the BGP peers are in the same AS (IBGP Peers), and the destination network being advertised in the update message is in an external AS, then the NEXT_ HOP IP address that will be sent in the update message will be the IP address of the external peer router which sent the advertisement to this AS.

Below are some examples for each of these scenarios.

NEXT_HOP BGP UPDATE between Different Autonomous Systems

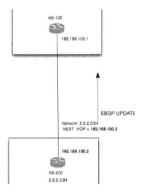

In this example, the EBGP update is pretty straightforward. As the rule states If the BGP Peers are in different Autonomous Systems then the NEXT_HOP IP address that will be sent in the update message will be the IP address of the advertising router.

NEXT_HOP will always be advertised by the router, which is sending an update to the BGP peer on how to reach a particular network.

The router in AS-200 sends in its update that network 2.2.2.0/24 is reachable via its IP address of 192.168.100.2

The router in AS-100 when needs to reach the network 2.2.2.0/24, it will always use the next hop ip address of 192.168.100.2 which is advertised by the router in AS-100 as a NEXT_HOP Attribute to reach this network.

Since NEXT_HOP is a well-known Mandatory Attribute, the router in AS-100 will have to accept and honor this value.

In this scenario where there are two routers in different AS and have formed the EBGP relationship, the NEXT_HOP attribute is pretty simple and straightforward.

The command "show ip bgp neighbor 192.168.100.1 advertised-routes" when executed on the router in AS-200 will show the network prefix it is advertising and the NEXT_

HOP it is advertising. Both these values will be network: 2.2.2.0/24 and the NEXT_HOP as 192.168.100.2

NEXT_HOP BGP UPDATE Within Peers in Same Autonomous System

NEXT_HOP address for the BGP peers in the same Autonomous Systems is the address of the advertising router, which in this case is RTR-A. RTR-A and RTR-C is IBGP Peers, When RTR-A sends an update message indicating the reachability information for network 10.10.10.0/24, it puts its own IP address in the NEXT_HOP. For RTR-C to reach the network 10.10.10.0/24, it will have the NEXT_HOP IP address of RTR-A and not RTR-B to which it is directly connected.

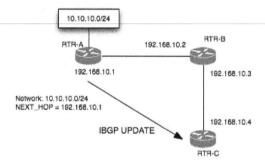

Also, this applies to the routers on the same-shared IP segment; the NEXT_HOP will always be the IP address of the advertising router.

In this scenario, the router is AS-100 is advertising the network 172.16.30.0/24 and specifies the next hop ip address of its own as 172.16.10.1, the router in AS-200 receives this update and has the next hop to reach this network as the IP address of the router which advertised the network which is the router in AS-100.

Within AS-200 now RTR-A advertises this network to its IBGP peers and advertises the NEXT_HOP as the IP address of the router in AS-100.

RTR-C, which is the IBGP peer of RTR-A, now knows to reach the network 172.16.30.0/24 it has to use the next hop ip address of 172.16.10.1 (which is the ip address on router in AS-100).

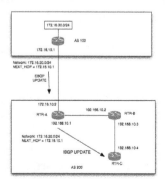

This could cause an issue because RTR-C does not know how to reach the address 172.16.10.1 and the packets for the destination in 172.16.20.0/24 is dropped. The route 172.16.30.0/24 is installed in BGP table but it is not installed in the IGP as the next hop IP address specified is not reachable and is considered as an invalid address. This issue can be resolved in one of the three ways.

1. Use static routes to link external addresses to internal routers, not a very feasible solution to use.

2. Run IGP is passive mode on the external interfaces.

3. BGP implementation gives a more practical solution called as "Next_Hop_Self" this when configured on the local RTR-A it will cause RTR-A to set its own IP address in the NEXT_HOP attribute. The internal peers RTR-B and RTR-C will now have a NEXT_HOP IP address of 192.168.10.1 to reach the network 172.16.30.0/24 in AS-100. Since the internal routers already have the RTR-A's address in IGP they know how to reach the external network through RTR-A.

Local Preference (LOCAL_PREF):

LOCAL_PREF is only used in updates sent to the IBGP Peers. This is a well-known discretionary attribute and as the name suggests it is used locally within an AS to update the internal BGP peers. It is not passed on to the BGP peers in other autonomous systems.

LOCAL_PREF specifies the BGP Speaker's degree of preference for an advertised route.

The higher the value of Local Preference attribute the more preferred the route is.

Remember: For Local Preference: Higher Value = More Preference.

Note that the Local Preference will only affect the traffic leaving the AS.

For an example on how LOCAL_PREF influences BGP routing, take a look at the diagram below.

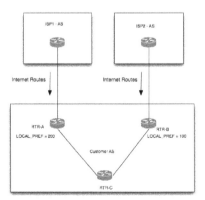

In this example, the customer is peering with two ISPs to get the internet routing table, assuming that the connection to ISP-1 is a Gig connection and the connection to ISP-2 is only a T1, the customer wants to use ISP-1 and keep ISP-2 as a backup in case the link to ISP-1 fails.

From the diagram, RTR-A is connected to ISP-1 and it advertises the routes received from ISP-1 with a local preference of 200 to other internal BGP peers.

RTR-B is connected to ISP-2 and is advertising the routes received from ISP-2 with a local preference value of 100 (which is the default value of LOCAL_PREF).

Assuming that both the ISPs are advertising the same destination routes then RTR-C, the internal BGP Peer receives the routes from both RTR-A and RTR-B and will select RTR-A because the LOCAL_PREF value is higher on the routes advertised by RTR-A.

Also note that RTR-B will also prefer the routes advertised by ISP-1 connected to RTR-A. that is all internal routers within the customer AS in the diagram will now prefer Routes received from ISP-1.

LOCAL_PREF affects the traffic leaving the AS, the traffic leaving the Customer-AS in this example will prefer the routes from ISP1 to reach the destination networks. If there are any destination routes that ISP2 is advertising which are not being advertised on ISP1 for some reason, then traffic destined for those routes which are missing in ISP1's advertisements will leave from RTR-B to ISP2 in order to reach those destinations network prefixes.

ATOMIC_AGGREGATE and AGGREGATOR

ATOMIC_AGGREGATOR path attribute does route aggregation on the routes that are non identical but point to the same destination. In effect if summarizes the routes when advertising them to the BGP peer.

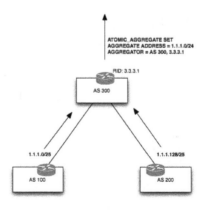

When a router receives routes for the same destination, it makes the best path decision by selecting the more specific path. When aggregation is performed the BGP Speaker starts advertising the less specific routes to its peers but the path detail information is lost in this process. Anytime a BGP speaker does this aggregation by summarizing more specific routes into a less specific route it has to inform its down stream BGP peers that aggregation has been done, this is done by attaching the ATOMIC_AGGREGATE attribute to the update message.

When the downstream BGP speakers receive the route with ATOMIC_AGGREGATE attribute set, then they cannot advertise the more specific routes for this aggregated route, and they will have to keep the ATOMIC_AGGREGATE attribute attached when advertising this route to their BGP peers.

In some instances not all routes in a network can be aggregated, and in others all of them can be aggregated but still there might be an need to advertise both aggregate-address and the more-specific routes. In both the cases the router can advertise both the more specific routes as well as the aggregate address. Aggregation is done by the command "aggregate-address <network-prefix> <mask> and individual network statements" if the same command is used with the keyword "summary-only" then only the aggregate address is advertised and not the more-specific prefixes.

ATOMIC_AGGREGATE is a well-known discretionary attribute and informs its down stream routers that a loss of path information has occurred.

AGGREGATOR

When the ATOMIC_AGGREGATE attribute is set, the BGP speaker has an option of attaching the AGGREGATOR attribute. AGGREGATOR i optional transitive attribute and gives information on where the aggregation was performed by including the AS number and the IP address of the router that originated the aggregate route. Cisco uses the Router ID as the address of AGGREGATOR.

AS_SET

When aggregation is done on the BGP route, the AS_Path information is lost. One of the purposes why AS_Path is used is to avoid any loops, and if the BGP speaker does not see its own AS number in the AS_Path, it will accept the route and can create a potential loop in the routing.

AS_SET is used to avoid this; AS_SET gives an unordered list of AS numbers when aggregation is done.

When a BGP speaker does aggregation for an NLRI leant from other autonomous systems, it can include all the AS numbers in the AS_Path as AS_SET, including AS_SET will still give a list of AS numbers, though unordered it will still let the BGP speaker know if its own AS number was there somewhere in the path and it can reject the NLRI if its own AS number was seen for this NLRI advertisement.

MULTI_EXIT_DISC Attribute: (MED)

MED is an optional non-transitive attribute and it is used to influence how the incoming traffic comes into an AS.

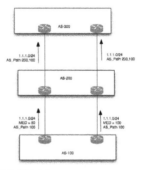

MED allows the AS to inform its immediate neighbor AS of its preferred entry points. MED is also called as metric and the lowest value of MED is the most preferred one.

Note that MED is not passed beyond the receiving AS. It is only used to influence traffic between two directly connected autonomous systems. Also MEDS are never compared when the routes to the same destination are received from two or more different AS. MED only applies to the routes advertised by a single AS.

In this example, AS-100 advertises the route from two different entry points with the MED value of 50 on one router and a value of 100 on another. The Preferred entry point will be the router, which is advertising the routes with the MED value of 50, since this is the lower value. Also notice that AS-200 will not advertise the AS-100 MED values to AS-300 in its outgoing route advertisements, since MED is an optional non-transitive attribute.

Also in this example the MED attribute will only take affect if AS-200's BGP implementation recognizes the MED attribute, or else setting these MED attribute values on the routes for a preferred entry point into, AS will not have any affect.

Note: By default MED values are not compared for routes to the same destination received from two or more different autonomous systems. There is however a way for enabling this by using the command "bgp-always-comapre-med". When this command is used, MED values on the received routes for same destination from different autonomous systems are compared. If this command is configured then it needs to be configured on every BGP router in the AS.

COMMUNITY Attribute

COMMUNITY attribute allows sharing a common policy across multiple BGP peers who can be identified to be in a same group.

This is an optional transitive attribute so it needs to be passed on to other BGP peers.

This attribute simplifies the policy enforcement by grouping a set of BGP peers with common properties to share a common set of policy.

An AS can set a COMMUNITY attribute for some of its BGP peer routes, and set the LO-CAL_PREF and MED attributes based on the COMMUNITY rather than setting these values individually for each of these Peers. This helps in simplifying the process of policy enforcement.

Community attribute is always represented in Hex Format and is a set of 4 Octets.

As per RFC 1997 the first 2 octets are AS-number and the last two octets are an administratively defined identifier, resulting in the format of AA:NN.

The default Cisco format is the reverse of this as NN:AA, but this can be changed by the command "ip bgp-community new-format".

Community values in these ranges are reserved.

0 – 65535 [Hex: 0x00000000-0x0000FFFF] and

4294901760 – 4294967295 [Hex: 0xFFFF0000-0xFFFFFFFF]

Some of the well-known communities fall into these reserved ranges, as below.

1. INTERNET: The Internet community is the default community. it has no value. All routes by default to belong to this community and all of the routes in this category are advertised freely.

2. NO_EXPORT: Routes received carrying this value cannot be advertised to EBGP Peers. That is these routes must not be advertised outside the AS. The value is 0xFFFFFF01. If there is a confederation defined and this value is received then the routes cannot be advertised outside the confederation.

3. NO_ADVERTISE: Routes received carrying this value cannot be advertised at all, that is they cannot be advertised to IBGP or EBGP peers. The value is 0xFFFFFF02.

4. LOCAL_AS: Routes received carrying this value cannot be advertised to EBGP peers and peers in other AS within a confederation. The value is 0xFFFFFF03. As per RFC 1997 this attribute is called as NO_EXPORT_SUBCONFD.

Apart from these well-known community attributes, private community attributes can also be defined for certain uses, but these private community attributes will only be significant to the AS that has defined it in context to its BGP peers.

A route can carry more than one community attribute, and the BGP peer that receives such a route with multiple community attributes can act based on one, some or all of the community attributes. A router can also add or modify the community attributes before passing them to other BGP peers.

Routing Schemes

A routing scheme is a mechanism enabling to deliver messages from any source to any target in a network. The latter is typically modeled as an undirected connected weighted graph G = (V, E) where V models the set of routers and E models the set of communication links between routers. All edges incident to a degree-d node are labeled from 1 to d, in an arbitrary manner, and the label at a node u of an incident edge e is called the port number of edge e at u. A routing scheme consists of a way of assigning a routing table to every node of the given network. These tables should contain enough information so that, for every target node t, each node is able to compute the port number of the incident edge through which it should forward a message of destination t. The routing tables must collectively guarantee that every message of any source s and any target t will eventually be delivered to t.

Unicasting

A unicast transmission is a one-to-one communication that passes from a single source to a single receiver or destination. One of the simplest everyday examples of unicast transmission would be a phone call between two people.

In computing terms, unicast transmission is the most common method of information transfer, which takes place on networks. Traffic in the form of streams of data packets typically moves from a single host (such as a web server) to a single endpoint (such as a client app, computer, or browser).

Though a unicast transmission is point to point, the same information may be passed from the source node to any number of other nodes on the network, in a succession of one-to-one communications. A replica of each packet in the data stream goes to every host on the network that requests it.

More technically, unicast transmission employs Internet Protocol or IP provision techniques such as transmission control protocol (TCP) and user datagram protocol (UDP). These are session-based protocols, which allow a communication to be set up, completed, and terminated as a single operation. A unicast transmission is sent to a single node on the network, which is identified by a unique 64-bit address.

Benefits of Unicast

Unicast transmission has been in use for a long time, with well-established protocols and easy to deploy techniques. Well-known and trusted applications such as http, smtp, ftp and telnet all use the unicast standard and employ the TCP transport protocol.

On a network, transmission takes place from host to host, which can reduce the traffic burden on a Local Area Network (LAN), as a whole.

Drawbacks of Unicast

If a network device is called upon to send a message to multiple nodes, it has to send multiple unicast messages, each addressed to a specific device. This first requires the sender to know the exact IP address of each destination device.

In addition, each unicast client that connects to the host server uses up some network bandwidth. If multiple clients are involved, this may introduce scaling issues as far as network and server resources are concerned. The problem becomes even more pronounced if many hosts are transmitting via unicast to many receivers, at the same time.

Broadcasting

Any form of communication in which a single sender transmits messages to many receivers at once, the most familiar examples being the television and public radio systems. The opposite of broadcast is POINT-TO-POINT or narrowcast communication, between just a single transmitter and a single receiver - a telephone conversation for example. When such a multiple connection is made via a network cable as opposed to wireless, such communication is often called MULTIPOINT, as opposed to a point-to-point or UNICAST. Communication channel is shared by all the machines on the network in broadcast network.

In broadcast networks, each receiving station receives all the signals sent by the transmitters. The routing of the signals is effected passively. Each station may transmit on a separate wavelength. The receiver receives the desired signal to be placed on the right wavelength. The two most conventional topologies are the star and bus, as shown in figure. In both cases, each station transmits towards the area, which makes a wavelength-division multiplexing of all waves reaching it.

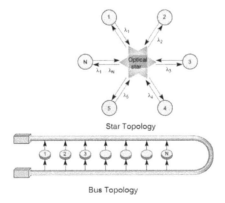

Star Topology

Bus Topology

When all the signals come directly to all stations without passing by electric forms, the network is said single-hop. This is the case of the two structures illustrated in Figure. If you have to go through intermediate steps to perform routing, we have multi-hop network (multi-hop), such as those described in Figure below.

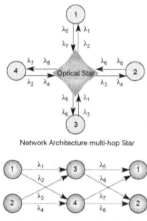

Network Architecture multi-hop Star

Network Architecture Shufflenet Multihop

As an example of a broadcast network and single jump, we have already mentioned the Lambdanet Bellcore. The difficulty of this type of network is to have sufficient wavelength and receivers with components capable of adapting to rapid changes in wavelength optical signals. In view of this major difficulty, of diffusion and multihop networks have been developed by several companies. In these networks, the transmitter and the receiver usually have only two wavelengths. To go from an input to an output port, the information is routed in the form of a data packet. As switching is done at the intermediate node, there are passing through an electronic element, which is a fragile item to be secured.

The above Figure shows that to move from node 1 to node 2 must be issued, for example, the wavelength of 2 to node 4, which forwards on the wavelength of 8 to node 2, or issue on the wavelength 1 to the node 3, which transmits to the station 2 of the wavelength 6. It is seen that two paths are possible, which secures the communication process.

The figure below illustrates a router, which has sent a broadcast to all devices on its network:

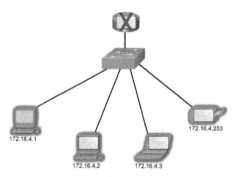

Normally, when the computers on the network receive a packet, they will first try to match the MAC address of the packet with their own and if that is successful, they process the packet and hand it to the OSI layer above (Network Layer), if the MAC address is not matched, then the packet is discarded and not processed. However, when they see a MAC address of FF:FF:FF:FF:FF:FF, they will process this packet because they recognize it as a broadcast.

But what does a "broadcast" look like?

The image below shows the basic information contained within a network broadcast:

MAC source addr	MAC dest. addr	Frame	Protocol	Addr. IP src	Addr. IP dest
00:80:C8:F9:72:F3	FF:FF:FF:FF:FF:FF	IP	UDP->bootps	192.168.0.1	255.255.255.255

Let's now have a closer look at the above captured packet.

The image above shows a broadcast packet. You can clearly see that the "MAC destination address" is set to FF:FF:FF:FF:FF:FF. The "Address IP destination" is set to 255.255.255.255, this is the IP broadcast address and ensures that no matter what IP address the receiving computer(s) have, they will not reject the data but process it.

Now you might ask yourself "Why would a workstation want to create a broadcast packet ?"

The answer to that lies within the various protocols used on our networks.

Let's take for example Address Resolution Protocol, or ARP. ARP is used to find out which MAC address (effectively, which network card or computer) has a particular IP address bound to it. For a network device such as a router to ask "Who has IP address 192.168.0.100?", it must "shout" it out so it can grab everyone's attention, which is why it will use a broadcast address to make sure everyone on the network listens and processes the packet.

In the example image above, the particular machine was looking for a DHCP server (notice the "bootps" protocol under the UDP Header - Layer 4, which is basically DHCP).

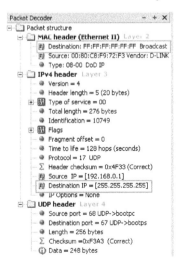

Subnet Broadcast or Direct Broadcast

A Subnet or Direct broadcast is targeted not to all hosts on a network, but to all hosts on a subnet. Since a physical network can contain different subnets/networks e.g. 192.168.0.0 and 200.200.200.0, the purpose of this special broadcast is to send a message to all the hosts in a particular subnet.

In the example below, Router A sends a subnet broadcast onto the network. Hosts A,B,C and the Server are configured to be part of the 192.168.0.0 network so they will receive and process the data, but Host D is configured with a different IP Address, so it's part of a different network, it will accept the packet cause of its broadcast MAC address, but will drop the packet when it reaches its Network Layer, where it will see that this packet was for a different IP network.

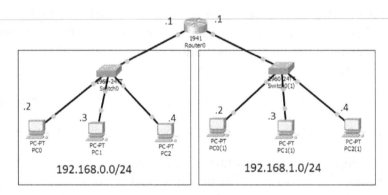

It is very similar to the network broadcast we just talked about but varies slightly in the sense that its IP broadcast is not set to 255.255.255.255 , but is set to the subnet broadcast address. For example, my home network is a Class C network: 192.168.0.0 with a subnetmask of 255.255.255.0 or, if you like to keep it simple, 192.168.0.0/24.

This means that the available valid hosts for this network are from 192.168.0.1 to 192.168.0.254. In this Class C network, as in every other network, there are 2 addresses, which we can't use. The first one is preserved to identify the network (192.168.0.0) and the second one for the subnet broadcast (192.168.0.255).

No.		MAC source addr	MAC dest. addr	Frame	Protocol	Addr. IP src	Addr. IP dest	Port src	Port dest
36	2	00:02:B3:3C:32:68	FF:FF:FF:FF:FF:FF	IP	UDP->Netbios-NS	192.168.0.6	192.168.0.255	137	137

The above packet, captured from my packet sniffer, shows my workstation broadcasting to the subnet 192.168.0.0. From the broadcast address you can tell that we are using a full Class C network range, otherwise the Destination IP wouldn't be 192.168.0.255.

The Packet decoder on the right shows you the contents of each header from the above packet.

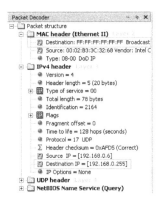

Looking at the MAC Header (Datalink Layer), the destination MAC address is set to FF:FF:FF:FF:FF:FF and the IP Header (Network Layer) has the Destination IP set to 192.168.0.255 which is the Subnet Broadcast Address. Again, all computers on the network which are part of the 192.168.0.0 subnet will process this packet, the rest will drop the packet once they see it's for a network to which they do not belong.

Multicasting

Some broadcast systems also support transmission to a subnet of the machines. This is known as multicasting. In other words, Multicast is a communication system between a single sender and multiple receivers on a network. One address bit is reserved for multicasting and the remaining (n - 1) address bits can hold a group number. Any machine can subscribe to any or all of the groups. The IP (Internet Protocol) address supports concept of classes. This architecture is called Classful addressing. In Classful addressing, the IP address space is divided into five classes: classes A, B, C, D and E. Each class occupies some part of the whole address space.

Multicast Address

- Addresses in class D are for multicast communication from one source to a group of destinations.

- If a host belongs to a group or groups it may have one or more multicast addresses.

- A multicast address can be used only as a destination address but never as a source address.

Multicast Communication

- Unicast communication is one source sending a packet to one destination.

- But multicast communication is one source sending a packet to multiple destinations.

- Such a communication takes place using multicast packets.

Applications

Multicasting has many applications such as access to distributed database, information dissemination, distance learning and multimedia communications.

Anycast

Anycast, also known as IP Anycast, is a networking technique that allows for multiple machines to share the same IP address. Based on the location of the user request, the routers send it to the machine in the network that is closest. This is beneficial since, among other things, it reduces latency and increases redundancy. If a particular data center were to go offline, an Anycasted IP would choose the best path for users and automatically redirect them to the next closest data center. The following outlines some of the pros and cons that are associated with configuring Anycast.

Pros

- Speed: Traffic going to an Anycast node will be routed to the nearest node thus reducing latency between the client and the node itself. This ensures that speeds will be optimized no matter where the client is requesting information.

- Redundancy: Anycast improves redundancy by placing multiple servers across the globe using the same IP. This allows for traffic to be rerouted to the next nearest server in the case that one server fails or goes offline.

- DDoS mitigation: DDoS attacks are caused by botnets, which can generate so much traffic they overwhelm a typical Unicast machine. The benefit of having an Anycast configuration in this situation is that each server is able to "absorb" a portion of the attack resulting in less strain on the server overall.

- Load balancing: Load balancing can be utilized in the case that there are multiple nodes all within the same geographic distance from the request. This takes some of the resource requirements off of a singular node and disperses them across multiple nodes.

Cons

- Difficult to Implement: Implementing IP Anycast is a complex endeavor that requires additional hardware, reliable upstream providers, and proper traffic routing.

Border Gateway Protocol and Autonomous Systems

Border Gateway Protocol (BGP) and Autonomous Systems (AS) are integral parts in the way IP Anycast functions. The BGP exchanges routing and reachability information between AS. It makes routing decisions based on paths, policies, and rule sets, which is a key component of what IP Anycast offers. Within BGP routing there are multiple routes for the same IP address, which are pointing to different locations.

An Autonomous System is a single or collection of networks all administered by the same administrator. Autonomous Systems each have a unique ASN, or Autonomous System Number, for use in BGP routing since each ASN identifies each network on the Internet.

Tools like ExaBGP can be used to transform BGP messages into text or JSON, which can then be handled by simple scripts. This allows administrators to easily detect and handle network or service failures.

Working of Anycast

Anycast directs user requests to the nearest node in order to reduce page latency. It does this by following these steps:

1. Multiple service instances announce they share the same IP address.

2. When the user's browser makes a request, the router receives that request and simply chooses the route with the shortest distance to the nearest server based on the AS path.

Using Unicast, the path would only lead to one destination no matter the distance. Using Anycast, the route is optimized due to it always selecting the best path. In the case that a server is down, the BGP will simply find the next best path and route the request there.

It should be noted however that anycast can be configured not only to route request based on distance but also other factors for example:

- Availability of server

- Number of connections

- Time to response.

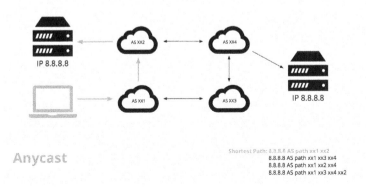

Geocast

Geo-cast Routing in Vanet

It is basically location based multicast routing. The objective of geo-cast routing is to deliver packets from source node to all other nodes within a specified geographical region, also called Zone of Relevance.

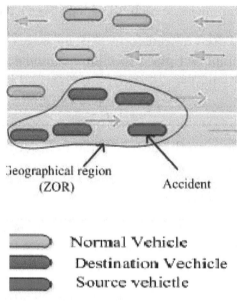

Figure: Geo-Cast Routing

Initial Efforts towards Geocasting

The first idea of geocast goes back to attempt to relate IP address to geographic locations in the UUMAP project. The project maintained a database in which geographic locations of Internet host were stored. Later two similar projects tried to relate DNS names to geographic locations. They extended the DNS data structure with geographic longitude and latitude information, which makes it possible to return geographic location of a host, based on IP address or DNS names. However, both these approaches were notable to support the reverse function, that is, they were not able to return the IP address or DNS name based on geographic information.

Therefore, such systems made it possible geographic destination location was first presented in Cartesian Routing. Cartesian Routing uses latitude-based and longitude-based addresses. Each network node, that is, source node, destination node, or intermediate node, knows its geographic address and the geographic addresses of its directly connected routers to relate data flows with geographic areas, but they were unsuitable to direct data flow to a given geographic area. Routing packets to a geographic destination location was first presented in Cartesian Routing. Cartesian Routing uses latitude-based and longitude-based addresses. Each network node, that is, source node, destination node, or intermediate node, knows its geographic address and the geographic addresses of its directly connected routers.

Geocast Routing Motivation

Emerging inter - vehicles communication based on mobile networks has sparked considerable curiosity about the intelligent transport systems (ITSs). Wireless ad-hoc network communication plays a vital role in ITS. By using the global positioning system (GPS), VANETs have overcome the limitation of traditional systems, like radar and video cameras and make possible more advanced services in ITS. Most of the ITS services require sending messages to all nodes in a certain geographical area, called geocasting, a subclass of multicasting. Unlike multicast, which sends a packet to arbitrary nodes, geocast enables transmission of a packet to all nodes within a pre-defined geographical region. The goal of geocasting is to guarantee delivery while maintaining a low cast.In vehicular ad-hoc networks, the major challenge for routing protocol is to find a route from the sender to the destination without any preconfigured information and under constantly varying link circumstances. Topology based routing is strictly avoided because of dynamic changes in topology. The approach of position based routing relies only on geographic position information to deal with the problem of dynamic topology changes. This means, that all routing decisions, to which node packet should be forwarded, are based on the geographic destination data that is included in the packet. Position based routing is a suitable candidate for vehicular ad-hoc networks since position information is already available from navigation systems.

Different Techniques of Geocast Routing

There are three different techniques of geocast routing: Routing with simple flooding, direct flooding and no flooding.

Simple Flooding

This algorithm works: vehicle relays a received packet to all neighbors vehicle. In order to avoid loops and endless flooding, this packet was not already received before. A vehicle broadcasts a packet if the own whereabouts is within the specified destination province, which is comprised in each geocast packet. This is a straight forward and resilient but not efficient approach. Direct flooding trying to limit the message overhead and network congestion. In this flooding whole the network without trying to limit the flooding area. But we are trying to limit the message overhead and network congestion by applying the forwarding zone. But forwarding zone protocol is different from the direct forwarding method. So we use direct flooding and simple flooding with routing.

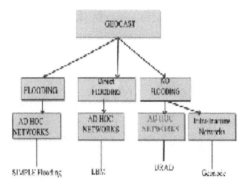

Figure: Geocastrouting taxonomy

Routing with Directed Flooding

In Location based multicast (LBM) algorithm, a forwarding of packet is describing by specified vicinity called "Forwarding Zone". Simple Flooding is altered by defining a forwarding zone that includes somewhat the destination region and a path between the sender and the destination region. An intermediate node forwards a packet only if it resides to the forwarding zone. Overhead is increased, by increasing the forwarding zone because the probability for reception of a geo cast packet at all destination nodes could be increased. Two types of forwarding zones are described. One is the rectangular forwarding zone and the other one is distance-based forwarding zone as shown in figures below respectively. In the rectangular type, the vehicles that are inside the forwarding zone forward the packets only. If the packet is delivered to the vehicles that are outside the forwarding zone, the packet is discarded. In Second Distance based type, the distance is measured from the sender to the center of destination region. The vehicles having distance less than this distance from source to the center of destination region is used in broadcasting, otherwise the nodes with larger distance drop the packet as shown below.

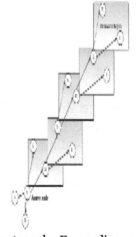

Rectangular Forwarding zone

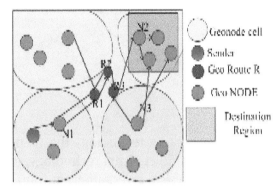

Figure: Geocast example with GeoNode

It is also called Geonode. Geo Node encompasses an infrastructure system. In this advent, there are three basic essentials: Geo-node, Geo-router Geo-host. Each Geo-router has a circular range. The transmission of packet in this advent is completed by multicast routing. In figure the packet is sent to N1 by the source S. N1forwards the packet to its router R1. Now according to the circular range of router, the destination region is covered byR3, so R1 forwards the packet to R2 from where it is forwarded to R3. R3 delivers it to N2 and N3, both of which interconnect with the destination region.

References

- How-does-routing-table-work: grandmetric.com, Retrieved 20 June 2018

- What-is-ip-routing, reference, knowledge-center: metaswitch.com, Retrieved 11 July 2018

- Routing-algorithms, computer networking notes: ecomputernotes.com, Retrieved 24 May 2018

- Routing-decisions-best-path-selection: globalknowledge.com, Retrieved 11 July 2018

- Bgp-path-attributes-and-the-decision-process: netcerts.net, Retrieved 17 April 2018

Ethernet

Ethernet refers to a computer networking technology that is used in LAN, MAN and WAN. In order to completely understand ethernet technology, it is necessary to understand the chief aspects of ethernet physical layer, ethernet frame, power over ethernet, ethernet over PDH, ethernet over SDH, etc. which have been extensively detailed in this chapter.

Ethernet is a computer network technology, which is used in different area networks like LAN, MAN, WAN. Ethernet connecting computers together with cable so the computers can share information. Within each main branch of the network, "Ethernet" can connect up to 1,024 personal computers and workstations.

Ethernet provides services on the Physical (Layers 1) and Data Link Layer (Layers 2) of OSI reference model. The Data Link Layer is further divided into two sublayers that are Logical Link Control (LLC) and Media Access Control (MAC), these sublayers can be used to establish the transmission paths and format data before transmitting on the same network segment.

Systems that use Ethernet communication divide their data into packets, which are also known as frames. These frames further contain source and destination address, a mechanism, which was used to detect errors in the data and retransmission requests.

Ethernet was developed over several years in the early 1970s by group researchers within the company Xerox Palo Alto Research Center (Xerox PARC) including, in particular, Robert Metcalfe (who founded later 3Com company). The goal the research project was to connect networked computers and laser printers. Xerox Corporation filed a patent on this technology late 1977. In 1979, companies Digital Equipment Corporation (DEC), Intel and Xerox combined to improve Ethernet and together published the first standard in 1980: Ethernet Blue Book sometimes called TEN (after the initials of the three companies). Finally, this technology became standard in 1983: 802.3 was born well before the 802.11. A little abuse of language, it is called Ethernet 802.3 standard. The format of DIX Ethernet packets is slightly different from the 802.3 Ethernet packets, but the two can coexist on the same network. The invention of single-chip Ethernet controllers has made Ethernet cards very cheap, and many modern PCs have it built-in on the Motherboard.

Wired Ethernet

Initially, Ethernet can be designed to run over coaxial cables, twisted pair cables, fiber optic cable.

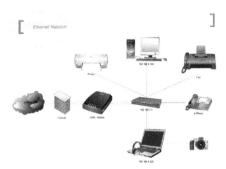

Wired Ethernet network, devices are connected with the help of a fiber optic cable, which connects the devices within a distance of 10km. For this, we have to install a computer network interface card (NIC) in each computer. A unique address is given to each computer that is connected. So, for sharing data and resources like printers, computers, and other machines, Ethernet networking is used as it establishes a communication system.

Ethernet is a shared medium network technology, where all the workstations are connected to the same cable and must connect with one another to send signals over it. The algorithm used to resolve collisions - that is, when two workstations try to speak at the same time - is called CSMA/CD, and works by forcing both workstations to back off for random (and hence probably different) intervals before trying again.

Advantages of using Wired Ethernet Network

- It is very reliable.

- Ethernet network makes use of firewalls for the security of the data.

- Data is transmitted and received at very high speed.

- It is very easy to use the wired network.

Disadvantages of using Wired Ethernet Network

- The wired Ethernet network is used only for short distances.

- The mobility is limited.

- Its maintenance is difficult.

- Ethernet cables, hubs, switches, routers increase the cost of installation.

Wireless Ethernet

In this, wireless NICs are used for connecting the computer instead of a cable and these wireless NICs make use of radio waves for communicating between the systems and furthers these NICs are connected with a wireless switch or hub.

This technology requires maintenance, but it is more easy to use.

Advantages of using Wireless Ethernet

- These types of networks can handle a large number of users.

- It is less expensive than wired Ethernet network.

- In wireless Ethernet, we can easily add new devices to the network, as no new cable is needed for the connection.

- A wireless network allows laptops, tablets and other mobile devices to move freely within a network without losing the connection in the network.

Disadvantages of using Wireless Ethernet

- The speed of wireless Ethernet is slower than the wired Ethernet network.

- Wireless networks are less secure as compare to the wired Ethernet network.

- Wireless network connections get obstructed by the structure of the building like walls, ceilings etc.

- Setting up of a wireless Ethernet network is difficult for the non-experienced users.

Types of Ethernet Network

The maximum data rate of the original Ethernet technology is 10 megabits per second (Mbps), but a second generation fast Ethernet carries 100 Mbps, and the latest version called gigabit Ethernet works at 1000 Mbps. Ethernet network can be classified into 3 types.

Fast Ethernet

This type of Ethernet can transfer data at a rate of 100 Mbps. Fast Ethernet makes use of twisted pair cable or fiber optic cable for communication.

There are three types of fast Ethernet, which are as follows:

- 100BASE-TX

- 100BASE-FX

- 100BASE-T4

Gigabit Ethernet

This type of Ethernet network can transfer data at a rate of 1000 Mbps. Gigabit Ethernet also makes use of twisted pair cable or fiber optic cable. 48 bits used for addressing in Gigabit Ethernet.

Nowadays gigabit Ethernet is very popular. The latest Gigabit Ethernet is a 10 Gigabit Ethernet, which can transfer data at a rate of 10 Gbps.

Gigabit Ethernet was developed so that it can meet the needs of the user like faster communication network, faster transfer of data etc.

Switch Ethernet

Switched Ethernet involves adding switches so that each workstation can have its own dedicated 10 Mbps connection rather than sharing the medium, which can improve network throughput - it has the advantage over rival switched technologies such as asynchronous transfer mode that it employs the same low-level protocols, cheap cabling, and network interface cards as ordinary Ethernet.

When we use a switch in a network, then we use a regular network cable rather than using a crossover cable. The crossover cable is made up of a transmission pair at one end and a receiving pair at the other end.

The main task of the switch in a network is to transfer the data from one device to another device in the same network without affecting the other devices.

It supports different data transfer rates like 10Mbps to 100Mbps for fast Ethernet and 1000Mbps to 10 Gbps for the latest Ethernet.

This type of Ethernet makes use of star topology.

Features of Ethernet

- Through Ethernet network, data can be sent and received at very high speed.
- Ethernet network is less expensive.
- With the help of Ethernet networking, your data is secured as it protected your data. Suppose that someone is attempting on your network, and then all of the devices in your network stop processing instantly and wait until the user attempts to transmit it again.
- Ethernet facilitates us to share our data and resources like printers, scanners, computers etc.
- Ethernet network quickly transmits the data. That's why; nowadays most of the universities and college campuses make use of Ethernet technology, which is based upon the Gigabit Ethernet.

Coaxial Cable

Coaxial cable is a type of cable that has an inner conductor surrounded by an insulating layer, surrounded by a conductive shielding. Many also have an insulating outer jacket the diagram below illustrates the construction of a typical cable. Electrical signal flows through the center conductor.

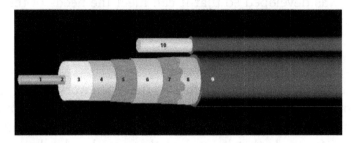

1. Center conductor - copper-clad steel.

2. Center conductor bond - clean stripping polymer is utilized to block moisture migration.

3. Dielectric - polyethylene providing mechanically stable, closed cell foam with high VP.

4. First outer conductor - shield with an aluminum-polymer aluminum tape securely bonded to the dielectric core.

5. Second outer conductor - an additional aluminum-polymer-aluminum tape is used in tri-shield and quad-shield constructions to further enhance HF shield isolation before and after flexure.

6. Third outer conductor - an additional aluminum-polymer-aluminum tape is used in tri-shield and quad-shield constructions to further enhance HF shield isolation before and after flexure.

7. Fourth outer conductor - an additional 34 or 36 AWG aluminum braid is used in quad-shield constructions to further improve LF shield isolation in extreme RF noise environments.

8. Corrosion resistant protectant

    ◦ Indoor and aerial - a non-drip material designed to eliminate moisture migration into the cable construction.

    ◦ Underground - a flowing compound able to seal small jacket ruptures.

9. Jacket - a UV stable outer jacket of either polyethylene (PE) or flame retardant polyvinyl chloride (PVC) is available to protect the core during installation and for the installed life of the cable.

10. Integral messenger - a galvanized, carbon steel wire support member attached to the cable by a separable web.

Ethernet over Twisted Pair

Twisted pair Ethernet is an Ethernet computer network that uses twisted pairs of insulated copper wires for the physical layer of the network, which is combined with the data link layer.

Twisted pair cable wires are twisted around each other to decrease obstruction from other twisted pairs in the cable. The two twisted wires assist in decreasing crosstalk that can disrupt signals and reduce electromagnetic induction, which produces voltage across a conductor transferring through a magnetic field.

Typically, twisted pair has less bandwidth than other Ethernet standards such as optical fiber and coaxial cable. Twisted pair Ethernet may also be known as Ethernet over twisted pair.

Ethernet is a standard for connecting computers to a local area network (LAN). Twisted pair is the most economical LAN cable and is often used by older telephone networks, although many networks have twisted pair wiring somewhere within the network.

Presently, two of the most common types of twisted pair Ethernet are:

- Fast Ethernet or 100BASE-TX with a transmission speed at 100 Mbps

- Gigabit Ethernet (1000BASE-T) running at 1 Gbps

Both the 100BASE-TX and 1000BASE-T use a standard 8P8C connector that has a male plug and female jack, each of which has eight evenly spaced conducting channels. Compared to 10BASE-T, the 100BASE-TX and 1000BASE-T are a lot more efficient.

The majority of twisted pair Ethernet standards can be wired directly by lining up the pins. Other twisted pair Ethernets are connected by using the crossover method, which joins the receiver to the transmitter and the transmitter to the receiver. Both the 100BASE-TX and 1000BASE-T are designed to use at least a Category 5 cable with a maximum cable length of 100 meters. Newer connections use a Category 5e.

Ethernet over Copper

Ethernet over copper, also known as EOC, is a fairly new technology of data packet transmission. It is also known as Ethernet in the first mile and is characterized by:

- Its usage of traditional copper wires also known as POTS or plain ordinary telephone service,

- Its ability to deliver symmetrical speeds,

- Flexibility of bandwidth,

- Being an extremely affordable solution for any business organization.

Limitations to Ethernet over Copper

Ethernet over copper is an extremely affordable solution primarily because it uses traditional copper cables. However, one of the biggest considerations that you will have to pay attention to if you are looking at Ethernet over copper is the distance. The speed of connectivity may reduce over greater distances between your business organization and the Central telecom office.

Speeds and Symmetry

Depending on the service provider that you go with, you can enjoy speeds ranging from 3 megabits per second and going on to even 45 megabits per second. Depending on the distance between your business organization or your office and the Central telecom office, you can also enjoy a really flexible amount of bandwidth that can be made available to you.

One of the biggest advantages offered by Ethernet over copper is that it delivers symmetrical speeds. This simply means that the user of this technology gets the same download and uploads speeds. This is huge advantage indeed because quite a few other options such as cable and DSL are asymmetrical. Typically, they offer greater download speeds and slower upload speeds.

Continuity of Service

Another advantage that you can enjoy with Ethernet over copper solutions is the fact that a service provider can deliver connectivity through the usage of multiple loops. The usage of customer premise equipment means that this connectivity can be installed through multiple pairs of POTS. This adds to redundancy and delivers continuity of service. Therefore, even if one line fails, the other lines will take over the functioning. This is important when an organization is looking at handling business critical operations, which will be derailed massively with even a small break in connectivity.

Installation and Scalability

Another big reason for the popularity of Ethernet over copper is the fact that it can be installed extremely easily. Since it uses ubiquitous and conventional technology, a business organization can be up and running in no time whatsoever. Once this solution has been installed, a business organization can also enjoy extreme scalability. This simply means that with the growth in business operations, the technology will also be scaled up to take care of higher demands of data connectivity.

Thus, looking at EOC or Ethernet over copper is an extremely practical solution for most business organizations. Its advantages of flexibility, scalability, cost effectiveness; fast installation and easy maintenance make EOC an extremely practical choice for business everywhere.

Ethernet Physical Layer

Ethernet provides services corresponding to physical layer and data link layer of the OSI reference model. Each Ethernet physical layer protocol has a three-part name that summarizes its characteristics. The components specified in the naming convention correspond to LAN speed, signaling method, and physical media type.

Characteristics	Ethernet Value	10Base5	10Base2	10BaseT	10BaseFL	100BaseT
Data rate (mbps)	10	10	10	10	10	10
Signaling method	Base-band	Baseband	Baseband	Base-band	Baseband	Baseband
Maximum segment length	500	500	500	500	500	500
Media	50-ohm coaxial	50-ohm coaxial	50-ohm coaxial	UTP cable	Fiber-optic	UTP cable
Topology	Bus	Bus	Bus	Star	Point-to-Point	Bus

The table above summarizes the differences between the various physical-layer specifications of Ethernet:

Ethernet Topology

Ethernet topology is based on following three categories:

- Ethernet 10 Mbps: A single LAN specification that operate at 10 Mbps over coaxial Ethernet 10base2 or 10base5 cable.

- 100-Mbps Ethernet: A single LAN specification, also known as Fast Ethernet that operates at 100 Mbps over UTP Ethernet cable.

- 1000-Mbps Ethernet: A single LAN specification, also known as Gigabit Ethernet that operates at 1 Gbps (1000 Mbps) over fiber optics and twisted pair Ethernet cables.

100BaseT Overview

100BaseT uses the existing IEEE 802.3 CSMA/CD specification. As a result, 100BaseT retains the IEEE 802.3 frame format, size and error-detection mechanism. In addition, it supports all applications and networking software currently running on 802.3 networks. 100BaseT maintains dual speeds of 10 and 100 Mbps using 100BaseT Fast Link Pulses (FLPs). 100BaseT hubs must detect dual speeds much like Token Ring 4/16 hubs, but adapter cards can support 10Mbps, 100 Mbps, or both.

100BaseT Signaling

100BaseT supports two signaling types:

- 100BaseX

- 4T+

Both signaling types are interoperable at the station and hub levels. MII (Media Independent Interface) which same like AUI interface provides interoperability at base level. The hub provides interoperability at the hub level.

The 100BaseX signaling scheme has a convergence sublayer that adapts the full duplex continuous signaling mechanism of the FDDI Physical Medium Dependent (PMD) layer to the half duplex, start-stop signaling of the Ethernet MAC sublayer. 100BaseTX's use of the existing FDDI specification has allowed quick delivery of products to market. 100BaseX is the signaling scheme used in the 100BaseTX and the 100BaseFX media types.

The 4T+ signaling scheme uses one pair of wires for collision detection and the other three pairs to transmit data. It also permits 100BaseT to work with existing Category 3 cabling while all four pairs are installed on desktop. 4T+ is the signaling scheme used in the 100BaseT4 media type, and it supports half duplex operation only.

100BaseT Hardware

Components used for a 100BaseT physical connection include the following:

- Physical medium: This device caries signals between computers and can be one of three 100BaseT media types:

  - 100BaseTX

  - 100BaseFX

  - 100BaseT4

- Medium Dependent Interface (MDI): The MDI is a mechanical and electrical interface between the transmission medium and the physical layer device.

- Physical Layer Device (PHY): the PHY provides either 10 or 100 Mbps operation and can be a set of integrated circuits (or a daughter board) on a Ethernet port, or an external device supplied with an MII cable that plugs into an MII port on a 100BaseT device (similar to a 10 Mbps Ethernet transceiver).

- Media Independent Interface (MII): It is used with a 100 Mbps external transceiver to attach a 100 Mbps Ethernet device to several of these three media types. The MII has a 40 pin plug and cable that stretches up to 0.5 meters.

Cables and Connectors

AUI

Ethernet is usually implemented a network interface card on a primary circuit board. Ethernet cabling standards indicates that how to utilize a transceiver to connect a cable to the physical network medium. The transceiver performs a lot of the physical layer functions, as well as collusion discovery. Transceiver cable is connected end station to a transceiver.

Ethernet provides for a verity of cabling options such as 10Base2, 10base5 and 10baseT. The 10base2 Ethernet connection is very rare nowadays because the 10base2 drivers are not so longer available while the 10base5 cable is referred as an AUI (Attachment Unit Interface) and the network attachment device is called a MAU (Media Attachment Unit), instead of a transceiver.

AUI Cable

The AUI connector is connecting with AUI to AUI cable. The AUI to AUI interface cable can be connected with the switch AUI port with the help of AUI and transceiver.

Gigabit Ethernet Physical Layer Implementation

The Gigabit Ethernet specification addresses three forms of transmission media: long-wave (LW) laser over single-mode and multimode fiber (to be known as1000Base LX), sort-wave (SW) laser over multimode fiber (to be known as 1000BaseSX), and the 1000BaseCX medium, which allows for transmission over balanced shielded 150 ohm copper cable. The IEEE 802.3ab committee is examining the use of UTP cable for Gigabit Ethernet transmission (1000BaseT).

The 1000BaseT draft specification would be used to enable Gigabit Ethernet to extend distances up to 100 meters for category 5 UTP cables, which is widely used for cabling in buildings.

The Fiber Channel PMD specification currently allows for 1.062 gigabit signaling in full duplex, Gigabit Ethernet will increase this signaling rate to 1.25 Gbps. The 8B/10B encoding allows a data transmission rate of 1000 Mbps. existing type of connector for Fiber Channel and for Gigabit Ethernet is SC connector for both single and multimode fiber. The Gigabit Ethernet specification calls for media support for multimode fiber-optic cable, single-mode fiber-optic cable, and a special balanced shielded 150 ohm copper cable.

Ethernet Frame

When transmitting data over Ethernet, the Ethernet frame is primarily responsible for the correct rulemaking and successful transmission of data packets. Essentially, data sent over Ethernet is carried by the frame. An Ethernet frame is between 64 bytes and 1,518 bytes big, depending on the size of the data to be transported.

In the OSI model the frame is on the data link layer and is responsible for the error-free transmission and separation of the bit stream into blocks. The first version of Ethernet (Ethernet I) was still based on 16-bit data fields without defined bytes. Modern Ethernet frames were first used in the Ethernet II structure, before the IEEE (Institute of Electrical and Electronics Engineers) developed the standard protocol IEEE 802.3 (first IEEE 802.3raw) in 1983.

Following technical advancements, the frame structure was adapted several times so that the frames could carry more defined data. With the IEEE 802.3 format, the basic MAC frame and the SNAP frame were created for the multiplexing process and for manufacturer-related identification data. For the development of the VLAN, the Ethernet II frame and the Ethernet IEEE 802.3 frame were developed as "tagged" variants. These tags contain control data that can assign the frame to a specific VLAN.

Ethernet II

Bit Sequence 1010101010...		Ethernet Frame, 64-1518 Bytes					Inter Frame Gap
Preamble	SFD	Dest. Addr.	Source Addr.	Type	Data	FCS	
8 Bytes		6 Bytes	6 Bytes	2 Bytes	46 - 1500 Bytes	4 Bytes	9.6 µs

Figure: The Classic Frame Structure of Ethernet II, with a special feature being The Type Field.

An Ethernet frame must be at least 64 bytes for collision detection to work, and can be a maximum of 1,518 bytes. The packet starts with a preamble that controls the synchronization between sender and receiver and a "Start Frame Delimiter" (SFD) that defines the frame. Both values are bit sequences in the format "10101010 ..." in which the actual frame contains information about source and destination addresses (MAC format), control information (in the case of Ethernet II the type field, later a length specification), followed by the transmitted data record. A frame check sequence (FCS) is an error-detecting code that closes the frame (except for the preamble and SFD). The packet is completed by an "Inter Frame Gap," which defines a 9.6 µs transmission pause.

Ethernet II uses the classic frame structure with a type field ("Type") which defines various protocols of the network layer. In the OSI model, the network layer is important for connecting and providing network addresses. The type field was replaced by a length specification in later frame formats.

The Ethernet II frame was defined in 1982 and has formed the foundation of all subsequent frame developments. However, the format still enjoys great popularity, primarily because it gives the data field the most space (up to 1,500 bytes).

Ethernet 802.3Raw

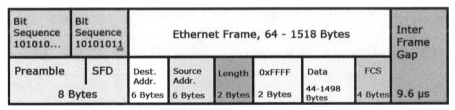

Figure: The classic frame structure of Ethernet 802.3raw

This rough version of the 802.3 packet, given the unfortunate name "Ethernet 802.3," was brought out by Novell before widespread establishment of IEEE 802.3 standards and the popular IPX/SPX protocol, unfortunately leading to frequent confusion with the IEEE standard. Consequently, Novell added "raw" to the name. In contrast to the classic Ethernet II model, this frame defines an exact end to the bit sequence for the SFD. This identifies the data packet as the 802.3 standard for the receiver. 802.3raw frames do not contain a protocol identifier, as they are only usable for Novell IPX. In addition, the data to be transmitted is always prefixed with 2 bytes, which always consist of ones. This is the only way to distinguish a "raw" frame from other frames in the 802.3 family.

The IEEE 802.3raw frame can only be used for the IPX protocol, because the type field's protocol ID is missing. The name "IEEE 802.3raw" is also slightly misleading, since Novell used the protocol name without involving the IEEE in the development of the frame. The use of this frame means extra work for the user, because compatibility issues can arise between devices. From 1993 onwards, Novell itself recommended the "Ethernet 802.2" standard, which used the IEEE 802.3 frame, to avoid the likelihood of confusion with the "raw" frame.

Ethernet IEEE 802.3

Bit Sequence 101010...	Bit Sequence 1010101	Ethernet Frame, 64 - 1518 Bytes							Inter Frame Gap
Preamble	SFD	Dest. Addr.	Source Addr.	Length	DSAP	SSAP	Control	Data	FCS	
8 Bytes		6 Bytes	6 Bytes	2 Bytes	1 Byte	1 Byte	1 Byte	42 - 1497 Bytes	4 Bytes	9.6 µs

Figure: The standardized frame structure of Ethernet 802.3. New features are "DSAP" and "SSAP," which replace the type field and the control field containing the LLC frame

This standardized version of the Ethernet 802.3 frame can define up to 256 compatible protocols, with important protocol information integrated into the data field. In addition, the "Destination Service Access Point" (DSAP) and "Source Service Access Point" (SSAP) are included. The new control field defines the "Logical Link" (LLC) of the protocol. This point ensures the transparency of the media sharing procedures and can control the data flow.

Ethernet IEEE 802.3 is by far the most popular and widely used LAN frame structure today. However, some networks and protocols require more space for specific information. Consequently, there are variants of the IEEE 802.3 frame that provide additional data blocks for specific information, among them the SNAP extension and the VLAN tag.

Ethernet IEEE 802.3 SNAP

Bit Sequence 101010...	Bit Sequence 1010101	Ethernet Frame, 64 - 1518 Bytes								Inter Frame Gap
Preamble	SFD	Dest. Addr.	Source Addr.	Type	DSAP	SSAP	Control	SNAP	Data	FCS	
8 Bytes		6 Bytes	6 Bytes	2 Bytes	0xAA	0xAA	0x03	5 Bytes	38 - 1492 Bytes	4 Bytes	9.6 µs

Figure: The classic frame structure of Ethernet 802.3 SNAP, with a special feature being the SNAP field

The SNAP field ("Sub Network Access Protocol") is useful for defining more than 256 protocols. To do this, 2 bytes are made available for the protocol number. In addition, the manufacturer can integrate a unique identifier (3 bytes). Unlike its predecessors, SNAP also ensures backward compatibility with Ethernet II. DSAP, SSAP, and Control are firmly defined here.

With the newly added space for protocol information, IEEE 802.3 SNAP is extremely versatile and makes compatibility between numerous different protocols in a network possible. However, the space for the actual data is slightly less.

VLAN 802.1q - Ethernet II Tagged and IEEE 802.3 Tagged

Tagged frames contain a so-called VLAN tag for them to be assigned to a virtual local area network (VLAN), which separates the network structure into physical and logical levels. This means that with the help of VLANs, subnetworks can be implemented without having to install hardware. The subnetwork is then virtual and not physically realized. Identifying Ethernet frames within a VLAN requires the "Tag" field. On a physical level, VLANs work through switches.

Bit Sequence 1010101010...		Ethernet Frame, 68 - 1522 Bytes						Inter Frame Gap
Preamble	SFD	Dest. Addr.	Source Addr.	Tag	Type	Data 46 - 1500 Bytes	FCS	
8 Bytes		6 Bytes	6 Bytes	4 Bytes	2 Bytes		4 Bytes	9.6 µs

Figure: The classic frame structure of Ethernet II tagged. The tag field contains important information for the VLAN integration

In the OSI model, a VLAN works on the data link layer (layer 2) and controls the data flow control. With VLAN, networks can become more efficient by being divided into subnets. For the information that the switch handles, the tagged frames are responsible. In the Ethernet II frame, the "Tag" field is implemented before the "Type" field and uses 4 bytes. This increases the minimum size of the Ethernet II frames by 4 bytes.

Bit Sequence 101010...	Bit Sequence 1010101		Ethernet Frame, 68 - 1522 Bytes								Inter Frame Gap
Preamble	SFD	Dest. Addr.	Source Addr.	Tag	Length	DSAP	SSAP	Control	Data	FCS	
8 Bytes		6 Bytes	6 Bytes	4 Bytes	2 Bytes	1 Byte	1 Byte	1 Byte	42 - 1497 Bytes	4 Bytes	9.6 µs

Figure: The classic frame structure of Ethernet 802.3 tagged. The tag field contains important information for the VLAN integration

VLAN tags can also be installed in today's most popular IEEE 802.3 frame format. Within this frame, the "Tag" field uses 4 bytes and is implemented before the length specification. The minimum size of the frame is now increased from 4 bytes to 68 bytes.

Point-to-Point Protocol over Ethernet (PPPoE)

Point-to-Point Protocol over Ethernet (PPPoE) combines PPP, which typically runs over broadband connections, with the Ethernet link-layer protocol that allows users to connect to a network of hosts over a bridge or access concentrator. PPPoE enables service providers to maintain access control through PPP connections and also manage multiple hosts at a remote site.

The working standard for the PPPoE protocol was published by the IETF in 1999. The IETF specification for PPPoE is RFC 2516. PPPoE expands the original capability of PPP by allowing a virtual point to point connection over a multipoint Ethernet network architecture. PPPoE is a protocol that is widely used by ISPs to provision digital subscriber line (DSL) high-speed Internet services, of which the most popular service is ADSL. The similarity between PPPoE and PPP has led to the widespread adoption of PPPoE as the preferred protocol for implementing high speed Internet access. Service providers can use the same authentication server for both PPP and PPPoE sessions, resulting in a cost savings. PPPoE uses standard methods of encryption, authentication, and compression specified by PPP.

PPPoE is configured as a point to point connection between two Ethernet ports. As a tunneling protocol, PPPoE is used as an effective foundation for the transport of IP packets at the network layer. IP is overlaid over a PPP connection and uses PPP as a virtual dial up connection between points on the network. From the user's perspective, a PPPoE session is initiated by using connection software on the client machine or router. PPPoE session initiation involves the identification of the Media Access Control (MAC) address of the remote device. This process, also known as PPPoE discovery, involves the following steps:

- Initiation - The client software sends a PPPoE Active Discovery Initiation (PADI) packet to the server to intitiate the session.

- Offer - The server responds with a PPPoE Active Discovery Offer (PADO) packet.

- Request - Upon receipt of the PADO packet, the client responds by sending a PPPoE Active Discovery Request (PADR) packet to the server.

- Confirmation - Upon receipt of the PADR packet, the server responds by generating a unique ID for the PPP session and sends it in a PPPoE Active Discovery Session (PADS) confirmation packet to the client.

When a PPPoE session is initiated, the destination IP address is only used when the session is active. The IP address is released after the session is closed, allowing for efficient re-use of IP addresses.

PPPoE Stages

PPPoE has two stages, the discovery stage and the PPPoE session stage. In the discovery stage, the client discovers the access concentrator by identifying the Ethernet media access control (MAC) address of the access concentrator and establishing a PPPoE session ID. In the session stage, the client and the access concentrator build a point-to-point connection over Ethernet, based on the information collected in the discovery stage.

PPPoE Discovery Stage

To initiate a PPPoE session, a host must first identify the Ethernet MAC address of the remote peer and establish a unique PPPoE session ID for the session. Learning the remote Ethernet MAC address is called PPPoE discovery.

During the PPPoE discovery process, the host does not discover a remote endpoint on the Ethernet network. Instead, the host discovers the access concentrator through which all PPPoE sessions are established. Discovery is a client/server relationship, with the host (a device running Junos OS) acting as the client and the access concentrator acting as the server. Because the network might have more than one access concentrator, the discovery stage allows the client to communicate with all of them and select one.

The PPPoE discovery stage consists of the following steps:

1. PPPoE Active Discovery Initiation (PADI)—The client initiates a session by broadcasting a PADI packet to the LAN to request a service.

2. PPPoE Active Discovery Offer (PADO)—Any access concentrator that can provide the service requested by the client in the PADI packet replies with a PADO packet that contains its own name, the unicast address of the client, and the service requested. An access concentrator can also use the PADO packet to offer other services to the client.

3. PPPoE Active Discovery Request (PADR)—From the PADOs it receives, the client selects one access concentrator based on its name or the services offered and send it a PADR packet to indicate the service or services needed.

4. PPPoE Active Discovery Session-Confirmation (PADS)—When the selected access concentrator receives the PADR packet, it accepts or rejects the PPPoE session:

   ∘ To accept the session, the access concentrator sends the client a PADS packet with a unique session ID for a PPPoE session and a service name that identifies the service under which it accepts the session.

   ∘ To reject the session, the access concentrator sends the client a PADS packet with a service name error and resets the session ID to zero.

PPPoE Session Stage

The PPPoE session stage starts after the PPPoE discovery stage is over. The access concentrator can start the PPPoE session after it sends a PADS packet to the client, or the client can start the PPPoE session after it receives a PADS packet from the access concentrator. A device supports multiple PPPoE sessions on each interface, but no more than 256 PPPoE sessions per device.

Each PPPoE session is uniquely identified by the Ethernet address of the peer and the session ID. After the PPPoE session is established, data is sent as in any other PPP encapsulation. The PPPoE information is encapsulated within an Ethernet frame and is sent to a unicast address. Magic numbers, echo requests, and all other PPP traffic behave exactly as in normal PPP sessions. In this stage, both the client and the server must allocate resources for the PPPoE logical interface.

After a session is established, the client or the access concentrator can send a PPPoE

Active Discovery Termination (PADT) packet anytime to terminate the session. The PADT packet contains the destination address of the peer and the session ID of the session to be terminated. After this packet is sent, the session is closed to PPPoE traffic.

The PPPoE session is not terminated for the following configuration changes:

- Changing idle time out value
- Changing auto rec timer value
- Deleting idle time out
- Deleting auto rec timer
- Add new auto rec time
- Add new idle time out
- Change negotiate address to static address
- Change static ip address to a new static ip address
- Changing default chap secrete.

The PPPoE session is terminated for the following configuration changes:

- Add ac name
- Delete chap ppp options
- Add new chap ppp options
- Configure uifd mac.

Power over Ethernet

Power over Ethernet (POE) is a networking feature that lets network cables carry electrical power over an existing data connection with a single Cat5e/Cat6 ethernet cable.

PoE technology relies on the IEEE 802.3af and 802.3at standards, which are set by the Institute of Electrical and Electronics Engineers and govern how networking equipment should operate in order to promote interoperability between devices.

PoE-capable devices can be power sourcing equipment (PSE), powered devices (PDs), or sometimes both. The device that transmits power is a PSE, while the device that is powered is a PD. Most PSEs are either network switches or PoE injectors intended for use with non-PoE switches.

Common examples of PDs include VoIP phones, wireless access points, and IP cameras.

Advantage of PoE

Power over Ethernet (PoE) allows for installation of remote or outside equipment without having to connect to AC power. This allows power to be delivered to more areas without the need to install additional electrical infrastructure or to have power outlets at every endpoint. Equipment can be installed without the need for an electrician and because ethernet cable costs less and is often already installed in buildings, PoE-based systems are far more cost-effective and efficient.

Benefits of PoE

PoE benefits organizations in 5 primary ways—reduced installation costs, installation safety, responsive deployments, data-gathering capabilities, and productivity enhancements. End users can plug PoE capable devices into existing networks or start from scratch with ease.

Reduction in Installation Costs

PoE installation costs are far less than the cost of installing traditional wiring, and the operating costs are far more efficient. One twisted pair cable delivers both data and power to devices. Existing copper from legacy phone systems can also be re-purposed.

Safety of PoE Installation

PoE Type 3 voltages are typically less than 60 volts, and Type 4 less than 90. Conduits and metal cladding are not required. Fewer steps and hazards and the straightforward use of one Cat5e or Cat6 Ethernet cable, remove the need for a licensed electrician.

Reasons for PoE Deployments more Responsive

PoE devices adapt to changing environments. They can be easily moved and reconnected at the switch level and easily integrate into changing network configurations. PoE is plug and play. An entire network does not need to be brought-down to add or subtract devices.

PoE Data-gathering Capabilities

PoE technology is perfect for data collection. For example, analytics software can help facilities groups to determine when an area is occupied and when LED lighting and HVAC components may be turned off. Operational costs can be much lower based on actual usage.

PoE Enhances Productivity

LED lighting systems, because of 2-way data capabilities, can be programmed to follow spectrum and frequencies found in nature. Employees can enjoy greater health, alertness, creativity, collaborative opportunities, and a sense of well-being while on the job.

All of these features allow organizations the ability to control and limit costs without sacrificing quality of life.

Some Limitations of PoE

The limitations of PoE are few but should be taken into account when adopting for the first time:

1. Simple PoE only transmits signals 100m;

2. Non-compliant devices require additional equipment;

3. Power budgets may only achieve levels available on legacy equipment.

This part will further expand these 3 limitations and how to adjust for them:

- Transmission distance

- Device compatibility workarounds

- Power delivery rates

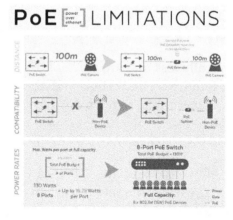

Maximum Distance of PoE

PoE can transmit 100 meters from the switch or hub to the NIC, regardless of where the power is injected. The limitation is not the power; it's the Ethernet cabling standards that limit the total length of cabling to 100 meters. The furthest distance a PoE switch can transmit simple data over Ethernet is a distance of 100 meters. A PoE Ethernet Extender, however, can lengthen that span up to 4000 feet.

For networks spanning enterprises, campuses, and large retail operations like shopping malls, extended reach allows centralized control across a wide area.

Device Compatibility

Legacy devices, those that are not PoE compliant, require either an injector or a splitter. PoE delivers power AND data over one cable and therefore one input. Legacy devices receive data and power separately.

- A PoE Injector sends power to PoE equipment that receives data through existing non-POE switch.

- A PoE Splitter also supplies power, but it does so by splitting the power from the data and feeding it to a separate input that a non-PoE compliant device can use.

Amount of Power Delivered by PoE per Port

When purchasing, administrators want to be sure the maximum power budget of a switch is sufficient for the devices it supports. Identify the manufacturer power spec/budget per port to know if the end device will receive required power through that switch.

Power Suppied by PoE Devices

PoE devices supply power according to the device IEEE 802.3 generation. The life-cycle generation is indicated by the extension: "af," "at" or PoE+, and "bt" or "UPoE". The following chart provides side-by-side comparison of maximum power each PoE Type delivers at the port level.

IEEE Extension	Type	Power Budget per Device
IEEE 802.3af	Type 1	15.4W
IEEE 802.3at / PoE+	Type 2	30.8W
IEEE 802.3bt / UPoE	Type 3	60W
IEEE 802.3bt	Type 4	90-95W

Devices using PoE

The devices using PoE to receive data and power known are smart technologies, those found in the Internet of Things (IoT). A list of examples follows. Keep in mind this list keeps expanding as more people adopt PoE and manufacturers continue to prioritize development of these products.

• Ethernet Extenders	• PoS Kiosks	• LED Lighting SystemsRound
• Security Access Controls	• Industrial Controls	Robin Queue • Digital Signage
• Smart Clocks	• Network Switches	• Routers
• Wireless Access Points	• IP/Pan-Tilt-Zoom Cameras	• VoIP Phones

PoE+

Power over Ethernet Plus (PoE+) is the 2009 Ethernet standard amendment released by the Institute of Electrical and Electronic Engineers, also known as (IEEE) 802.3at. PoE+ delivers 30W at the port level over an Ethernet twisted pair cable.

PoE vs. PoE+

The original PoE IEEE 802.3af, completed in 2003, delivers 15.4W. Never ratified, this version was more-or-less an informal working version of its successor, the 802.3at. The big difference is 802.3at delivers more power per device.

Practicality of Mixing PoE and Non-PoE Devices in any Network

PoE and non-PoE devices can mix in the same network. Non-PoE devices require a separate power source. A PoE splitter may also be required if the device does not support PoE. This will split power and data from the PSE.

Power over Ethernet Applications

PoE applications power an increasing percentage of 8.4 Billion IoT connected devices, which number is up 31% from the previous year. Higher-powered IEEE 802.3bt supports: thin client computers, VoIP phones and wireless networks, IP security cameras, facility monitoring controls, digital signage, point of sales kiosks, and LED lighting and sensors.

PoE Switch

A PoE switch is a network switch with the ability to provide power over Ethernet from each interface while still being able to forward frames. Both managed and unmanaged PoE switches are available. A PoE switch requires one Uplink to an existing network to further expand and increase ports.

PoE Switch   PoE Camera

PoE Hub

A PoE hub can be viewed as a stack of PoE injectors. Example, a 4 port PoE hub will have 4 data-in interfaces and 4 PoE interfaces. Each PoE interface requires a data connection with the corresponding data-in side. A 4 port PoE hub will require 4 data ports from your network switch. Data ports on the PoE hub will not forward frames within the hub (frames received on port 1 cannot be forwarded to ports 2-4).

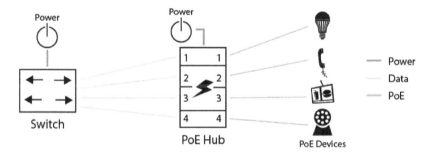

PoE Splitter

A PoE splitter supplies power to non PoE compatible devices by splitting power from data and feeding it to a separate input. Splitters are used on legacy and low power devices like IP cameras, to split PoE power from data signal, and convert to lower voltage requirements for the camera.

PoE Injector

A PoE injector is a device that sends power to signals sent from a non-compatible PoE switch to PoE equipment. Though current switch purchases tend to be of PoE compatible models, PoE injectors are required in situations where existing equipment is older and will be cycled out at a future date.

Poe Extender

A PoE extender is a device used to extend Ethernet network devices beyond the basic 100m-distance limit for twisted pair Ethernet cable. Extenders unite networks that span large distances in settings such as, hotels, shopping malls, business and academic campuses, and sporting venues.

Fiber Channel over Ethernet

FCoE (Fiber Channel over Ethernet) is a storage protocol that enables Fiber Channel communications to run directly over Ethernet. FCoE makes it possible to move Fiber Channel traffic across existing high-speed Ethernet infrastructure and converges storage and IP protocols onto a single cable transport and interface.

The goal of FCoE is to consolidate input/output (I/O) and reduce switch complexity as well as to cut back on cable and interface card counts. Adoption of FCoE been slow, however, due to a scarcity of end-to-end FCoE devices and reluctance on the part of many organizations to change the way they implement and manage their networks.

Traditionally, organizations have used Ethernet for TCP/IP networks and Fiber Channel for storage networks. Fiber Channel supports high-speed data connections between computing devices that interconnect servers with shared storage devices and between storage controllers and drives. FCoE shares Fiber Channel and Ethernet traffic on the same physical cable or lets organizations separate Fiber Channel and Ethernet traffic on the same hardware.

FCoE uses a lossless Ethernet fabric and its own frame format. It retains Fiber Channel's device communications but substitutes high-speed Ethernet links for Fiber Channel links between devices.

FCoE works with standard Ethernet cards, cables and switches to handle Fiber Channel traffic at the data link layer, using Ethernet frames to encapsulate, route, and transport FC frames across an Ethernet network from one switch with Fiber Channel ports and attached devices to another, similarly equipped switch.

FCoE is often compared to iSCSI, an Internet Protocol (IP)-based storage-networking standard.

Connection-oriented Ethernet

Historically, Ethernet has been a connectionless technology by design. In classic LAN environments, the connectionless capabilities of Ethernet MAC bridging and CSMA/CD provided considerable flexibility, simplicity, and economy in networking latency-insensitive traffic within a single, well-bounded administrative domain.

To bring the cost and flexibility benefits of Ethernet into the public network, the industry has made enormous modifications, enhancements, and extensions to classic Ethernet protocols. The result is "Carrier Ethernet." Most of these enhancements have focused on extending the connectionless classic Ethernet protocol to a service provider environment. This has brought about new capabilities in:

- OAM (IEEE 802.1ag, IEEE 803.2ah, ITU-T Y.1731)

- Survivability (ITU-T G.8031, IEEE 802.3ad, IEEE 802.1s)

- Scalability (IEEE 802.1ad, IEEE 802.1ah)

- Speed and distance (e.g., IEEE 802.3ae).

In addition to the above standards, equipment vendors "beefed up" enterprise-class Ethernet hardware and software platforms to provide a number of carrier-class features.

The next step forward is to make Ethernet connection- oriented. Connection-oriented Ethernet is a high-performance implementation of Carrier Ethernet that is optimized for aggregation infrastructure and EVPL, EPL, and E-Tree services

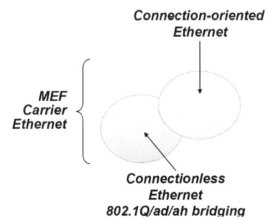

Figure: Connection-Oriented Ethernet: A High-Performance Implementation of Carrier Ethernet

Essential Functions of Connection-oriented Ethernet

The three essential functions that make Ethernet connection-oriented are:

- Predetermined EVC paths

- Resource reservation and admission control

- Per-connection traffic engineering and traffic management.

The ability to predetermine the EVC path through the Ethernet network is fundamental to making Ethernet connection-oriented. In classic connectionless Ethernet bridging, Ethernet frames are forwarded in the network according to the MAC bridging tables in the learning bridge. If a destination MAC address is unknown, the bridge floods the frame to all ports in the broadcast domain. Spanning tree protocols like IEEE 802.1s are run to ensure there are no loops in the topology and to provide network restoration in the event of failure. Depending upon the location and sequence of network failures, the path EVCs take through the network may be difficult to predetermine.

Predetermining the EVC path—either through a management plane application or via an embedded control plane—ensures that all frames in the EVC pass over the same sets of nodes. Therefore, intelligence regarding the connection as a whole can now be imparted to all nodes along the path.

Resource reservation and CAC is the next critical function. Now that the EVC path through the network has been explicitly identified, the actual bandwidth and queuing resources required for each EVC are reserved in all nodes along the path. This is vital to ensure the highest possible levels of performance in terms of packet loss, latency, and jitter. CAC ensures that the requested resource is actually available in each node along the path prior to establishing the EVC.

Once the path has been determined and the resources allocated, the traffic engineering and traffic management functions ensure that the requested connection performance is actually delivered. After packets have been classified on network ingress, a variety of traffic management functions must be provided in any packet-based network. These include:

- Policing

- Shaping

- Queuing

- Scheduling

Packet classification is the processes of identifying to which EVCs the incoming frames belong. The ingress equipment can examine a variety of Ethernet and IP layer information to make this decision. Once the incoming frame is classified, policing is then applied to ensure that all frames coming into the network conform to the traffic contract, known as the bandwidth profile, agreed to upon connection setup. Two-level, three-color marking allows incoming frames that conform to the CIR to be admitted to the network. Frames that exceed even the EIR are discarded immediately, and frames that exceed the CIR, but not the EIR, are marked for possible discard later, should the network become congested. An EVC can be subject to a single such policer if the bandwidth profile is applied to the entire EVC. EVCs can also include bandwidth profiles for each of many CoS classes within the EVC. In this case, a single EVC can be subject to multiple policers.

Heart of Connection-oriented Ethernet

The shaping, queuing, and scheduling granularity determines whether each individual EVC enjoys the significant performance benefits of connection-oriented Ethernet, or is essentially connectionless from a performance point of view.

Every time an Ethernet frame in any Ethernet packet network waits for a transmission opportunity on an egress port, it is queued along with other connections that are also bound for the same egress port and a scheduler determines which frame goes next and possibly there is a shaping function. The critical question is how these frames are queued, scheduled and shaped and at what level of granularity. Several possibilities exist within a connection:

- Per card
- Per port
- Per EVC connection
- Per CoS

On many Carrier Ethernet traffic management implementations, Ethernet frames from many EVCs are placed into a single set of egress queues and therefore visibility into individual EVCs becomes lost. When this happens, the network begins to play "priority roulette" where, essentially, all EVCs in a single priority class get random access to transmission opportunities; the service quality of individual connections consequently goes down.

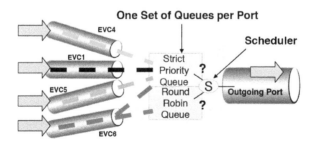

Figure: Priority Roulette": Individual EVC Visibility Lost to Scheduler in Per-Port Queuing

Connection performance can, therefore, only be guaranteed by providing policing, scheduling, and hierarchical egress shaping functions down to the granularity of an individual CoS class within an EVC.

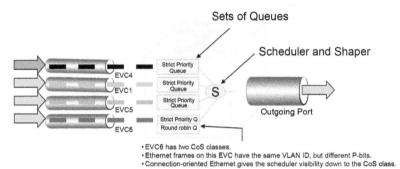

Figure: Per-EVC Queuing, Scheduling and Shaping

By providing the previously discussed three essential functions of connection-oriented Ethernet, Ethernet connections can now enjoy levels of service quality on a par with Ethernet over SONET/SDH—along with the aggregation flexibility of native Ethernet.

A Word about Protection

Once Ethernet frames flow in a connection-oriented manner across the network, it becomes possible to provide dedicated, deterministic, automatic protection switching functionality equivalent to that provided by SONET/SDH—with 10 ms failure detection and 50 ms protection switching speed.

ITU-T G.8031 and IEEE 802.1Qay standards both offer methods to create dedicated protection resources with the same deterministic characteristics as the working path resources (bandwidth profile and loss, latency and jitter performance). Upon Ethernet layer or lower-layer failure or degradation, protection switching logic (located in the originating and terminating nodes of a protection domain) performs rapid 10 ms failure detection and switches to the protection resource in 50 ms. This allows service providers to provide availability guarantees similar to TDM, over arbitrary Ethernet network topologies and large distances.

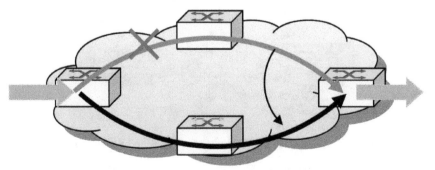

Figure: Automatic Protection Switching for Connection-Oriented Ethernet

Technology Choices

Several existing and emerging technologies can realize connection-oriented Ethernet. These technologies include:

- VLAN switching
- 802.1Qay (PBB-TE)
- MPLS-TP
- T-MPLS
- PW/MPLS

There are two important considerations when choosing a connection-oriented Ethernet approach for metro aggregation and transport infrastructure:

- How many layers are required in the network?
- Is a routed IP data plane and associated complexity required?

Ethernet-only approaches, such as VLAN switching and PBB-TE, do not require additional pseudowire or MPLS layers. They are therefore simpler to integrate into OSS systems and require fewer layers of OAM for fault and performance management.

Furthermore, Ethernet-only approaches do not require deployment of a software intensive IP-routed data plane deep into the metro aggregation network. This is vital, because there are often thousands of remotely deployed elements in this network; the introduction of an IP-routed control plane would greatly increase the complexity of software maintenance, troubleshooting and provisioning, and therefore raise the operational cost of the network.

Important Applications for Connection-oriented Ethernet

There are several important applications that will drive deployment of connection-oriented Ethernet. These include:

- Wireline backhaul for 4G mobile wireless networks
- Infrastructure scaling for enterprise Ethernet services networks
- Private-line-equivalent quality EPL services
- Triple play network optimization
- General Ethernet infrastructure.

Fast Ethernet

Fast Ethernet is traditional CSMA/CD (carrier sense multiple access/collision detection) access control at 100 Mbits/sec over twisted-pair wire. The original Ethernet data rate was 10 Mbits/sec.

During the early development of Fast Ethernet, two different groups worked out standards proposals-and both were finally approved, but under different IEEE committees. One standard became IEEE 802.3u Fast Ethernet and the other became 100VG-Any-LAN, which is now governed by the IEEE 802.12 committee. The latter uses the "demand priority" medium access method instead of CSMA/CD.

100VG-AnyLAN has not caught on, while Fast Ethernet enjoyed great success in enterprise LAN environments. At about the same time, switching technologies came on the scene to further improve network performance. More recently, Gigabit Ethernet has come on the scene to provide a high-speed upgrade path for Fast Ethernet users. It provides high-speed backbones that interconnect Fast Ethernet LANs.

Fast Ethernet takes advantage of the scalability of CSMA/CD hierarchical networking. It is designed after the 10Base-T standard and can be built into hierarchical networking topologies. This type of configuration is compatible with structured wiring strategies".

The primary concern of Fast Ethernet developers was to preserve the CSMA/CD medium access method of 802.3 Ethernet while boosting the data rate. In addition, the developers kept the frame format. Because of this, Fast Ethernet fits in well with traditional Ethernet installations. One version of the Fast Ethernet standard will run on older Category 3 cable installations. Multiple Ethernet types (10 and 100 Mbits/sec) may coexist. A Fast Ethernet-compatible hub simply needs to perform speed matching when exchanging frames. An autonegotiate feature allows devices to detect the speed of incoming transmissions and adjust appropriately.

There are four Fast Ethernet schemes:

- 100Base-TX Runs on two pairs of Category 5 data-grade twisted-pair wire with a maximum distance of 100 meters between hub and workstation.

- 100Base-T4 Runs on four pairs of cable, including Category 3 cable, with a maximum distance of 100 meters between hub and workstation.

- 100Base-FX Runs on optical cable at distances up to 2 kilometers, and is used to connect hubs over long distances in a backbone configuration (e.g., a building in a campus environment).

- 100Base-SX Called Short Wavelength Fast Ethernet, this is a proposed standard (as of this writing) for a Fast Ethernet over fiber-optic cable using 850 nm wavelength optics.

The higher frequency used in the Fast Ethernet standard is prone to attenuation, so cable distance is more limited than in the Ethernet 10Base-T specification. If the encoding scheme of traditional Ethernet were used with Fast Ethernet, the high-end frequency would be above 200 Mhz. That is double the maximum frequency rating of Category 5 cable. To get around this, new encoding schemes were implemented to allow higher-frequency transmissions.

Note that the collision domain is 1/10th the size of the collision domain in 10-Mbit/sec Ethernet. This is because of the 10-times increase in speed of the network. It also means that Fast Ethernet networks can only be one-tenth the physical size of a 10Base-T network.

Fast Ethernet can support full-duplex switched networking modes to provide even better performance. A full-duplex nonshared link (i.e., workstations are attached to switches, not hubs) doesn't even need CSMA/CD, because no other stations are trying to use the link, and each end system has its own channel to transmit on. Collision detection and loopback functions can be disabled. This arrangement is especially useful for backbone connections. If both end systems are transmitting at the same time, the combined data rate is 200 Mbits/sec.

100Base-TX

100Base-TX works with two pairs of UTP (unshielded twisted pair) or STP (shielded twisted pair). Transmission takes place on one pair of wires and collision detection takes place on the other pair of wires. Two types of cable can be used with this specification: Category 5 UTP and IBM's Type 1 STP. Category 5 cable has four pairs of wire. Since only two of the pairs are used, the other two are available for other uses or future expansion. However, it is not recommended that another high-speed network be used on the pairs.

Category 5 cable is designed to cancel out the effects of EMI and, therefore, has very stringent installation requirements. All the components in the cabling system must be Category 5 compliant, including connectors, patch panels, punchdown blocks, and hubs/switches. The twists in the cable must be maintained all the way up to within 1/2 inch of a connector. The twists in the cable help maintain proper signaling, especially at high data rates. Other 100Base-TX requirements are:

- Cable distance: A link segment is the connection between a workstation and a hub or switch. The maximum link segment distance is 100 meters; but if faceplates are used, the specification recommends not exceeding 90 meters from hub to faceplate. This allows 10 meters for the faceplate-to-station connection.

- Maximum collision domain size: First, understand that a collision domain is a segment of a network in which all the stations on that segment hear the same broadcast. The maximum end-to-end distance between two systems within a 100Base-TX twisted-pair broadcast/collision domain segment is approximately 205 meters. This is illustrated in Figure F-2. These distances are flexible as long as the maximum is not exceeded. For example, the inter-repeater distance could be increased if the workstation-to-repeater distance is decreased.

- Repeater hubs: Fast Ethernet repeaters are relatively sophisticated devices compared to standard Ethernet repeaters. They detect improper signals, perform data translations between different types of Fast Ethernet, monitor the network for faults, disconnect faulty ports, and partition off part of a network that is having problems so that the network can continue running. There are two types of repeater hubs in the 100Base-TX scheme:

  ○ Class I repeaters should be used if the network has mixed Fast Ethernet types (100Base-TX, 100Base-FX, and 100Base-T4) because they will change the data encoding between network types on different ports. One class I repeater is allowed per collisions domain.

  ○ Class II repeaters are strictly devices that send all incoming signals to all other ports without translation. They should be used when all the ports are supporting the same network type. Two class II repeaters are allowed per collision domain, but the link between the repeaters cannot exceed 5 meters.

- Switching hubs: To get around the hub count limitation just described, you can install switching hubs, which basically segment the network as a bridge would segment a network. Beyond plain switching is multilayer routing, which builds high-speed inexpensive routing right into the switches and allows network managers great flexibility in designing their networks.

- Full-duplex mode: Full-duplex mode allows simultaneous data transmission between two end nodes without collisions. A 100Base-TX link operating in full-duplex mode has an effective bandwidth of 100 Mbits/sec. All components, including the hubs, must be full duplex capable.

100Base-T4

The 100Base-T4 standard has the same cabling specifications as 100Base-TX in terms of distances and hub configuration. The difference is that 100Base-T4 uses all four wires in a half-duplex signaling scheme. Three pairs are used to either transmit or receive data, and the other pair is used for collision detection. 100Base-T4 also uses a special three-level encoding scheme (as opposed to two levels in other media) to reduce the clock rate. Spreading the 100-Mbit/sec signals over three pairs reduces the signal frequency and allows it to run on older Category 3 cable. Basically, 33.33 Mbits/sec is transmitted over each of the three pairs.

Higher-grade cable such as Category 5 is recommended for future expansion. Like 100Base-TX, the 100Base-T4 specifications have a maximum hub-to-station cable length of 100 meters and an end-to-end maximum of 250 meters. 100Base-T4 also uses the same repeater-classing scheme as 100Base-TX. Class I hubs allow a mix of different Fast Ethernet network types, and class II hubs allow only one scheme.

100Base-FX

100Base-FX is the fiber-optic cable implementation of the Fast Ethernet standard. It is ideal for building backbone connections. Cable distance is limited to 412 meters; but if full-duplex mode is used, cable runs may be as long as 2 km. While fiber-optic cable can span longer distances, the limit is imposed to account for packet round-trip timing.

Fiber-optic cable is not prone to interference. It does not emanate a signal, so it is more secure (especially for wiring across public areas). In addition, fiber-optic cable can scale up to higher transmission rates for future expansion.

100Base-FX requires a cable with two strands of 62.5/125-micron fiber. One strand is used for signal transmission while the other is used to receive and detect collisions. 100Base-FX also uses the same repeater-classing scheme as 100Base-TX. Class I hubs allow mixed Fast Ethernet networks, and class II hubs allow only one scheme.

Ethernet Exchange

Interconnections have always been a key focus for data centers located in areas with high concentrations of network service providers. Some of these data center providers are now investing in specialized exchanges to support Carrier Ethernet services.

An Ethernet Exchange, a form of an External Network-Network Interface (ENNI), is "an interconnect point among service providers where Carrier Ethernet Services are exchanged." From an end user's point of view, you want your service provider to supply this service so you can have a direct Ethernet connection from end-to-end.

End users see Benefits of Ethernet

Today, most enterprises are still encapsulating their native Ethernet data into TDM/SONET/SDH then de-encapsulating it at the other end. However, more and more, end users are seeing the benefits of Ethernet Services and perhaps eventually, the entire public network may be running native Ethernet.

There are currently just a few vendors of Carrier Ethernet Exchange services: CENX, Equinix, Neutral Tandem and Telx.

- CENX: Carrier Ethernet Neutral Exchange (CENX) was the first Carrier Ethernet Exchange. CENX has Carrier Ethernet Exchange services currently available in Chicago, Los Angeles, London, Miami, New Jersey, New York and Hong Kong. The system is resilient and supports high availability with Gigabit and 10-Gigabit Ethernet connections. MemberLink is a new service from CENX that allows customers to connect to any remote Ethernet Exchange through member companies.

- Equinix: Most widely known for its co-location and managed services business, Equinix was an early entrant as a Carrier Ethernet Exchange as well. It has a global footprint on four continents: North America, South America, Europe, Asia and is not only servicing carriers, but has started to open its exchange to cloud companies.

- Neutral Tandem: Its Carrier Ethernet Exchange was launched in early 2010. Since then, the company acquired Tinet and has made recent progress with its new EtherCloud offering. With this, Tinet can provide end-to-end international connectivity to any company. It allows global coverage using VPLS through Juniper equipment in the core and Cisco in the access.

- Telx: While Telx is best known as a leading colocation provider, it was also at the forefront of Ethernet exchanges. Telx is a carrier-neutral data center colocation provider and has several facilities around North America, which enables it to supply seamless Ethernet connection not only between carriers, but between any of its enterprise colo customers as well. Its Ethernet Exchange services have a range of options depending on customer's needs. It charges by the port and can connect customers at 100 Mbps, Gigabit or 10G data rates through its Cisco ASR 9000 equipment. Telx expects to incorporate 40G as needed – probably not until 2012/2013 timeframe, though. No equipment is oversubscribed and low latency options are available for premiums.

Ethernet over PDH

Ethernet transport over non-Ethernet networks has existed for decades. A myriad of technologies, protocols, and equipment have been created to accomplish one seemingly simple task: connect network node A with network node B over distance X. The set of solutions to that simple equation has thus far been unbounded. From the first computer gateway with a 300-baud acoustic FSK modem, to today's advanced Ethernet-over-SONET/SDH systems, the task has remained essentially the same. However, varying forces over the years have caused the evolution of technological implementations used to solve this task and shaped them to the needs of the day. Some of the evolutionary "branches" have been miserable failures. Others have seen extensive global deployments, such as DSL. How does one identify an emerging evolutionary branch that will endure? Using hindsight as a guide, the enduring technologies struck an optimal balance of service quality, dependability, available bandwidth, scalability, interoperability, ease of use, equipment cost, and cost of operation. Technologies that perform poorly in any of these areas are not selected for widespread usage, and eventually disappear or are relegated to niche environments. With this perspective in mind, the emerging Ethernet-over-PDH (EoPDH) technology can be evaluated.

In a broad stroke, EoPDH is the transport of native Ethernet frames over the existing telecommunications copper infrastructure by leveraging the well-established Plesiochronous Digital Hierarchy (PDH) transport technology. EoPDH is actually a collection of technologies and new standards that allow carriers to make use of their extensive networks of legacy PDH and SDH (Synchronous Digital Hierarchy) equipment to provide new Ethernet-centric services. In addition, the collection of EoPDH standards paves the pathway for interoperability and the gradual migration of carriers to Ethernet networks. The standardized technologies used in EoPDH (in simple terminology) include frame encapsulation, mapping, link aggregation, link capacity adjustment, and management messaging. Common practices in EoPDH equipment also include the tagging of traffic for separation into virtual networks, prioritization of user traffic, and a broad range of higher layer applications such as DHCP servers and HTML user interfaces.

Frame encapsulation is the process by which Ethernet frames are placed as payload inside an auxiliary format for transmission on a non-Ethernet network. The primary purpose of encapsulation is the identification of the beginning and ending bytes of the frame. This is known as frame delineation. In actual Ethernet networks, a start of frame delimiter and length field performs the frame delineation function. A secondary role of encapsulation is to map the sporadic ("bursty") Ethernet transmissions into a smooth, continuous data stream. In some technologies, encapsulation also performs error detection by appending a Frame Check Sequence (FCS) to each frame. Many encapsulation technologies exist, including High-Level Data Link Control (HDLC), Link Access Procedure for SDH (LAPS/X.86), and Generic Framing Procedure (GFP). Although any encapsulation technology could theoretically be used for EoPDH applications, GFP has significant advantages and has emerged as the preferred encapsulation method. Most EoPDH equipment also supports HDLC and X.86 encapsulation for interoperability with legacy systems.

GFP is defined in ITU-T G.7041, and makes use of Header with Error Control (HEC) frame delineation. In some other encapsulation protocols that use start/stop flags, such as HDLC, bandwidth expansion occurs when start/stop flags occur in the user data and must be replaced with longer escape sequences. By making use of HEC frame delineation, there is no need for GFP to perform flag substitution in the data stream.

This gives GFP the significant advantage of having a consistent and predictable payload throughput. This is critical for carriers needing to provide customers with a guaranteed throughput. In, the frame format of Frame-mapped GFP (GFP-F) is shown, along with HDLC for comparison. Note that the octet count is the same for native Ethernet and GFP-F encapsulated Ethernet. This small detail simplifies rate adaptation. Once the Ethernet frames are encapsulated in a higher-level protocol that performs frame delineation, they are then ready to be mapped for transport.

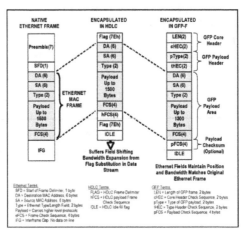

Figure: Comparison of HDLC and GFP frame encapsulation

Mapping is the process by which the encapsulated Ethernet frames are placed in a "container" for transport across a link. These containers have various names across technologies. To generalize the term "container" for purposes of discussion, a container's primary purpose is to provide alignment of information. Some containers also provide management/signaling paths and link quality monitoring. Containers normally have rigid formatting with predefined locations for overhead and management traffic. Some examples of containers in the SDH include C-11, C-12, and C-3. The terms "trunk" and "tributary" are commonly used to refer to PDH containers. Some examples in the PDH include the DS1, E1, DS3, and E3 framing structures. In most cases, one or more lower data-rate containers can be placed inside ("mapped") into a higher data-rate container. In SONET/SDH networks, virtual channels (VCs) and tributary units have also been defined, which work around some of the rigid requirements of the basic containers to provide greater flexibility.

Frame formats for the basic DS1 and E1 tributaries are shown in figure below. Note that each frame has a reserved location for framing information. The purpose of the framing bit (or byte) is to provide alignment information to the receiving node. The structured frame format is repeated every 125ms. A group of 24 DS1 frames is an Extended Super Frame (ESF). A group of 16 E1 frames is an E1 multiframe. By using the framing information, the receiving node can separate the incoming bits into individual time slots or channels. In traditional telephony, each time slot (or channel) carries the digitized information for a single telephone call. When transporting packetized data, all time slots can be collectively utilized as a single container.

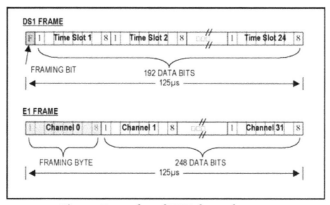

Figure: Examples of PHD frame formats

When encapsulated Ethernet frames are transported over PDH, the time between Ethernet frames is filled with an idle pattern. When GFP encapsulation is being carried over DS1 or E1, the information is byte-aligned. Alignment is slightly more complicated when a DS3 link is used. Nibble alignment is specified for DS3 links in ITU-T G.8040. Figure below shows an example of GFP-encapsulated Ethernet over a DS1 link. Note that the positioning of the encapsulated Ethernet frame is independent of the DS1 framing pattern bits ("F") and is byte-aligned. Though not shown in the diagram, the payload information has an X43+1 scrambling algorithm applied prior to transmission. Similar mapping and scrambling techniques are utilized for SDH transport containers. The complete specification for mapping Ethernet frames directly over SDH can be found in ITU-T G.707.

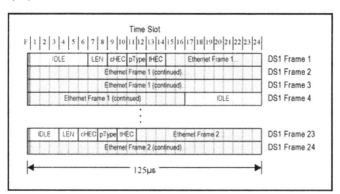

Figure: GFP Encapsulated Ethernet frames mapped into a DS1 extended super frame (ESF)

Link aggregation is functionally the combination of two or more physical connections into a single, virtual connection. Link aggregation is actually a structured methodology for distributing data across multiple signal paths, aligning information received from paths with dissimilar latencies, and recompiling the data correctly for a transparent handoff with higher-level protocols. Link aggregation is also not new. Multi-Link Frame Relay (MLFR), Multi-Link PPP (MLPPP), Multi-Link Procedure (X.25/X.75 MLP), and Inverse Multiplexing over ATM (IMA) are just a few examples of link-aggregation technologies. Of these, IMA and MLFR are the most widely deployed.

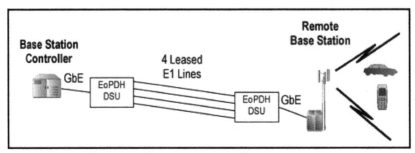

Figure: Link aggregation application example

Link aggregation has typically been used to increase bandwidth between two network nodes, as shown in the Figure above, allowing deferral of a migration to a higher throughput PDH or SDH tributary. One form of link aggregation, Ethernet in the First Mile (EFM, defined in IEEE 802.3ah) bonds multiple DSL lines together to either increase throughput at a given distance or, often more importantly, to effectively increase the distance able to be served at a given throughput.

The primary link aggregation technology used in SONET/SDH networks today is called Virtual Concatenation (VCAT) and is defined in ITU-T G.707. The standard makes use of existing overhead paths for VCAT overhead. However, when VCAT the concept was extended to PDH networks, the existing management paths were insufficient and a new field was assigned for the VCAT overhead path. Figure below shows the location of the VCAT overhead for a DS1 connection. The overhead byte occupies the first time slot of the ESF on each of the concatenated DS1s.

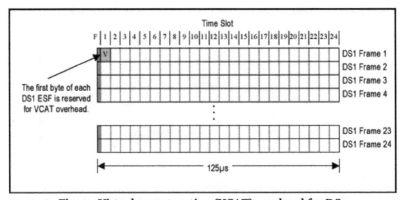

Figure: Virtual concatenation (VCAT) overhead for DS1

The management channel created by the VCAT overhead byte is used to convey information about each link. With each transmitted DS1 ESF or E1 multiframe, one byte of VCAT overhead is placed on the link. Thus, 1/576th of the available DS1 bandwidth is used for VCAT overhead.

The VCAT overhead definition is shown in Figure 6. The 16 bytes shown in the figure are transmitted one byte at a time over 16 consecutive DS1 ESFs. Every 48ms, the bytes are repeated.

The lower nibble of the VCAT overhead byte contains a Multi-Frame Indicator (MFI), used to align the frames from links with varying transmission delays. The high nibble contains a uniquely defined control word for each of the 16 values of MFI. This upper nibble is called the VLI, for Virtual Concatenation and Link Capacity Adjustment Scheme (LCAS) information.

ESF/MF#	MSB	VLI CONTROL				MFI1 SEQUENCE			LSB
1		MST (7-4)				1	0	0	0
2		MST (3-0)				1	0	0	1
3	0	0	0	RS-ACK		1	0	1	0
4		RESERVED (0000)				1	0	1	1
5		RESERVED (0000)				1	1	0	0
6		RESERVED (0000)				1	1	0	1
7		RESERVED (0000)				1	1	1	0
8		SQ Bits 7-4				1	1	1	1
9		MFI2 MSBs (7-4)				0	0	0	0
10		MFI2 LSBs (3-0)				0	0	0	1
11		CTRL / LCAS				0	0	1	0
12	0	0	0	GID		0	0	1	1
13		RESERVED (0000)				0	1	0	0
14		RESERVED (0000)				0	1	0	1
15	C_1	C_2	C_3	C_4		0	1	1	0
16	C_5	C_6	C_7	C_8		0	1	1	1

* Source: ITU-T G.7043

Figure: VCAT overhead byte definition for DS1/E1

Collectively, the concatenated links are referred to as a Virtually Concatenated Group (VCG). All members of a VCG have their own VCAT overhead path, as shown in the Figure below. The Figure below also diagrams the placement of data on the members of the VCG. The complete EoPDH link bonding specification can be found in ITU-T G.7043.

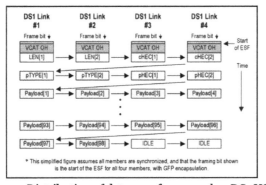

Figure: Distribution of data on a four-member DS1 VCG

Link capacity adjustment is used to change the aggregate throughput by the addition or removal of logical connections between two nodes. When members of a VCG are added or need to be removed, the two end nodes negotiate the transaction using the LCAS. LCAS makes uses of the VCAT overhead path to perform the negotiation. By using LCAS, bandwidth can be added to the VCG without interrupting the flow of data. In addition, failed links are automatically removed with minimal impact on traffic. The complete standard for LCAS can be found in ITU-T G.7042/Y.1305.

Management messaging is primarily used to communicate status, report failures, and test connectivity between network nodes. In carrier Ethernet networks, this is typically referred to as Operation, Administration and Maintenance (OAM). OAM is important because it eases network operation, verifies network performance, and reduces operational costs. OAM contributes greatly to the level of service received by the subscriber by automatically detecting network degradation or failure, automatically implementing recovery operations when possible, and ensuring that the length of downtime is recorded.

The messages exchanged are known as OAM Protocol Data Units (OAMPDUs). More than 16 OAMPDUs have been defined for many purposes: monitoring status, checking connectivity, detecting failures, reporting failures, localizing errors, looping back data, and preventing security breaches. The International Telecommunication Union (ITU) has defined layers of management domains, allowing a user's network-management traffic to pass through the network while the carrier's OAM manages each point-to-point link. The ITU has also defined interaction between management entities, allowing multiple carriers to seamlessly manage end-to-end flows. The format and usage of OAMPDUs has been jointly defined by the IEEE, ITU, and the Metro Ethernet Forum (MEF). Applicable standards are IEEE 802.3ah and 802.3ag, as well as ITU-T Y.1731 and Y.1730.

Tagging allows the carrier to uniquely identify a customer's data traffic at any location in the carrier's network. Several techniques are used for this purpose: VLAN tagging, MPLS, and GMPLS. All of these techniques insert several bytes of identification into each Ethernet frame at the ingress point (when traffic first enters the network), and remove the information when the frame leaves the network. Each of these techniques also provides functions other than just tagging. For example, VLAN tags also include fields for prioritizing traffic, and MPLS/GMPLS was designed to be used to "switch" traffic (i.e., to determine a frame's destination, and forward it only to the applicable part of the network).

Prioritization can be used when Ethernet frames are buffered at any point in the network. While the frames are waiting in a buffer, the highest priority traffic can be scheduled to be transmitted first. One could visualize prioritization as the rearranging of cars at a stop light. Buffering must occur when the output data rate from a node is less than the input data rate. Usually, these conditions are transients due to network congestion and exist only for very brief periods. If the long-term output rate of a node is less than the input data rate, flow control must be used to exert "backpressure" to slow data from the data source. The latter condition is common at nodes where Local Area Network (LAN) traffic enters a Wide Area Network (WAN) connection, due to the relatively higher cost of bandwidth over long distances. This node is usually called the "Access Node" and plays the most important role in prioritizing traffic. These two concepts, prioritization and flow control, are the cornerstone of what is commonly called Quality of Service (QoS). Many people have the misconception that using prioritization provides a guaranteed "clear pipe" for high priority traffic. In actuality, prioritization and scheduling merely allows "more important" traffic to be delayed the least at buffered nodes. There are several other dimensions that must be considered for properly implemented QoS.

Higher level applications performed by a network node can cover a wide range of purposes. Layer-2 (Data Link Layer) and Layer-3 (Network Layer) applications are most common. Layer-2 applications include protocols that impact node-to-node communications. These include protocols such as Address Resolution Protocols (ARP/RARP/SLARP/GARP), Point-to-Point Protocols (PPP/EAP/SDCP), and Bridging Protocols (BPDU/VLAN). Layer-3 applications include protocols for inter-host communication. These include protocols such as the Bootstrap Protocol (BOOTP), Dynamic Host Configuration Protocol (DHCP), Internet Group Management Protocol (IGMP), and Resource Reservation Protocol (RSVP). Layer-4 (Transport) protocols are occasionally implemented, but normally only to service higher-level applications.

Layer-7 (Application Layer) protocols are occasionally utilized in EoPDH equipment. These include the Hyper-Text Transfer Protocol (HTTP) for serving a HTML user-interface web page, and the Simple Network Management Protocol (SNMP) for providing automated equipment monitoring by the subscriber's network management tools.

EoPDH technology provides a method of transporting native Ethernet frames over the existing telecommunications infrastructure by leveraging the well-established PDH transport technology. The long-term outlook for EoPDH can be evaluated on several metrics:

Service Quality and Dependability Advanced Ethernet OAM increases service quality above that of the underlying DS1/E1 or DS3/E3 transport. Links are monitored, performance degradation and link failures are automatically reported, and recovery operations can be automated. Because the underlying transport is PDH, existing PDH management tools can also be utilized. Over time, the PDH and Ethernet management tools may merge, providing transparency and a single management interface.

Bandwidth Needs and Scalability EoPDH link aggregation allows scaling of bandwidth utilized for transport in increments as small as 1.5Mbps, from 1.5Mbps to 360Mbps. This range covers all access applications on the near horizon, including bandwidth-hungry applications such as IPTV. The use of Committed Information Rate (CIR) circuits at the ingress point allows even finer granularity for bandwidth served to the end customer.

Interoperability and Ease of Use Because EoPDH leverages existing PDH technology, a large infrastructure of knowledge and equipment already exists for PDH tributaries. Trained craftspeople already understand provisioning and maintenance of PDH tributaries, and PDH test equipment is readily available. Legacy equipment can be used to transport, switch, and monitor the PDH tributaries. Because of interoperability, significant cost advantages exist when EoPDH is used in conjunction with legacy SONET/SDH networks. The combination of these technologies is called Ethernet-over-PDH-over-SONET/SDH, or EoPoS. EoPoS reduces cost by allowing reuse of legacy TDM-over-SONET/SDH equipment. Rather than replacing existing SONET/SDH nodes with "next-generation" Ethernet-over-SONET/SDH (EoS) boxes, PDH tributaries can be dropped from legacy ADMs to lower cost CPE or demarcation devices that perform EoPDH VCAT/LCAS link aggregation.

Equipment Cost and Cost of Operation Because existing equipment can be used in the transport network, only access nodes need to be EoPDH enabled. Often, enabling an access node for EoPDH requires adding only a small DSU (modem/media converter). Advanced Ethernet OAM reduces operational cost through link monitoring and rapid fault location. Future equipment may make use of Ethernet-based protocols for self-configuration, greatly simplifying installation. EoPDH not only saves the carrier money, the subscriber service fee for multiple (aggregated) DS1 or E1 connections is usually much less than the service fee for a higher speed connection, such as DS3, saving the carrier's customer money as well.

Applications for EoPDH technology span the realm of telecom equipment. All equipment that places Ethernet frames on a PDH, TDM, or other serial links is able to benefit from the advantages of EoPDH technology. Example equipment types include remote DSLAMs, cellular backhaul, WAN routers, Ethernet access, multi-tenant access units, and EFM equipment.

Ethernet over SDH

Although there are various predictions regarding future trends, there is no question that today's communications landscape is dominated by two networking technologies: Ethernet in the local area network (LAN) and SONET or SDH in the public telecommunication companies' (PTTs') wide-area networks (WAN). Connecting remote sites via a single high-speed LAN for employee access to corporate servers, remote storage sites, and Web hosts represents a critical reason for Ethernet LANs to be extended over metropolitan, nationwide, or even international distances.

A number of technologies have been employed to transport LAN traffic over the PTT network frame relay, ATM, packet over SONET/SDH, multilink-PPP, and others each requiring inter-working the native Ethernet traffic to the transport protocol prior to transmission. In some service models, customers are required to inter-work their network traffic prior to handing it off to the public network; in others the carrier takes complete responsibility for the function. Both approaches call for specialized equipment for inter-working, and both create network management issues.

The inter-working function generally must terminate the Ethernet and map the underlying Internet Protocol (IP) traffic into a new Layer 2 (L2) or, alternatively, encapsulate the Ethernet within another L2 technology.

One of the challenges of Ethernet over SONET/SDH is the differing rate between the two technologies. Ethernet rates are typically 10 Mbits/sec, 100 Mbits/sec, or 1 Gbit/sec, always increasing in factors of 10. On the other hand, SONET/SDH rates are optimized for voice traffic and do not match the optimal rates for transporting the Ethernet data stream. These rate mismatches, illustrated in table below, make carrying a single Ethernet connection over a SONET pipe bandwidth inefficient.

Table: Typical Ethernet Rates vs. SONET Rates

Data Bit Rate	SONET Rate	Effective Payload Rate	Bandwidth Efficiency
10 Mbit/sec Ethernet	STS-1	~48.4 Mbit/sec	21%
100 Mbit/sec			
Fast Ethernet	STS-3c	~150 Mbit/sec	67%
1 Gbit/sec Ethernet	STS-48c	~2.4 Gbit/sec	42%

To help optimize the transport of Ethernet over SONET/SDH links, two new technologies have been standardized. The first, virtual concatenation, allows for non-standard SONET/SDH multiplexing in order to address bandwidth mismatch. The second, Generic Framing Procedure (GFP), provides deterministic encapsulation efficiency and eliminates inter-working.

Virtual Concatenation

Virtual concatenation, based on International Telecommunication Union recommendation ITU-T G.707 (2000), is a technique that allows SONET/SDH channels to be multiplexed in arbitrary arrangements. This permits custom SONET/SDH pipes to be created that are any multiple of the basic rates.

Using virtual concatenation, the SONET/SDH transport pipes may be "right-sized" for Ethernet transport. For SONET, virtual concatenation rates are designated by STS-m-nv for high-order concatenation, where the nv indicates a multiple n of the STS-m base rate. Similarly, low-order virtual concatenation is designated by VT-m-nv (VT stands for "virtual tributary"). For SDH, the rates are designated by VC-m-nv. In effect, the SONET pipe size may be any multiple of 50 Mbits/sec for high-order virtual concatenation (STS-1 or VC-3), or 1.6 Mbits/sec (VT-1.5)/2.176 Mbits/sec (VC-12) for low-order virtual concatenation.

All the intelligence to handle virtual concatenation is located at the endpoints of the connections, so each SONET/SDH channel may be routed independently through the network. Equipment in the center of the network need not be aware of the virtual concatenation. This allows for deployment over existing SONET/SDH networks.

Table: Typical ethernet rates vs. SONET/SDH rates using virtual concatenation

Data Bit Rate	SONET Rate	Effective	Bandwidth
		Payload Rate	Efficiency
10-Mbit/sec Ethernet	VT-1.5-7v	~11.2 Mbit/sec	89%
10-Mbit/sec Ethernet	VT-2.0-5v	~10.88 Mbit/sec	92%
100-Mbit/sec			
Fast Ethernet	STS-1-2v	~96.77 Mbit/sec	103%
1-Gbit/sec Ethernet	STS-1-21v	~1.02 Gbit/sec	98%
1-Gbit/sec Ethernet	STS-3c-7v	~1.05 Gbit/sec	95%

Virtual concatenation provides flexibility in choosing the transport size to better match the desired bandwidth requirements. In addition to sizing the transport paths to handle the anticipated peak bandwidth, virtual concatenation may be used to create an arbitrary-sized transport pipe.

The pipe may be sized for the average bandwidth for a single connection or to provide a statistically multiplexed transport pipe. In virtual concatenation, data is striped over the multiple channels in the virtual concatenation group (VCG). Control packets, which contain the information required for reassembling the original data stream, are inserted in some of the currently unused SONET/SDH overhead bytes. This information contains the sequence order of the channels and a frame number, which is used as a time stamp. The receiving end-point is then responsible for reassembling the original byte stream. This includes compensating for differential delay that may have occurred by different routings or paths that the channels took through the network.

Dynamic Bandwidth Allocation

A specification for dynamically changing the bandwidth used for a virtual concatenated channel, the Link Capacity Adjustment Scheme (LCAS) is defined by ITU-T recommendation G.7042. Using this technique signaling messages are exchanged within the SONET/SDH overhead to change the number of tributaries being used by a VCG. The number of tributaries may be either reduced or increased and, in the absence of network errors, the bandwidth change may be applied without loss of data.

Under LCAS, bandwidth can be adjusted based on time-of-day demands and seasonal fluctuations. For example, businesses can subscribe to higher-bandwidth connections for backup or other applications when the demand for bandwidth, and hence the cost, is lower. LCAS can also provide "tuning" of the allocated bandwidth. If the initial bandwidth allocation is only for the average amount of traffic rather than for the peak bandwidth, and the average bandwidth usage changes over time, the allocation can be modified to reflect this change. This tunability can be used to provide (and charge for) only as much bandwidth as the customer requires.

LCAS is also useful for fault tolerance and protection, since the protocol has the ability to remove failed links from the VCG. As the data stream is octet-striped across the tributaries in the VCG, without such a mechanism if one of the tributaries has errors, the entire data stream has errors for the duration of the error within the tributary. The LCAS protocol provides a mechanism to detect the tributary in error and automatically remove it from the group. The VCG ends up operating at a reduced bandwidth, but the VCG continues to carry error-free data.

Generic Framing Procedure

GFP, based on ITU recommendation G.7041, is a protocol for mapping packet data into an octet-synchronous transport such as SONET/SDH. Unlike High Level Data Link Control (HDLC) -based protocols, GFP does not use any special characters for frame delineation. Instead, it has adapted the cell delineation protocol used by ATM to encapsulate variable length packets. A fixed amount of overhead is required by the GFP encapsulation that is independent of the contents of the packets. In contrast to HDLC, whose overhead is data dependent, the fixed amount of overhead per packet allows deterministic matching of bandwidth between the Ethernet stream and the virtually concatenated SONET/SDH stream.

The GFP overhead can consist of up to three headers: a core header containing the packet length and a cyclic redundancy check (CRC) that is used for packet delineation; a type header identifying the payload type; and an optional extension header. Frame delineation is performed on the core header, which contains the two-byte packet length and a CRC. The receiver would hunt for a correct CRC and then use the received packet length to predict the location of the start of the next packet.

Within GFP, two different mapping modes are defined: frame based and transparent.

Frame-based GFP is used for connections where efficiency and flexibility are key. To support frame delineation within GFP, the frame length must be known and prepended to the head of the packet. In many protocols, this forces store-and-forward encapsulation architecture to buffer the entire frame and determine its length, which may add undesirable latency. Frame-based GFP is good for sub-rate and statistically multiplexed services, as the entire overhead associated with the line coding and interpacket gap (IPG) is discarded and not transported.

In transparent GFP, all code words from the physical interface are transmitted, making it appropriate for applications that are sensitive to latency or for unknown physical layers. Currently, only physical layers that use 8B/10B encoding are supported. To increase efficiency, the 8B/10B line code is transcoded into a 64B/65B block code and then the block codes are encapsulated into fixed-size GFP packets. As all physical layer bits are transmitted, the transparent GFP requires more bandwidth than frame-based GFP but has lower latency. Transparent GFP is primarily targeted at storage area networks (SANs) where latency is very important and the delays associated with frame-based GFP cannot be tolerated.

Supported Service Models

Private leased-line services, typically provided via ATM, frame relay, or multi-link frame relay, are widely used to interconnect business locations.

An Ethernet-based leased-line service could be carried through the SONET/SDH network using GFP encapsulation and virtual concatenation. Ethernet private lines may be provisioned at various service rates from 50 Mbits/sec to 1 Gbit/sec utilizing STS-1 concatenation and from 1.6 Mbits/sec to 100 Mbits/sec utilizing VT1.5 concatenation. Ethernet private lines deployed over SONET/SDH offer the reliability and broad service area coverage associated with the carrier infrastructure. As a private line, data-rate guarantees and security are key offerings, as well as upgradeable bandwidth utilizing the LCAS protocol to adjust the bandwidth supplied.

Virtual leased lines or virtual private networks (VPNs) are services in which many customers share the same transport bandwidth. This leads to more efficient use of the transport bandwidth via statistical multiplexing, and thus lowers costs. Since the transport bandwidth is shared, this service is generally a more economical offering than a private leased line but does not necessarily offer the quality of service (QoS) provided by the private leased line. Instead, service parameters are controlled with service-level agreements (SLAs).

Add/Drop Multiplexers as the Customer Interface

The PTT networks are based on SONET/SDH rings. Rings are connected to provide complete connectivity around a metropolitan area and from city to city. The four basic building blocks, or types of equipment, used to provide this connectivity are shown in Figure below.

Of these four building blocks, three have customer-facing interfaces: add/drop multiplexers (ADMs), terminal multiplexers, and multi-service provisioning platforms (MSPPs).

Some forms of MSPPs are ADMs with data interfaces and some are routers with SONET/SDH interfaces and switching. ADMs have traditionally been used to provide PDH (T1/E1/T3, etc.) and SONET/SDH drops to connect to specific customers, and provide a good place for Ethernet over SONET/SDH customer interfaces.

With most applications at either end of a metropolitan- or wide-area network ring being IP- and Ethernet-based, some experts have predicted the replacement of SONET/SDH by gigabit-speed native Ethernet. Fortunately, the ITU-approved standards for virtual concatenation and GFP over SONET/SDH make it possible for long-haul carriers to offer Ethernet services over their TDM networks and should substantially extend the life of this mature transport technology. What's more, SONET/SDH offers features that native Ethernet doesn't, such as bandwidth guarantees and redundancy in the event of a cable break.

DCS, (Digital Cross -connect Switch) Provides grooming and connectivity between Rings.
Has no drops, only serves to provide connection between rings.

ADM, (Add Drop Multiplexer) Provides grooming and connectivity for access equipment.
Has interfaces to PDH and/or optical services. Typically layer 1 only, and closer to network edge than DCS

TM, (Terminal Multiplexer) Provides aggregation of optical and PDH services for transport on a typically unprotected Optical uplink to a higher order ADM

MSPP, (Multi-Service Provisioning Platform)
Adds layer 2 and/or Layer 3 functionality to the ADM.
Usually resides at the Metro Edge (might take the form of a POS card etc.)

Figure: Basic Equipment on SONET/SDH rings

References

- Ethernet, communication-networks, computer networking notes: ecomputernotes.com, Retrieved 29 June 2018

- Twisted-pair-ethernet-25741: techopedia.com, Retrieved 12 July 2018

- Ethernet-at-the-physical-layer: tech-faq.com, Retrieved 25 March 2018

- What-is-power-over-ethernet: versatek.com, Retrieved 14 April 2018

- Market-overview-carrier-ethernet-exchanges: datacenterknowledge.com, Retrieved 10 May 2018

- New-approaches-to-ethernet-over-sonetsdh-53450202: lightwaveonline.com, Retrieved 30 June 2018

Permissions

We would like to thank the editorial team for lending their expertise to make the book truly unique. They have played a crucial role in the development of this book. Without their invaluable contributions this book wouldn't have been possible. They have made vital efforts to compile up to date information on the varied aspects of this subject to make this book a valuable addition to the collection of many professionals and students.

This book was conceptualized with the vision of imparting up-to-date and integrated information in this field. To ensure the same, a matchless editorial board was set up. Every individual on the board went through rigorous rounds of assessment to prove their worth. After which they invested a large part of their time researching and compiling the most relevant data for our readers.

The editorial board has been involved in producing this book since its inception. They have spent rigorous hours researching and exploring the diverse topics which have resulted in the successful publishing of this book. They have passed on their knowledge of decades through this book. To expedite this challenging task, the publisher supported the team at every step. A small team of assistant editors was also appointed to further simplify the editing procedure and attain best results for the readers.

Apart from the editorial board, the designing team has also invested a significant amount of their time in understanding the subject and creating the most relevant covers. They scrutinized every image to scout for the most suitable representation of the subject and create an appropriate cover for the book.

The publishing team has been an ardent support to the editorial, designing and production team. Their endless efforts to recruit the best for this project, has resulted in the accomplishment of this book. They are a veteran in the field of academics and their pool of knowledge is as vast as their experience in printing. Their expertise and guidance has proved useful at every step. Their uncompromising quality standards have made this book an exceptional effort. Their encouragement from time to time has been an inspiration for everyone.

The publisher and the editorial board hope that this book will prove to be a valuable piece of knowledge for students, practitioners and scholars across the globe.

Index